GROWING UP: ATTACHMENT PARENTING FROM KINDERGARTEN TO COLLEGE

by

Isabelle Fox, Ph.D.

GROWING UP: ATTACHMENT PARENTING FROM KINDERGARTEN TO COLLEGE

For information about this book, its author and publisher, and for business, educational or promotional use contact:

SUN PUBLISHERS
15233 Ventura Blvd., Suite 1111
Sherman Oaks, CA 91403
Telephone: Toll-free (866) 369-6283
Fax: (818) 788-8369
Email: foxbethere@aol.com

Visit our web site at www.growingupattached.com

ISBN 0-9712149-2-1
Library of Congress Control Number 2003093987

Library of Congress Cataloging in Publication Data
Fox, Isabelle
GROWING UP: ATTACHMENT PARENTING FROM KINDERGARTEN TO COLLEGE
Includes bibliographical references
1. attachment 2. child development 3. parenting 4. adolescence

First Edition
Cover by Carolyn Fox and David Reeser

Dedication

To my husband, children and grandchildren.

ACKNOWLEDGMENTS

I feel enormous gratitude to my husband, Robert M Fox, for his unwavering encouragement and support. His enthusiasm as a parent, as well as grandparent, served as a great inspiration.

A big "thank you" to Barbara Nicholson and Lysa Parker, founders of Attachment Parenting International, who enunciated the need for this book and made valuable suggestions and comments. I would be remiss in failing to recognize their effort and dedication in establishing world-wide support groups for young families and their children.

I also appreciate the support of members of my Bowlby Study group; Pat Sable, Diana Taylor, Robin David, Nick Stefanidis, and Miranda Clinco, who shared ideas and concepts related to attachment theory.

Sybil Sosin was most helpful; her editing made my book much more concise and organized.

I am indebted to my clients and workshop participants who have provided me with much insight into the stresses and concerns of today's families.

Finally I want to thank my own children; Michael, James and Carolyn, for practicing "Attachment Parenting" and raising seven wonderful grandchildren.

Isabelle Fox
11/20/02

Growing Up: Attachment Parenting from Kindergarten to College

Contents

PREFACE

This book was written in response to the many requests from parents who practiced attachment parenting with their infants and young children and wanted a consistent approach to relating to their school age and adolescent children.

Attachment parenting is a philosophy which advocates the importance of developing secure, empathic, and loving relationships. It stresses the importance of continuity, protection, and responsiveness of caregiving. In turn, this develops trusting and enduring attachments and bonds between parent and child.

Attachment parenting, with infants and children, encourages breast feeding, holding, rocking, being emotionally sensitive to the baby's day and night needs, as well as creating a close, protective and predictable environment for the infant and young child. However, as the child develops, concepts involving nonviolent methods of discipline are recommended. In addition, prolonged separations or frequent changes of environments or caregivers are discouraged since such events can cause lifetime negative consequences.

Growing Up: Attachment Parenting from Kindergarten to College is both focused on the normal developmental issues faced by parents yet is consistent with attachment theory which promotes the continuity of secure bonds and positive relationships.

Many parents often wish that they had responded to their infants and preschoolers with more sensitivity and understanding. They are concerned about the negative effects of their parenting on their school aged child. But, we know children are resilent and that a positive change in attitude and behavior by parents can be reparative—especially if an early attachment was established.

Parents can feel reassured that altering their behavior and their relationship toward their offspring can improve the emotional wellbeing of their child.

Having children can be difficult, frustrating, uncertain, and inconvenient, and at times it feels downright oppressive. Most parents have had little or no practice at it, and often they do not want to parent their children the same way they were parented. But they have few models other than their own parents. In other jobs, training is a prerequisite to entry or performance. But this is not the case with parenting. There is little training to be had; people don't take lessons, aren't licensed, and don't have to pass exams to be parents. The new parent is seldom apprenticed to a skilled parent or nurturer.

This book is written as a guide for parents from an attachment theory prospective. It is meant to be picked up and put down as needed. It is designed to support mothers and fathers in the complex and important job of being a parent from an attachment theory point of view. It explores the development of children from age five through late adolescence as well as how best to respond to these changes. Hopefully, this book will help you be the parent you want to be—and enjoy the process as well. After all, what job is more important? We can't all be top executives, famous artists, or fabulously rich. But all of us, if we try, can learn how to parent successfully. In doing so, we will make an enormous contribution to our children and to society. We will also insure our own immortality and live on through the strengths we have created in our children and their children for generations to come.

Many parents do not fully enjoy their first child. It is not because this child is more difficult. It is because this child is a totally new experience. People react to the unknown with excitement, but also with tension and anxiety. The more we know, the more we can enjoy and love. It is similar to the way we respond to a familiar melody in contrast to a new tune.

It is also true that if you understand what can be expected and what is normal as your baby grows from infancy through childhood and adolescence, you won't blame yourself for feeling inadequate or respond by being critical of the child. In other words, if you are aware of the physical, emotional, and social development of your child, you can more easily see the situation as normal growth, not as a problem. With increased understanding, you won't feel so vulnerable, disappointed, depressed, angry, critical, or guilty. This is especially true when your child behaves in a way that is hard for you to handle. For example, if you recognize that a baby's dropping food from a highchair is an important step in the development of the grasp-and-release response, you may not feel as angry as you would if you perceive the mess as the work of a malevolent child.

You may also feel distress when your six-year-old flips the game board over just as it is clear that the child is loosing. Children learn to play by the rules during the school-age years. At age six or seven they may not have mastered the concepts of playing fair. It is typical for children this age to become upset or even enraged when losing. Understanding this behavior as normal may help you respond with good humor. You may also need to respect the fact that teenagers often need to spend hours in the bathroom or on the phone as they learn to know themselves more intimately.

Many adults feel that parenting should flow naturally and intuitively. This book addresses the times when it doesn't. It can help you understand and enjoy this very tough job, a job that is more difficult in hard economic times or when few support systems are available. Parents that have practiced Attachment Parenting have an advantage in that most have given their children a warm welcome into this world. They have most likely provided a nurturing environment that respected the needs of infants, toddlers, and young children for protection, continuity, and predictability of responsive care. The goal in these formative years is to provide secure attachments and a positive feeling that the world is safe and trustworthy.

One of the difficulties of the parenting process is remaining responsive to the constant shifts and changes of your child's development and behavior. Therefore, another objective of this book is to enable you to appreciate each stage of your child's growth and to respect its particular developmental tasks. The exploratory needs of toddlers may be just as important as the academic struggles and pressures of the school-age child. Appreciating the importance of close physical contact with the newborn and allowing the teenager privacy from parental intrusion are both valuable. They are examples of the need for parents to respond differently at various stages.

The needs of children change as they grow and develop. Children require less continuous contact with parents in the school years. At this time mothers and fathers have more freedom and time to return to work. However, even older children need adequate supervision and appropriate emotional supports to ensure optimal development.

I recognize that parenting is difficult and not instantly rewarding. Because I believe that daily interactions between parent and child are important, I encourage responsive parenting and secure bonding. In this book I hope to rededicate and reaffirm the vital importance of the nurturing process as well as to explore the developing relationship and attachments between mother, father, and child.

It is because children can provide enormous pleasure, wonder, laughter, and awe that I wish to enable mothers and fathers to participate fully in the parenting process. I also want to emphasize that these commitments to the developing child are as important as any career for the limited time we are privileged to be parents.

A pervasive theme throughout this book is to help you provide a positive and loving relationship with your child from age five through the young adult years. Its goal is to help you deal responsibly with developmental changes and normal stress. You may also benefit from insight on how such events as death, divorce, separation, and illness can affect the school-aged child, the adolescent, and the young adult.

This book is based on my thirty-five years of clinical experience helping children and parents deal with their concerns, worries, and problems. It is developmental in approach. Although my basic frame of reference tends to be eclectic, I have been influenced by many of the current themes in psychology and child development, principally the work of Dr. John Bowlby, other attachment theorists, and attachment study groups.

The concepts of attachment parenting are neither revolutionary or new. Its practices are as old as parenting itself, but I have been concerned that many contemporary mothers and fathers have lost sight of what it takes to be a responsive parent.

It is my intention to encourage parents to empathize and be sensitive to their child's changing needs as they move through childhood to adulthood.

Although parents should help children to become self reliant and competent, Attachment Parenting also recognizes the desirability of maintaining a continuing relationship and sustaining affectionate bonds.

Part I
The School-Age Child

Chapter 1

The Importance of Being There

Martha was wide awake at two in the morning. In a few hours, her twins were going off to elementary school for the first time. She couldn't stop thinking about her children's anxiety about starting "real" school, even though they had attended a morning preschool program. Perhaps they would cry at separating. Who would comfort them? Will they be placed in different classrooms? What should she fix for their lunch? Will they feel relaxed in their new school clothes? And what would she do during the five hours she was free of childcare responsibilities? Could she and her friend Joan start working on creating a landscape consulting business?

Martha came from a relatively stable family, but she often experienced her mother as distant, absent, and depressed. Martha wanted to nurture her children differently, and she was not certain how to be both available and responsive to her twins as they grew older. She grew up with watching "Leave It to Beaver" and the "Brady Bunch" on television. But she was also influenced by the women's movement. She realized the importance of empathic nurturing to form secure attachments to her twins. Yet she was inspired to create an identity besides the role of mother as well as to contribute to the family income.

As Martha tossed and turned, her husband Josh awoke. He, too, was excited about his children's adventure. The fact that they were entering school for full days would not alter his daily routine as dramatically as it would Martha's. Nevertheless, he wanted to be a more participating parent than his own father had been. Josh felt that he was loved by both of his parents, but he could remember only a few family events, outings, and celebrations. He wanted to create a more playful, interactive, and varied home environment so that his children would have rich memories and meaningful experiences.

Both Martha and Josh were there, supporting each other during their twins' earliest years. They created continuity, predictability, protection, and responsive care for their children. During these years, of course, there were days when neither was an ideal parent. There were times when they were rushed, irritable, explosive, or preoccupied. But, generally, the twins felt tremendous warmth and commitment from mom and dad.

Even though they were apprehensive, Martha and Josh felt that their twins were ready for their new school adventure. They were anticipating their own entry into a new era of parenting with pleasure as well as some anxiety.

The parent of a school-age child is no longer involved twenty-four hours a day. Teachers, siblings, friends, relatives, and other adults can become important supports and influences for children from the age of approximately four through adolescence. However, in spite of these other relationships, the developing child will usually benefit from an understanding parent who is there when needed—a parent who knows when to help, when to be quiet, when to say no, and when not to intrude.

The words "I am there for you" or "he is there for me" have become expressions that permeate our everyday language. But "being there" involves far more than physical presence. It connotes the feeling that someone cares, is invested in you, and can be relied on to provide trust and support, to empathize and encourage. The words often imply that someone is there to serve as a secure base, and to facilitate exploration and adventure. Having a parent or other adult available allows the child to concentrate and process new experiences. This is in contrast to the young person or child who senses that no one is there for him or her. Such a child may feel stress, anger, loneliness, isolation, or depression. These negative emotions take their toll on the child's ability to learn in school and to develop social and moral behavior patterns.

Our society pays a heavy price for early parental neglect. This is especially true during adolescence, when many children experience emotional extremes and upheavals. They often need parental support, understanding, and guidance to weather disappointments, rejections, or unrealistic adult expectations.

Parents as Models

Being there serves an important function. It helps your child feel protected, accountable, and valued. But another profound effect of parental presence is that you become the model to influence your child's behavior.

Children imitate their parents because parents are the most important people in their world. Therefore, you must be aware that your own behavior is an essential part of your children's learning and acquiring the disciplined behavior desired.

- You cannot expect a child to stop hitting others if you hit or spank the child.
- If you use profanity, you cannot expect your children to control their use of toilet talk and profane language.
- If you don't always fasten your seatbelts, it will be harder for your child to learn to do so.
- It is hard to teach children to respond promptly to shifts in the days' activities if you do not pick them up from school, practices, or a friend's house on time.
- You should teach and encourage your children to use words to express their angry feelings. But this can be accomplished only if this is what they see in the home: that parents resolve differences by calm discussion, and not by yelling or physical abuse.

- You need to respect stop signs, red lights, and parking restrictions if you want you children to develop respect for society's rules.
- You should understand the consequences if you brag or joke about successful legal violations, if you lie, or if you grossly exaggerate events. These actions not only set a bad example but also communicate a double message about morality.
- If you allow your child to remain hungry, become overtired, or have no time for play, you are not modeling disciplined behavior. Predictable daily routines of eating, sleeping, and play model your commitment to order and discipline.
- If you want your child to listen to you, take the time to listen to your child. It may not be easy to stop what you are doing, but if you frequently respond to your child's signals with "in a minute" or "later," you are modeling nonresponsiveness, and you should not be surprised if your child fails to respond to and listen to you.

Parents, who are regularly away from home are not active models, and their children may be deprived of observing their disciplined behavior. Disciplined behavior is best learned from caretakers with whom the child has a close relationship on a regular basis. An absent parent may not be aware of behavioral difficulties and cannot follow through with appropriate teaching or appropriate consequences. Both quality and quantity time are needed in order to model disciplined behavior. Dr. Bruno Bettleheim wrote, "It takes what seems to be an infinite number of parental examples of self-control and patience to teach the values of this kind of behavior and to influence the child to internalize these values."

An available parent also demonstrates a commitment to the child and family. Feeling valued and cherished, children will respect themselves and will be more likely to respect the parent's requests. Children who do not feel this commitment have a harder time with parents' and society's demands. They may be more likely to have difficulty living with rules, expectations, and discipline.

The Undersupervised Child

It appears that more and younger children are returning from school to homes in which there are no adults present. If this happens once in a while, the child may feel a sense of recognition of his or her increasing maturity and independence. However, most school-age children still need adult supervision and still need to feel not only protected, but also cared for and valued. When they are regularly left unsupervised for the many after-school hours, they may feel deprived and neglected. This in turn may add to tension and stress from a demanding school day.

Stress is further increased if the child is expected to perform household chores. Many parents hope to ease some of their own burdens when they return from a day at work by assigning chores to their children. In this situation, the children may not only feel unprotected and alone, but may also feel pressured by household responsibilities. They may not be able to participate freely in relaxed, restorative play after their own hard day at school. They indeed have to "parent the parent" in that they are expected to please and help out their tired mother and father. Fulfilling these expectations may be too much stress for a school-age child, especially a child who is left alone in the house for many hours.

By contrast, coming home from school to a parent or caring adult and a welcoming snack can diminish and dissolve some of the tensions of the day as well as lessen the anxiety of separation from the parent and home. Children are relieved, reassured, and comforted when a parent is at home, even though they may not want to spend time with the parent. Tommy, a nine-year-old boy, said "When I walk in the door, I yell out, 'Mom. I'm home.' When I hear her voice, I go about my business. I often don't even talk to her, but I feel good inside to know she is home for me." Ann, on the other hand, waits for her working mom to return. She feels tension and anger build up. She feels unappreciated, lonely, unprotected, and vulnerable.

Because of their angry or fearful feelings, children may get into trouble, engage in destructive behaviors, and break or destroy their own or others' possessions. They may create messes, get into fights, play with matches, or have more accidents, all as an indirect way of crying out for the attention and supervision they need. Lonely after-school hours may prove to be a dangerous time in which lack of adequate supervision may set the stage for early experimentation with alcohol and/or drugs. Feelings of sadness and isolation may also be underlying a child's overeating or sitting passively glued to the television.

Inadequate supervision combined with uncomfortable feelings may leave the child vulnerable to contact with less-than-desirable companions and may contribute to the child's being exposed to inappropriate sexual activity.

> Jennifer, age nine, wished for some companionship. Her next-door neighbor was retired, and she spent many after-school hours with him. Sexual play and eventual seduction occurred. Jennifer was terrified by the experience but told no one about it. As much as the intimate contact frightened her, she enjoyed the companionship and was getting the attention she longed for.

Having a parent there decreases the opportunity for such emotionally damaging experiences to occur.

Often, children who are unsupervised may be reluctant to return to their own homes after school. They may begin to hang out with other friends at homes or other places in which there may or may not be an adult present.

Some children return home to a parent or adult caregiver who does not provide adequate supervision. The adult may not understand the needs of school-age children for supervision or may be too busy, on the phone, preoccupied, or depressed. Where is the child playing? With whom is he or she playing? What is the child is watching on television?

Just as school-age children need some casual supervision in the classroom or on the playground, they also need a caring presence while playing outside or at home. This presence does not need to be intrusive or oppressive. It should simply be a quiet support system. If chores or homework are part of the expected after-school routine, it often takes a friendly adult to see that these activities are begun and attended to. Few children regularly turn off the television by themselves, plow into their math problems, empty the trash, or wash dishes independent of adult support and structure.

If there is little warmth and emotional support from an adult for the child in the after-school hours, it is difficult for the child to become replenished and nourished, ready to deal with a demanding school day and concentrate on the assigned homework. The quality of afternoon and evening hours sets the stage for the next day at school. Parents therefore, have the task of creating an atmosphere at home that will diminish tensions and increase the child's sense of security and well-being, thereby allowing the child to function effectively and with pleasure.

The Family Meal

Eating together provides parents with an opportunity to model appropriate behavior for children. When successful people talk about their early lives, they often mention the importance of family mealtime in their early years. They recall how family meals provided a window into their parents' lives and the outside world. They also learned to listen to their brothers or sisters; they observed and practiced table manners, and they were witness to a variety of family interactions.

At mealtime, the tensions of hunger and fatigue are lessened. Most family members feel better. No wonder this is a good time for children to learn. They may be exposed to new vocabulary, problems, conflicts, solutions, as well as world and neighborhood events. They may hear expressions of values and feelings from parents, other adults, and siblings. Dinner also provides an opportunity for parents to find out about the child's day. The child can practice relating an event using verbal skills, and can expand vocabulary. The child can also feel that someone is listening.

To a child, no single breakfast, lunch, or dinner may be that significant, but the consistent ritual of eating and sitting together as a family plays an important part in the child's life. This family ritual becomes meaningful when it regularly occurs during the child and adolescent years.

It is sad to observe the many families in which parents grab a plate of food from the kitchen and plop down alone in front of television. Children often watch their own programs in another room and eat in isolation from the parent, not even sharing the television experience. If they do watch the same program, the focus is on the tube. There is little or no family discussion or interaction (except perhaps a battle over what to watch). Thus, a great opportunity is lost, and family members are deprived of a valuable social and educational experience.

At mealtime, parents and children can talk about current events, including world and local news and neighborhood gossip, sports, political candidates, issues, and elections, the weather, and what happened at work or school during the day. They can plan and evaluate trips, moves, hospitalizations, vacations, parties, purchases, and all the other events of life. Adults can reminisce about family lore and their own childhood experiences. Family problems, stresses, and complaints can be aired and solutions suggested and decided. Children can be taught table etiquette—how to hold a knife, fork, and spoon, to chew with the mouth closed, the use of napkins, the importance of not interrupting each other and of passing food to one another. Mealtime is also a good time to use anecdotes to teach values such as honesty, loyalty, friendship, generosity, and compassion. Of course, these subjects should not be presented in a grim and unpleasant manner. Discussions should be casual and friendly. Humor adds to the enjoyment of the meal.

Family meals require work. They involve planning, shopping, preparing food, setting the table, doing the dishes, and general cleanup. Most important is coordinating schedules so that all members are there. Some families may not be able to organize daily family meals. However, it is certainly an important parental responsibility to have three, four, or more sit-down dinners or breakfasts together as a family during the week.

At times, there may be so much fighting between siblings

that the parents feel it isn't worth the effort to create a sit-down dinner. A child who acts up must be asked to leave the table until he or she can behave in a more suitable manner. Two or three minutes away from the scene can help the child regulate the out-of-control behavior and return to the table able to act appropriately.

It may be helpful to have the children share the work of the sit-down meal with the adults. Each child can have a turn deciding on the menu. Children can rotate participating in cooking, setting the table, and washing dishes. Making mealtime a cooperative effort can reinforce its importance.

At times, a family member may not be able to attend. Perhaps a parent must work late or one child must participate in a school activity. Nonetheless, the remaining family members should eat together and experience the many advantages discussed.

Reestablishing the structure and formality of the family meal can be the first step in consolidating family traditions and values. A sit-down family meal can be a vital social and educational force. Most families can easily restore this simple tradition. It is well worth the effort, even if it takes place "only on Sunday."

Chapter 2

Development of a Conscience and Values

Children are not born with a conscience, and they do not automatically grow up to be honest, fair, generous, and kind. Most values are learned at critical times in the child's development.

A conscience is a set of values, prohibitions, and rights and wrongs. Its origin is in the child's early bonds and attachments with the parents. Nurturing and protecting the child allows him or her to feel loved, respected, and cherished. The child in turn will begin to respond positively to the parent's attitudes and to identify with their values and standards. It is mainly during the school-age years that parental values and prohibitions are incorporated by the child. Eventually, the values become the child's own.

If a child feels neglected or abused by the parents, it is more difficult for the child to accept and incorporate parental values. The anger and the stress that is built up between the parent and child stand in the way of the child's wanting to take in and identify with the parent's beliefs and morality. When the child feels that the parent is not there or has not been nurturing, it is harder to want to gratify and please the parent. It follows that when there is stress in this significant relationship, the child may not as readily incorporate positive parental values but may instead find other people with whom to identify, such as sports figures or peers.

> At age six, Linda would often cheat at games. Jeremy would often bring home a neighbor's toy. (It is during

these years that most children begin to lie, steal, and cheat.) Fortunately, since infancy both children had developed close bonds with each parent. Both mother and father took an active role in teaching that this kind of behavior was not acceptable. In turn, such parental involvement helped their children to develop a conscience. In time their behavior became socially acceptable. *(See sections on Stealing and Cheating.)*

Kindness and Caring

It is uplifting for parents to observe their child showing acts of kindness and concern for a friend or a pet. These positive acts are a result of many small caring interactions between the parent and child as well as between the parent and the outside world. Children who have been treated respectfully, with sympathy and kindness, tend to take on these behaviors more readily.

The school-age child is responsive to discussions about how people treat one another: what is kind or cruel, sympathetic or rejecting. Parents as well as teachers have an obligation to stress the positive values of kindness and caring as part of the child's education. It may be easier to talk about competition and winning—who won, who is best, whom did you beat? Unfortunately, caring and generous behavior are seldom discussed, emphasized, or questioned.

Helping a child express positive feelings to another child may be a first step in teaching these values. This should include how to thank someone, how to praise someone, and how to try to express sympathy to a person in a difficult situation. For example, when your child sees another child crying, worried, or frightened, encourage your child to say, *"I am sorry that you feel bad. Maybe we can play together when you feel better."* This behavior can reinforce values of both sympathy and kindness, but it may need the encouragement of an adult before it will occur.

Children often treat pets, dolls, and stuffed animals as they are treated. Children who are treated kindly and with sympathy frequently reveal this by their conduct toward their own toys or pets. Likewise, neglected and abused children often act accordingly to siblings, friends, or pets. Bossy, non-empathic children often feel that they don't have control of the important aspects of their lives and therefore try to control the other children in their immediate environment. Adults must actively help bossy children by respecting their need to have their way in some areas and having them practice giving up control to others. For example, if a child is insensitive to the wishes of guests, it may help to talk about what the visitor might want to do or play with before the guest arrives. Supporting the bossy child's need for decision making can help the visit go smoothly and teach the values of sharing and consideration: *"What do you think Lisa would like to do after she plays your new game with you? Perhaps we can put away your doll that's hard for you to share."*

Adults can also encourage children to evaluate what a person did that was kind and generous or mean and hateful. Adults can also incorporate examples of caring behavior in their own discussions. For example, you could tell your child, *"Jennifer's mother was really kind today. She picked up some groceries for me when she heard I had a cold. It was a thoughtful thing to do."* Or you may mention that John at work was considerate: *"He took over an interview I had scheduled so I could leave the office to be at your game."*

When a child is able to truthfully acknowledge negative as well as positive feelings, the child has taken the first step toward being able to be sympathetic and empathic. Adults tend to discourage children from saying, *"I hate so and so."* But if children truly do feel intense reactions, it can be beneficial for them to acknowledge it. To inhibit this is equivalent to teaching an emotional lie. Adults can further help children by saying, *"It is okay to feel strongly and to hate, but we get along better when we don't always say what we feel out loud, but keep it in our own head or talk about it later privately."*

It is not easy for parents to teach values when they are away from their children for many hours. Such absences make it difficult to take advantages of the events and small incidents that occur during the day. Nonetheless, it is the responsibility of the adults in the child's world to actively teach and reinforce the values and behaviors that they hold dear. These values don't come out of the blue. If adults are not available to do the teaching during these critical years, values are learned from other children, television, or a baby sitter. When values are taught by other adults, parents have less control over what kind of morality is being stressed and communicated.

Working parents, especially, need to think about what they want to communicate in the little time they have with their children. Americans often complain that "values have gone to pot," and many of us lament that children and adults do not seem to distinguish right from wrong and lack concern for others. These are valid complaints that cause all of us deep concern. Teaching civility, caring, and generosity takes energy, planning, and time.

The quality of the parent-child bond as well as the intensity of the relationship with teachers or adults creates a climate in which positive values of kindness and caring can be communicated and learned. It follows that when parents are frequently absent for long periods of time either because of work commitments or divorce, or when the bond or relationship is complicated by feelings of abandonment and anger, the child will have more difficulty learning positive values. When children feel that parents don't really care about them and that parents are primarily concerned with their own adult world, the children may have a harder time responding in a caring, law-abiding way.

Generosity

Most young children need special recognition regularly. Satisfying a child with a toy or treat, or filling a yearning or desire, provides the young child with a sense of his or her own importance and uniqueness. All through childhood the many small acts of generosity in which a need or craving is met create a foundation that allows the child to later be generous and giving.

Young children are basically self-centered and seldom consider the needs of others. It is up to you to model concern for others and to set the stage for learning generosity. Children can be encouraged to help select presents for their friends or family members, even though they are not in a position to pay for them. Discussing what someone would like or enjoy helps the child identify with someone else's wants and to develop empathy. Initially, some children may have a hard time giving away the birthday presents they select for friends because they love the gifts so much!

Children engage in generous acts for various reasons, not all stemming solely from the pleasure of giving. Some children tend to give away their possessions too freely. Such children hope to generate good feelings and cement their relationships through these acts of generosity. This may be a sign that the child needs some alternative social skills, a way to encourage friendships not solely based on the exchange of material possessions. If your child is overly generous, it may indicate an attempt to "buy" friendship. It might be helpful to arrange a special visit or outing with a playmate to facilitate closer ties, without the exchange of gifts.

Parents need to protect their children from spontaneously giving away important possessions. You could tell your child, *"It is nice to give things to our friends, but it feels better when children learn to play together and have fun without always having to give each other presents."* You might add, *"We can look over your toys and decide which ones you may give away or trade, and which ones are too important to you or our family to part with."*

If another child is giving your child inappropriate gifts, you might say, *"I know Janie wants to give you these clothes, but these are not to give away, they are to stay in Janie's house. You can use them and try them on all you want when you are there."*

Gratitude

Parents often expect children to show gratitude and express thanks. This may be a long time in coming. Often, your expenditure of money and energy to delight your children is met with irritability, disappointment, or whining for something more. You may not have fulfilled their exact expectations and fantasies; they may have had a particular brand, color, shirt, doll, or skateboard in mind. They seem to feel that you have failed them. They don't appreciate the time it took to get to the store, select the gift, stand in line to pay for it, assemble it (following directions only an engineer can understand), and wrap it.

Young children sometimes express spontaneous appreciation, but often they will not do so again until they are close to being adults. You might feel anger over the child's lack of enthusiasm about and gratitude for expensive presents. It is not realistic to expect regular appreciation. Using or playing constructively with a gift is an appropriate sign of thanks from the child.

Thanksgiving, the Fourth of July, and Easter are truly enjoyed holidays because they are not complicated with issues of giving, getting, and thanking. On the other hand, Christmas, birthdays, Valentines Day, Mother's Day, and Father's Day tend to be more emotionally loaded. Scale down your expectations and control the amount of time and money you spend on gifts during the holidays.

Children can be taught to say *"thank you"*. At the same time, they need to know that it is okay to be disappointed and to dislike a gift they received. Here again, you need to model polite behavior. You should thank your children for gifts they give you and control your own disappointment with them. Use or display a homemade gift to show your child that you value his or her effort, even if the gift has little appeal for you. Also encourage your child to write a simple thank-you note when presents arrive by mail or to phone an acknowledgement for a special gift when the giver cannot be thanked in person.

The goal here is to teach children appropriate social skills: how to say thank you, how to present a gift, and how to identify what other people may want. At the same time, help your children recognize that they have a right to their own feelings of disappointment and anger. School-age children can be taught to control these negative feelings during social interactions. They can also learn that they may acknowledge, in private, what they dislike and what was upsetting.

Politeness

It takes time and effort to teach a child appropriate ways of behaving in the outside world. Saying *"thank you"* at appropriate times smoothes and lubricates social interactions. Saying *"please,"* chewing with the mouth closed, using appropriate eating utensils, and not interrupting are all learned during the school-age years. City children need to be taught etiquette for getting on and off elevators and relinquishing seats on busses. Of course, the underlying lessons are consideration, sensitivity, and treating others as we want to be treated.

Children need to be given a vocabulary and some practice on how to behave on specific occasions. For example, Jonathan was told to say, *"Thank you for a very nice time"* to his friend's mom after attending a birthday party. However, he waited until he was in the car, and then mumbled it to himself. For Jonathan, this was a first step in learning to express polite behavior. Later, he can be reminded to directly thank the person.

After playmates visit, it may be helpful to tell your child, *"Jennifer was polite when she asked permission to get some juice from the refrigerator,"* or *"Susan shouldn't have opened up the cupboard and taken food without requesting permission. Maybe her mother never explained to her how it is customary to ask before you take something in other peoples houses."*

It is not necessary for children to practice appropriate behavior all the time at home. Eating manners can be relaxed during most meals. Children do not have to say "please" and "thank you" every time they want something. If parents feel strongly about it, they need to consistently model "please" and "thank you" themselves. Children do need to learn how to use a knife and fork when they cut meat and what utensil to use for salad or soup, but the goal is to help the children feel relaxed when they are visiting or at a restaurant or when there is company for dinner. In other words, the teaching manners and etiquette should be done in a relaxed fashion without nagging, and certainly not at every meal. Otherwise the learning process can become unpleasant and counterproductive.

Tolerance

Racial and religious prejudice has its roots in the early years. Verbal and nonverbal communications about people, places, and religion begin to set the stage for negative or positive feelings about certain groups. The preschool child will begin to notice differences and question why someone looks the way they look. That person could be obese or missing a limb, have a different skin color, or look ugly to the child. Differences bother children; they feel more comfortable in a predictable environment where everyone looks and talks much the same.

It is up to you to help your child acknowledge what is different about the person they are observing and to confirm the child's perceptions. However, also point out the similarities and make positive statements about the person's character and conduct. For example, Janie's mother mentioned, *"Dim does look different from you and your other friends in class. He seems a little shy and doesn't talk very much. His mother told me he really likes his new school and would like to know his classmates better. Do you think we could invite him over for a play date next week? You could show him your card collection."*

Prejudice also is learned from name-calling. When parents call each other negative, denigrating names or use negative epithets when speaking about groups of people, they set the stage for prejudice to develop. Words like *lazy, selfish, fatso, grumpy, stubborn mule, hippo, four eyes, gimpy,* and *sloppy*, and racial slurs and stereotypes are shortcuts that communicate judgments about people, especially when we are feeling angry and hostile. When you are trying to communicate displeasure, it is important to be specific about what you are upset about and to not fall into the trap of condemning someone with a negative stereotype. Rather than calling your child "lazy" or "stubborn," it is better to say, *"I am upset because you haven't put your clothes in the hamper, and when we get into a discussion about it you stick your fingers in your ears instead of doing it. That makes me mad, too."*

Another problem with name-calling is that it tends to label the child, and children tend to fulfill the prophecy by becoming what we call them. Children also think about themselves with these "brands" in mind. It follows that they learn how to think of others the same way, rather than examining what specifics they do or do not like about the person.

When children spontaneously use derogatory words and names, a parent can say, *"It sounds like when you call me stupid, you are mad at me. Let's talk about what I do that makes you so angry. Then I'll know how I can behave differently."*

Children aged five to eleven can be helped to see that some of the ways they express themselves about people's appearance, the color of their skin, or the religion they practice can be hurtful and are not socially appropriate. Children should be encouraged to talk about such observations privately rather than saying, for example, *"My, that lady is fat,"* or pointing to someone with one leg and asking, *"What happened to him?"* Since five- to eleven-year-old children are beginning to develop sensitivity and the ability to empathize with the feelings of others, you can explain that they would not like to be called a name or embarrassed by having people point or stare at them, and other people feel the same way.

It is important to model tolerance for other races and religions and at the same time to recognize certain differences. It is better to talk in specifics than to use stereotypes and prejudiced remarks. Name-calling often occurs when adults are angry and upset with someone, and often adults don't realize what messages they are communicating to their children.

School-age children are also influenced by their friends and by other adults. It is up to you to defuse these negative comments and attitudes by saying, *"It is a shame that when Billy gets mad he uses racial slurs. He assumes that all people of one race or religion are the same. Someone should teach him to express what make him angry, rather than resorting to name-calling."*

The elementary school years are critical in the formation of tolerance and in learning to avoid expressions of prejudice. Such attitudes must be taught over and over again. Gradually, through casual repetition, the message is appropriately communicated. Doing so is one of the important tasks of parenthood.

Lying

To the very young child, lying may seem a simple solution to an immediate problem. It is as if the words can perform magic; something is said not to be true, and the words are believed. Most preschool children are good witnesses and usually tell it like it is until they are about four years of age. Then they learn that "pretend" and "imagination" can be translated into words, creating their own reality. Initially, a child's reporting fantasy as truth can be beguiling and charming. Parents can even find pleasure in the fantasies that their children spin. For example, Vicky claims that her pretend brother does all the mischievous things at school and at home. He's the one who gets in trouble and should be blamed, leaving Vicky free of responsibility. Vicky's parents need to make sure that Vicky becomes accountable for the mischief, yet they also need to respect her ability to use her imagination to fantasize and pretend. Her mom can say, *"Your pretend brother sure gets you into trouble, but you still need to help me clean up this mess."* Or *"I like the stories you make up. It is fun to pretend, but we do need to fix the clock that was broken while you were playing with it."*

School-age children become more skilled at lying and conning. Because the child is spending more time away from home, the parents often have no idea what really happened at a particular time. They can't confront the child with the truth because they are often removed from the child's experiences. It is especially hard for parents who are working at full-time jobs and are away for large blocks of time to deal with children's lies, fibs, and exaggerations. It is also difficult for parents who have joint custody and are not part of the child's daily experience for part of the week to challenge the child's assertions.

Asking a direct question may or may not get at the truth. A sure way to limit lying is to ask few questions. However, if they ask no questions, parents may never learn the truth or be able to help their children develop honest responses and responsible behavior.

The school-age child who seems to be repeatedly lying, exaggerating, or bragging may be expressing frustration, longing, lack of self-esteem, anxiety, or feelings of inadequacy. It may be important to explore with the child these underlying causes and to let the child know that you are aware of the lies and exaggerations. Without making the child feel too guilty, reflect that it is okay to hope for or wish for things they want, but that everybody gets along better when they tell the truth and can trust each other. You should also help the child address the underlying problem and suggest what both you and the child could do differently.

The goal is to help your children respect their own ability to make up excuses, wish for, long for, and imagine all kinds of things. But at the same time, teach your children to differentiate the lie from the truth and to deal with reality. You may not be aware that when you react to the truth in a punitive, explosive, frightening, or overbearing manner, you are setting the stage for your child to lie or distort the truth. Lying, from the child's point of view, may be much simpler, safer, and quicker than dealing with your reactions to the truth. Many children who lie are often just afraid of adult responses.

Needless to say, when parents distort, exaggerate, or lie about events themselves, they are communicating a double message about the importance of reporting in a truthful and thoughtful manner.

Stealing

Stealing may also emerge at the end of the preschool years and may continue on and off through adolescence. It takes vigilance to be aware when children seem to suddenly have new playthings, candy, or extra coins that you did not provide.

Many early thefts take place when a child yearns for a toy or candy and impulsively grabs it or sneaks it. When you are aware that this has happened, tell the child that although he or she must have really wanted that toy or candy badly, that it must be returned to where it was taken. The child needs to know that he or she can get the toy or candy by asking you for it or buying it. Not everything can be supplied instantly, and it may be that if the child really wants a certain toy, he or she can look forward to getting it at a later time.

It is important to talk about what the child wants and wishes. Acknowledge that the child's desires are real, but explain that there are ways of obtaining what the child wants without stealing. For example, Daniel told his parents that he found a dollar and a quarter because he wanted a gun that cost more than a dollar. His parents knew that it was pretty unlikely that he found the money in the street and more likely that he found it in mom's purse. Dad told Daniel, *"You need to ask for what you want, and we can talk it over, but you also must respect our money as private property. Maybe you need to have your own allowance so that you can save the money to buy the squirt gun you want, or maybe you can wait until your birthday, when you might get the toy from mommy and me now that we know you want it."*

Sometimes children take candy and eat it or play with a toy, and no one discovers the theft. Nothing happens. If asked about it, the child provides a simple, believable explanation. Such stealing and lying may continue as the child finds that it can be a way to get something easily and not be involved in the consequences. Unfortunately, he or she is deprived of being held accountable, and the development of conscience is eroded. The child is not being taught what is right and wrong, what is true and what is not true.

When confronting and accusing your child, do not be excessively explosive or emotional. The goal is to teach respect for private property and to tell the truth without frightening or making the child too angry. Eventually, this can help to develop a conscience. Guilt feelings will develop as they introject your values, if they continue to take things that don't belong to them.

Returning stolen property to the store or the friend's house and making restitution is an essential part of the learning process. Children often need an adult to help them with this act. The adult and child together need to formulate some words to say to the storekeeper, for example: *"Here is the money for the candy bar I ate. I will not do this again, but will ask my mom to buy it for me next time I want it."* When returning a toy to a friend's home, the child could say, *"I like your toys a lot. I hope my mommy or daddy will get me some toys like yours. In the meantime, I know I can play with them at your house, not at mine."* If this is too hard for the child to say out loud, the parent can paraphrase it while the child listens.

Children can be present or help when a broken window is fixed or go to the store for materials to repair what they damaged to experience accountability. Not only must the child be accountable, but you must also model the very same things you expect of the child.

Suppose your child sees you break rules by parking in handicapped zones, lying about the child's age to pay less at the theater, or claiming that your child is sick in order to get out of a date or commitment. Suppose your child hears you brag about talking your way out of a traffic ticket where you were guilty of speeding. You would be communicating a double message about lying and stealing. Your children identify more with what they see you do than what they hear you say. Their ears are keenly attuned to the lies and exaggerations casually coming from the mouths of the adults in their lives. This can be confusing indeed.

Sometimes children confront their parents and embarrass them in front of other adults by saying, *"That's not true,"* or *"That didn't happen, mom."* The parent may respond, *"Don't talk to me that way,"* or *"Don't contradict me,"* and become angry at the child. It might be better to suggest that if the child doesn't agree with what is being said, you will talk about it after the company leaves. Or wink at the child to acknowledge that a little exaggeration is taking place. Thus, you and your child recognize that what was expressed is not quite true. It is validating for the child to know that the adult is admitting to distorting the truth.

Cheating

The game board suddenly flies up in the air, and there are cries of *"No fair!"* The five- to seven-year-old child will often fall apart at the threat of losing a game. Losing is painful for a child this age, who may feel that losing means being a failure, stupid, and incompetent. Winning means that all is well with the world and "I am an okay person who has success."

Cheating comes about when the need to win seems extremely important to the fragile ego. Sometimes losing or making a mistake appears so crucial to the child's self-esteem that the outcome is enormously important. When children lose too often or regularly feel that they are not doing well, many stop playing games or competing. The child who seldom gives a correct answer may stop contributing in class or may cheat on a test rather than risk the pain of failure.

It is easy for parents to play into the child's very real need to win and be successful. Parents commonly ask *"Who won the game?" "Who got the best grade?"* and *"What score did you get?"* All these questions emphasize the outcome of the activity rather than the child's pleasure in playing, learning a new skill, or accepting that something is difficult to master. This may result in communicating to the child that you are interested only in the outcome. In the child's eyes, the win becomes overvalued, and so does the loss.

You can let your children win when they are learning to play a new game, master a new sport, or develop an academic skill. The child must first learn to play the game, stick with it through the mastery stage, and feel the success and pleasure of winning and achieving competence. Once this has happened, the child can begin to focus on obeying the rules of the game and, at times, be confronted with disappointments. But this is only after the child achieves a certain level of competence.

Children themselves watch one another, and cries of outrage will erupt if a child is cheating. Five-, six-, and seven-year-olds are struggling to learn the rules and play fair. By eight, they seem to have a better attitude about losing. Team participation allows a group of children to face a loss together after a game is played. They support each other both in the joy of winning and the disappointment of losing. Children's teams show appreciation by a "cheer" (hollow though it may feel) to the losers. Children often need to know how to say "great game" or "good shot" to the winners, even though this praise may hide their own disappointment.

Adults play an important role in having children look at

how each and every person played the game, rather than who won and who lost. You might reflect on the difficulty a child can have playing a game by saying, *"It is hard for six-year-olds to lose; when you are eight it won't seem as hard, and you won't be so upset. As you grow older, it will be easier to handle these disappointments."*

Parents also need to be aware of the intensity of their own competitive feelings. Parents sometimes scream, *"No dinner unless you get a hit!"* at a Little League game, or they may be irritable and grouchy after a defeat. Some promise the child money if they bring home an A or kick a soccer goal. Children recognize that the " win" is all important to their parents. The same is the case when parents overreact to disappointing evaluations on a child's report card. If children are punished too severely or the parents explode too violently, children may be more willing to cheat to get the results they think their parents want. In the end, children may feel that their parents' show of pleasure is more important than what they learn in school or their playing experience on the field.

Materialism

We live in a highly materialistic society, and so do our children. Their wants become more sophisticated and costly, and they feel deprived if they don't get what they ask for. A trip to the toy store may end with the child's tears and disappointment and the parent's annoyance and horror about what the child wants and how much it costs. Preparation for the journey into "buying-land" is essential.

Generally, you should decide how much you are willing to spend, and you should tell your child what range of toys, clothes, or equipment you are going to buy. The common phrase *"We can't afford this"* has little meaning to a child, who either may feel anxiety that the family is starving and poor, or anger that the parents are mean because they spend money on other, less interesting things. You can say, *"It is hard to go into a store and not want to take the whole store home. We must leave some things for another trip,"* or *"We can look at everything today, but we can only buy some doll clothes, rain boots, and new tools."* When a child wants something that is too expensive, it is better to say, *"We need to save up our money to get these skates at another time,"* or *"Today we are not buying this item. Perhaps you will get it as a present on your birthday or holiday."*

The act of buying should not be the end of the process. Later, it can be helpful to talk over what pleasure the child felt when a desired item was purchased. Children need to begin to evaluate the quality and play value of their new possessions. They must be free to express disappointment as well as satisfaction. In other words, much can be learned even when mistakes are made.

If a child seems to be obsessed with the accumulation of toys and never appears to be satisfied for long, you may have to look deeper into what the child may really be feeling. Children find it easier to ask for a new toy or a treat than for a hug, some attention, or a kind word. Sometimes you can interrupt a stream of whines and requests and say, "Maybe what you really could use is a little special time with me." It may be hard for a parent to step back to deal with the underlying issue instead of thinking, *"How ungrateful the child is"* and *"Don't they remember how much I spent and how many clothes I bought them just yesterday?"*

Parents often succumb to the incessant materialistic demands of children when they feel guilty that they are not available because of work or other commitments to give the child their presence, their warmth, their conversation, their ears, or their strength and discipline. It may be easier to seduce a child with a gift than to invest time or effort to communicate important, nonmaterialistic values or spend special time. Give your child an added present on holidays and birthdays: a gift certificate for a private nature walk for just the two of you, or a visit to a museum, the zoo, a play, or a park, or a bike ride. This kind of gift communicates the value of the parent-child bond and focuses on nonmaterialistic values.

Chapter 3

Responsibilities

Defining responsibilities within the family is creative, difficult, and personal. Much depends on the size of the family, the ages of the children, and the number of adults present. We seldom think of responsibilities when things are going smoothly. It is only when homework is left at school, a pet has not been tended to, the jacket has been lost, or the bedroom looks like a disaster area that we question why children are not fulfilling their responsibilities. For each family, it may be important to define which responsibilities are the child's and which the parent's.

Parents' Responsibilities

Parents select and choose the environment in which the child is involved. Parents decide where the family resides and who lives with the family unit, such as other adults or extended family members. Parents are responsible for providing food and setting regular mealtimes. They also select a doctor for the child, choose a school and summer camp, and select and arrange after-school activities and car-pooling.

Parents need to provide input to the school to assist in obtaining the best match of child and teacher. Keep in touch with the teacher and attend parent-teacher conferences, back-to-school nights, open houses, and performances. Alert the teacher to critical or difficult events or situations the child is experiencing at home, in the neighborhood, or at school. Support the child's school experience. Demonstrate interest in the child's curriculum by finding out what is being studied, obtaining relevant pleasure books, reading with the child, and accompanying the child to the library, museums, farms, zoos, and the like.

Supervise your child so that he or she arrives at school on time. Make sure your child has appropriate clean clothes and lunch or lunch money. Arrange for transportation home from school, and make sure that the child is picked up on time.

Provide a place where the child can study and read at home, and schedule time for homework with the child. Don't schedule too many chores or activities that compete for the child's time and energy. The child may end up too exhausted and drained to focus on homework or concentrate at school. See to it that homework is attended to. You need not be involved directly with homework; it is not your responsibility to actively participate in doing or correcting homework. Most schools encourage the child to be responsible for doing and turning in homework. You can help the child get started, keep him or her company, and perhaps answer an occasional question. Also, you can provide moral support. But don't act as another teacher. Unfortunately, teachers often assign homework that is either so difficult or so extensive that parents feel they must rescue their children by participating in the assignment.

Avoid planning trips or events that conflict with school. Also avoid allowing the child to stay home as a "treat." A child who is kept at home is being denied full and regular participation in school programs. When these interruptions occur, the child receives a mixed message about the value and importance of school. Control the amount of television watched, and be an active participant in the selection of the programs. Support the child's new interests and activities. You can supply art materials, musical instruments, transportation to events, practices, lessons, and so on.

Provide time for the child to play, as well as time to do homework, activities, and chores. Make decisions about the child's growing independence. What streets can be crossed? What are the boundaries for bike riding, walking, and playing? What time is the child expected to return home? You are the one who decides when the child is ready to sleep over at a relative's or friend's home, to go to camp or on other outings.

Create birthday and holiday celebrations for the child. These can be simple, but they are important acknowledgements that the child is cherished and is special to you. These festive occasions also help establish fun-filled traditions and positive associations with the family.

Above all, be responsible for your own behavior and set appropriate examples for the child. The foundation of moral behavior is constructed in these early school-age years. Fairness, honesty, generosity, and living by the rules and by one's word are modeled by parents. Show affection and warmth. Create a positive atmosphere in your home, in spite of the normal stress and tension of family life.

The Child's Responsibilities

Children can be the bosses of certain aspects of their lives. Acknowledging each child's responsibilities and control in different areas can reduce the number of power struggles in the home. It is important for a maturing child to take control of more and more in his or her life. Being there so that the child is accountable is one of the hardest tasks for a parent.

School Responsibilities

Children can be responsible for selecting which of the available school clothes they will wear to school. Parents may think that they have more wisdom, taste, and judgment about what children should wear. However, the goal is to make children feel comfortable in the clothes they wear at school, as well as to give them practice in making decisions. In most situations, children should be allowed to select their own clothes within limits that you determine. For many parents, it is extremely difficult to step back in this area.

The child needs to remember to bring lunch or lunch money. If a child falls into the habit of forgetting, you may have to look at the issue of how often to rescue the child, and you may at some point decide to stop hand-delivering the lunch or money.

Children are responsible for getting along in class with their teachers and with the other children. Making and sustaining friendships is an ongoing task for the child. It is also the child's responsibility to be alert, to participate in class, and to complete schoolwork.

The child must remember to bring home books needed for homework, as well as the assignments and other notes to be given to the parents. The child, not the parent, is responsible for doing the homework and for returning it to school on time. The child is also responsible for practicing a musical instrument and preparing for team sports, drama, Sunday school activities, and so on.

Although you can support children in their efforts and see they are accountable, it is necessary for children to acknowledge their own responsibilities. If a child is having difficulty, especially with school tasks, parents need to explore what stress has been placed on the child and what might be the underlying reasons for the child's failure to assume age-appropriate responsibilities.

Responsibilities at Home

Whereas the teacher is primarily responsible for supervising children at school, and ensuring that they are accountable for homework, parents assume the job of monitoring accountability at home.

Although parents generally schedule bathing routines, school-age children can bathe independently and privately. The school-age child is responsible for caring for his or her toileting needs, usually without a parental presence, and is also responsible for keeping his or her bed dry.

Parents should be aware that simply because children can perform certain chores does not mean that these should become daily tasks. It is easy for parents to expect too much. It helps to supervise chores consistently, but without nagging, and see to it that they are completed. This can be difficult when angry feelings become part of the picture.

Parents need to be aware of the capacity and ability of each child as they mature throughout the school age years. Following are some appropriate chores for the school-age child. Of course, a ten-year-old can do more than a five-year-old.

- Feed and help care for pets.
- Help tidy the bedroom or playroom and pick up toys and clothes
- Make their own bed. They may need help when changing their bed linens.
- Set or clear the table.
- Help with the dishes.
- Take out the trash.
- Participate in cooking.
- Help clean up after the meal.

With many of these chores, you may need to give a helping hand and provide moral support or company. It may also provide some relief to rotate these jobs, allowing the child some choice, and to take give the child a day off occasionally or on a holiday. It will also help if you take a turn with the chores and, on special occasions, relax standards. The goal is to create a cheerful and pleasant atmosphere at home, as well as to help the child learn to participate actively as a member of the family.

More often than not, children enjoy joining their parents in washing the car, outside gardening and cleanup, and most household chores. Children usually object to doing chores alone or when they conflict with the more immediate pleasure of playing with a friend, or watching television.

Often, the parent is aware of a neglected chore, becomes angry, and "loses it." This loss of control may harden the child's opposition, generating more anger. It may increase the difficulty in getting the child to do what is expected. Parents also need to recognize their own deficiencies in motivating cooperative behavior and to apologize when their own responsibilities are not met.

Payment for Chores and Responsibilities

Linking money or rewards to chores or other responsibilities may lead to difficulties. It creates a connection in the child's mind between doing the task and getting paid, and the reward becomes the important goal. The child may not experience the intrinsic satisfaction of completing a task or contributing to the family. When money or rewards are introduced to pay for chores, the child may learn to expect monetary compensation for other work as well. Additionally, children may conclude that they can get out of having to do chores by giving up the money or reward. In other words, they may feel that they can buy their way out of their responsibilities.

This is not to suggest that children should never receive money or a present for a special job. But for the daily workings of the family, money should not be used as a motivator.

Motivation and Responsibility

Often, parents expect children to do their chores or jobs independently or after the first reminder. However, this seldom occurs, and family tension or power struggles are created.

Parents are responsible for setting or creating the organization of the household and for establishing a schedule. You can, of course, include all family members when developing this plan. You can formalize each child's responsibilities with a written schedule. This may be helpful to both you and the child, since both can look at the schedule to see what has and has not been accomplished. The agreement on a schedule itself becomes a motivator, shifting the focus away from the your constant verbal demands.

If children are having difficulty, sit down with them privately and explore what they feel might be some of the reasons for their difficulty. They may not be aware of what is bothering them, but in a safe and comfortable conversation, you or the child may discover a source of the difficulty. Then you and the child can begin to deal with it. The child can then be given another chance to follow through with the failed responsibility.

For example, if a child is failing to get dressed for school in the morning, talk about what may be bothering the child at school. Is it something about the car pool? a teacher? a bully? or academic pressure? Is the child worried about getting to school too early and having no one to play with?

> Linda, age 8, had trouble getting dressed in the morning and was always late for the car pool. Every one was aggravated. One evening, while they were having a snack, her father asked her what was upsetting at school. She admitted that she was afraid of some older girls who were mean to her on the playground.

Even after the problem is isolated and a plan is created, children may come up with excuses or make up reasons to avoid responsibilities. Or they may be afraid to explore the difficult issues bothering them. Parents need to take a firm stand, calmly and without anger. Explain that the child is expected to complete the agreed-on task. Continue to be supportive and even offer assistance, but make sure that the child is accountable. For example, set a time to see how the child is doing with getting dressed for school. During that discussion, evaluate and reassess the situation, acknowledging the child's positive progress or making a new plan that might work better. For example, a child's friend could be asked to arrive at school at the same time the child arrives.

These steps are difficult and may seem like too much to a busy, distraught parent. It may seem easier to explode, lay out a punishment, and hope for change. Unfortunately, the angry explosion only adds to the child's inner anger and stress. It doesn't deal with the underlying issues and doesn't demonstrate a respectful approach to the child.

Punishing children by grounding them, taking away television privileges, or denying them their allowance might seem a logical way to teach them to fulfill their responsibilities. The hope is that in the future, they will remember the pain or discomfort of the deprivation and complete the expected chore. Unfortunately, parents have to be well-disciplined themselves to see that the child stays grounded, that no television is watched, or that the child's allowance is systematically docked. Additionally, the unintended result is that the parent behaves like an ogre and becomes the target of the child's increased anger and frustration. This further erodes the relationship between the parent and child. Usually, the punishments or deprivations are completely unrelated to the chore and do not serve to focus on completing the task. For example, not being able to watch television has little to do with taking out the trash.

As difficult as it may seem, it is important for the parents to create a time to talk with their child. When the crisis is over, both parent and child can carefully explore the situation and determine what is it that their child needs to work on. What are the difficulties, and how can the parent or others be of help? This is certainly hard to do when the child has not fed the pet for two days! Finding the time may be the hardest part. When the household is in equilibrium and running smoothly, parents are reluctant to bring up troublesome matters.

It does not "just happen" that a child becomes accountable. Responsibilities must be taught by an adult and processed by the child. Unfortunately, this takes a certain amount of effort of your part. Becoming accountable is an important aspect of successful functioning. It allows your child to experience intrinsic satisfactions and mastery, and it positively influences social interactions at home, at school, and later in the community.

Pets

A dog or a cat may truly be a child's best friend. A pet is usually a great source of comfort to the school-age child. It is reassuring for children to return home and be greeted by an enthusiastic pet they can hug, cuddle, and cavort with.

School-age children often are shy about asking for physical contact. They may be reluctant to ask an adult to hold them or kiss them, yet at times they may truly need the warmth and contact. A dog or a cat will usually allow a child to spontaneously and affectionately hold and pet it. This is an enormous tension reducer at the end of a long school day.

Children can even express some aggressive feelings toward their pet without having it create a problem. Toddlers and preschoolers may need more supervision around pets since they have less ability to control their aggressive responses. Young children may unwittingly injure the animal, or the pet may snap or scratch in response to rough treatment by the child. However, school-age children are more in control of their hostile behavior and can truly find release and pleasure when relating to their own special animal.

Unfortunately, some children return from school to an empty house. They may enjoy the welcome presence of a dog or cat. Children may feel protected by their dogs. They may feel that nothing bad can happen to them when the dog is by their side. Therefore, working parents may want to re-evaluate their decision not to have a pet, especially if there is no adult supervision when the child returns from school.

Parents may also want to provide a pet to their only child. Children who have no siblings to torment, play with, and look forward to seeing may find a pet to be a substitute for brothers and sisters. It may be truly an act of love and understanding on the part of the parent to provide a pet for a child. Even before the child is able to take any responsibility, pets can be an important addition to their lives.

On the other hand, the addition of pets to families of five children or more may just add to the confusion and overwhelming responsibility of the parents. Caring for so many children is difficult enough, and having to feed and clean up after pets may be just too hard. So, the decision to have a pet may not be an easy one to make.

Children can be expected to handle appropriate chores to participate in their pet's nurturing and care. Older school-age children can be responsible for feeding the pet, providing it with fresh water, cleaning up after it, and playing with and exercising it. These chores are age-appropriate, although a child may need some help at times with cleaning up and bathing their pet.

Conflict between parents and children often arise over pet care. Parents may feel that a pet is an added responsibility, a drain on finances, and a general nuisance. Food must be brought into the house, excrement cleaned up and disposed of, and damaged furniture and shoes repaired. It may be hard for parents to understand the value to their child of having something alive and responsive, warm and cuddly, with which to interact and play, especially if the child does not consistently feed and care for the pet. For example, when June was driving her daughter, Kim, home from school, she said, *"A while back you took very good care of your cat Snowy, but lately she hasn't received her food regularly. Can I do something to help you with this responsibility?"* Kim thought that she could use help on Mondays, since she was so busy that day, but that she would take care of Snowy all the other days. Calmly discussing the problem, listening to a suggestion, then following through with a plan took care of her mother's irritation.

If parents are firmly against getting a dog or cat, or if someone in the family is extremely allergic to the fur, then hamsters, guinea pigs, fish, turtles, birds, rats, and rabbits can function as pets. They may not participate as actively in the child's play as a dog or a cat, but they are alive, they move, and they are interesting to observe and learn about. Of course, children in rural areas can make pets out of any number of farm animals.

The loss of a pet can be experienced by the child as a profound and painful blow. Parents often underestimate the companionship and sense of protection that the pet provided as well as its role as a participant in all kinds of fantasy play. How to handle the loss of a pet is covered in Chapter 6, "Dealing with Upsets."

Birthday Parties

Birthday parties are an important event for the school-age child. They provide an opportunity for family and friends to focus affection, attention, and material possessions on the birthday child. They are celebrations of the child's existence and importance in the family. This yearly rite brings good friends together to share an activity and enjoy special food, entertainment, and loving feelings.

Some children want large birthday parties so that they can get lots of presents. Others want a special experience they can share with just a few friends. Before the birthday, discuss and decide what form the celebration should take. Surprise parties are better planned during the teenage and adult years. Elementary school children may have specific fantasies about their birthday party, and it is important to acknowledge their wishes when possible.

Celebrations may take many forms. Children between ages five and seven could have a ballet party in which the children come dressed in ballet clothes and dance to the music of the *Nutcracker Suite.* Those between the ages of five and nine may enjoy a picnic at a park, beach, or lake with ball playing, swimming, or kite flying. For the age five to eleven crowd, a trip to the zoo, a museum, or an amusement park, complete with refreshments, can be a big hit, or a more quiet event can involve renting age-appropriate movies or tapes. Attending a baseball, basketball, or football game can thrill children between eight and eleven, as can holding a slumber party or a scavenger hunt in the neighborhood.

When planning a birthday party, you will need to consider the following issues:

- Number of guests
- Expense
- Ability to transport the children to the site
- Availability of sufficient adults or teenagers to supervise the children
- Size of home or facility in which the party will be held
- Emotional fortitude of the participating adults
- Length of time scheduled for the children to attend the party.

Even though birthday celebrations are a special anticipated event, children need to be reminded that parties are not without stresses, disappointments, and conflicts. For example, children want their special friends to come. At times, for various reasons, some do not. They may receive presents other than the ones they yearned for. The outing or experience may not turn out to be as exciting as the child dreamed it would be.

It may be important to remind children that after the party is over, there will be time to talk about how much fun it was or how disappointing it turned out to be. However, during the actual party, the birthday child needs to act pleasant and appreciative of the presents and function as a polite host. Later, there will be ample time to express negative feelings and complaints about the event and the guests.

When a whole class or a team is extended an invitation to a birthday party, there may be one child who is hated by the birthday child. It is important to discuss how that child would feel about being excluded and perhaps to suggest that the child be invited to make future relationship easier. A word or two of preparation before a birthday goes a long way to make the occasion a happy one.

It may not be easy for some children in the early elementary school years to attend parties without the presence of a parent. The child may not be familiar with a particular home or may not know the other friends and relatives of the party-giver. There are several supports that can be provided. You can take your child to the party and sit quietly until the child is comfortable and lets you know that it's okay to leave. Perhaps carpooling to the party with a friend will assure the child of having someone to talk to or play with at the party. The parent who drives can either drop the child off or remain temporarily. The parents of the birthday child can be asked to give special attention to the anxious child if needed. Finally, provide the child with a phone number where you can be reached or a cell phone to call home if upset.

Chapter 4

School

The early school experience can profoundly affect the child's future. If the child forms a strong bond with teachers and fellow students and responds to the curriculum in a positive way, the experience can provide an important support system in the stormy years of adolescence. School is a major part of a child's day well into adulthood, and it forms a significant part of the child's quality of life

The first day of kindergarten is a momentous occasion. Even though children may be accustomed to going off to nursery school, preschool, or a daycare center, entering elementary school is still a major event. Like all transitions and new experiences, starting school creates anxiety. The adjustment can be more difficult because the elementary school may be some distance from home, and the child may attend for more hours. The child is confronted with a multitude of children, most of whom are older. The child must deal with unfamiliar peers and teachers without the presence of a parent or a familiar caretaker. Siblings who attend the same school are seldom available for comfort. The child must make it on his or her own, truly a giant step in independence.

The primary grades, kindergarten through third grade, are critical in much the same way that an infant's first connections with a parent are important. If the child develops feelings of anxiety, disappointment, and inadequacy, he or she may have difficulty connecting and enjoying school in the years to come.

Most young children are excited about starting "big school." The kindergartner is usually a delight to parents. Five-year-old children seem to be more in equilibrium, more willing to follow rules and be cooperative. They are not as physically aggressive as four-year-olds, and they have the ability to be on their "best behavior."

Even securely attached children may find that the first days of school are stressful. Each child may handle separations differently, depending upon their own temperament and past preschool experiences. Kindergarteners often feel anxious. Not only are they the smallest in a large school and awed by bigger kids who seem like grown-ups to them, but they also need to form relationships with new teachers who are, in most cases, relative strangers. These relationships may take time to develop. Most children will experience some tension and anxiety the first month or so of the school year. But by Thanksgiving, they will feel that they belong and that the school has become their own.

Usually, five-year-olds who enter school have less difficulty separating from parents and home than three- and four-years-old, especially if they have already had a positive preschool experience. However, five-year-old Louise still worries about starting school. *"Who will pick me up?" "Where are my mom and dad during the day?" "How much attention are my baby brother and sister getting at home?"* A trip to the school before it opens may smooth the transition. Becoming acquainted with one other child who will be in the same class is also a comfort during the first days of school.

Typically, five-year-olds enjoy the predictability of rules, routines. and rituals. They are eager to take some responsibility, helping with clean-up, feeding pets, putting dishes in the sink, and remembering their lunch boxes. But they often still need a hand from a nearby friendly adult, either to start or to complete these tasks. Getting dressed in the morning can be an arena for power struggles—sometimes as a result of the child's anxiety about the coming school day and separation from the parent.

Five-year-olds have more control over their aggressive feelings, but their aggression erupts in angry or gleeful toilet talk and the use of sexual or four-letter words or expressions. Often, children don't have any idea what these words really mean! Such shocking words usually appear a few weeks into the school year.

At school, kindergartners may be teased, criticized, put down, bullied, or shamed by other children. Kindergarten children are frequently the butt or targets of older children or siblings who find kindergartners to be an easy mark for their own frustrations and tensions These upsetting experiences may be brought home in the form of irritability with younger siblings or other neighborhood children. The home becomes a laboratory for experimenting and trying out new and different behaviors, often aggressive in nature, that they experienced in school.

Many stressful experiences may occur in the process of getting to and from school, in car pools, in school busses, and in after-school care. These experiences can influence children's feelings and attitudes about school. Children may not want to go to school because they are unhappy about what happens to them before or after school.

The five-year-old may be concerned that their younger siblings seem to be getting more protection, affection, and attention from the parents. They may yearn to be back at home, where life seemed less complicated and more secure. Often, they are afraid of the dark, burglars, kidnapping, illness, older children, bullies, earthquakes, friendships, teachers, grades, and so on. Spending some time alone with your child may help you identify and deal with some of these normal but upsetting concerns.

School-age children also must cope with new freedoms and responsibilities. You, too, must shift gears and understand the part you play in the child's commitments. Expecting too much or too little will deprive the child of important growth experiences. In addition, you are responsible for creating a harmonious home life so that your children are free to immerse themselves in the process of learning and mastery without anxiety and stress.

Choosing a School

Most children attend the local elementary school. Usually these schools are reasonably close to the child's home, either within walking distance or on a school bus route. When relocating to a different home or a different city, look at the public schools in the area and consider moving to a district with a desirable public school.

Additional school options are available for parents who are financially able and willing to pay for private education. If you have some school choices, keep in mind that what ultimately counts is what goes on with the teacher in the classroom. Visit the school, if possible, and watch the prospective teacher in the classroom. Many schools will permit this. It is surprising how much you can learn about schools and teachers by watching and listening for thirty minutes! Remember in the area of Education, you need to be your child's advocate.

Clarify what you are looking for in a school. Begin by reflecting on your own early school days. Do you have good memories of your school years, and do you want a school that will give your child a similar experience? Should the school have the same kind of philosophy and structure as the one you attended? Or are you looking for a school with a different approach than the one you hated when you were in school? Ask:

- when and how reading, writing and math are introduced. How much is expected of the kindergarten child? of the third grader? of the sixth grader?
- What is the child-teacher ratio? Are the teachers competent, compassionate, and dedicated?
- Are learning experiences provided that are not just academic paper and pencil activities? For example, does the school provide blocks, puzzles, and other manipulative equipment, paints and clay, woodworking, construction, cooking, sewing, creative writing, nature study, science, and music, rhythm, and dance activities?
- Is there time for free play and socializing? for verbal expression? for dramatic play?

- Does the school take children on field trips into the community?

When considering a school for your children, it is also important to explore the policy concerning discipline. For example, is corporal punishment allowed or encouraged? If parents have a choice, such schools should be avoided. Physical punishment is abusive and counterproductive. It can and often does frighten all students-even those who are not so assaulted. Despite the fact that certain schools permit corporal punishment, most educators condemn these practices. Parents need to have the courage to switch teachers or schools if the child does not feel safe in the classroom. In some cases, home schooling may be an option.

Deskwork and Broader Learning

Many five- and six-year-olds cannot sustain extended intervals of sitting, listening, or doing paperwork. When mainly deskwork is offered and valued, these children end up feeling unsuccessful and stressed when they are unable to do what the teacher expects. For these young children, it may take participation in other activities—such as blocks, woodwork, clay, music, dramatic play, free outdoor play, and trips into the community— to create a positive connection with the school. These are appropriate and satisfying activities for five- and six-year-old children. They allow the children to associate school with pleasurable experiences, which helps create a bond to school and helps them with their later academic work.

Some parents may feel that experiences other than academics are not what school is about, that paperwork and right and wrong answers are what count in the school day. But for many children, the positive connection to school will not be established unless a variety of experiences are provided. In particular, five- and six-year-old boys may need more physical activity than is available and acceptable.

Children's self-esteem may be tied to how successfully they complete their paperwork. With a variety of experiences, many of which are not graded, the child can feel satisfaction from engaging in the activities that are not academic. If parents recognize the importance of providing many participatory learning experiences, they may not feel so disappointed over paperwork failures in these early years. The parents can take pleasure in the child's participation in a broad spectrum of school activities.

It is often assumed that a structured or formal school is required to control the behavior of highly active or aggressive children. But such a formal environment may create expectations for behavior that the child cannot fulfill. It may be preferable to select a school that provides more opportunities for productive play, giving the child an environment more attuned to his or her level of physical activity.

Development of a Connection to School

First, a bond or relationship must be established between child and teacher. The child must feel safe with the teacher. The teacher represents protection and caring as well as safety and order. This underscores the need to select a school, if possible, where the teachers are kind, compassionate, and nurturing.

The teacher also provides pleasure in the form of stimulation, new experiences, and the opportunity for the child to learn a variety of new activities. The teacher presents the ground rules and expectations which should be clear and appropriate to the developmental ability of the child. This includes a clean-up routine, the expectation that the child will raise a hand to request a turn to talk, and homework expectations.

The teacher must be able to create a balance, acknowledging each child's individual needs as well as modeling values of fairness and equality. Important leadership roles should be rotated so that each child experiences a turn. An upset or angry child may have to sit close to the teacher much of the day.

A bond to school is intensified when children feel comfortable taking risks in expressing their ideas, their solutions to problems, and their creative endeavors. Children need to risk making mistakes. Commitment to school is helped when children are free to participate courageously in the learning process rather than mastering only what the curriculum demands. The bond to school and teacher is further strengthened when the individual needs of the child are addressed and the child feels that the environment is caring, safe, and interesting.

It may take considerable time and effort to find a school or teacher that will supply all this, but it is worth the effort.

The Needs of Children in School

Children in school need appropriate structure and knowledge of the schedule and routine they are expected to follow. Learning tasks and the curriculum should be attuned to the child's level of comprehension. Time should be budgeted for individual creative expression so that children can draw their own pictures and make up their own stories. Children also need time to play and talk with other children. School should be a place for safe expression of feelings, worries, and anxieties.

When children are asked what they like best about school, they frequently answer "recess" or "lunch." These are the times when children are not evaluated or expected to be quiet. They can be themselves and are not expected to sit still, listen, or perform.

How Parents Can Help the School-Age Child

Schedule some special alone time with your child. This brief time of togetherness where no one else is involved may provide the best time to listen to your child's concerns about school.

It is not unusual for a child to complain that no one will play with him or her or that the teacher is mean. Be sympathetic and reflect that what happened was painful or difficult: *"It sounds like you felt unhappy when you thought your friends didn't want to play with you"* or *"If I heard someone say, 'Let's not play with Joan,' I'd feel hurt or mad too."* Don't cut off communication by saying *"That isn't true, the children do like you"* or *"You shouldn't feel that way about your teacher; she's very nice."* If you do, your children may stop talking because they conclude that you aren't affirming what they are feeling.

When children can express their feelings and share their worries and anger, they tend to feel better. It also help if they can identify the uncomfortable feelings, express them, and have them confirmed or acknowledged. It is only after they can express difficult feelings that they can move on. In addition, child and parent can talk about alternative ways to handle or deal with the troubling situation.

Children of this age still need to be supervised when playing both in and outside of the house, but it is important not to verbally frighten them with warnings about strangers and kidnappers during this time of increased independence and of heightened fearfulness. Parents who want their children to be confident and secure around adults face a dilemma between creating safe rules and allowing the child to feel relaxed, comfortable, and friendly with the adults they meet.

Children receive a mixed message if they are instructed to never talk to strangers, yet see their parents talk with strangers regularly and are expected to be friendly and responsive in many situations. It may be clearer to tell children they must not go by themselves in cars or houses of people they do not know. It is important to model this behavior for the child as well, by not hitching rides or entering strangers' homes. It is equally important not to go into gory details about what could happen to children who break the rules.

Five- and six-year-olds may become overstimulated and frightened by television or videos. It is important to create sensible rules about these media. Years ago, when young children were taken to the movies by parents, the experience was shared. Parents were aware of what their children were exposed to, and children could question and be reassured about what was fantasy and what was real. Today, children often watch television or videotapes without a parental presence. Some of what they watch may not be age-appropriate and may provoke excessive anxiety, which may intrude on their ability to concentrate in school. In addition, school tasks and experiences may seem dull in comparison. It has become increasingly important to monitor and control the young school-age child's exposure to television and other media.

School-age children must cope with new freedoms and responsibilities. Parents, too, must shift gears and understand what part they play in the child's commitments. Expecting too much or too little will deprive the child of important growth experiences. In addition, parents are responsible for creating a harmonious home life so that children are free to immerse themselves in the process of learning and mastery.

When children come home from school, allow them to unwind, fool around, and have enough free time to discharge the tensions of the day. It is easy to overschedule a child and overstructure the child's after-school time. In addition to extended day care, lessons and organized sports and activities are available for very young children. Because so much is available, parents may feel pressured to have their children participate, using up precious time for unwinding and relaxing. Children of five and six still need some lap time and cuddling, especially if there is a younger sibling at home. It may be helpful to spend a few minutes "playing baby" with the young school-age child. Most children can tolerate this for only a minute or two, but the intimate contact seems to provide an emotional boost or restorative experience.

Most parents are curious about the child's day at school. *"What did you do today?"* is usually answered, *"Nothing"*. This can be frustrating when you are eager to hear what has happened to the child. Unfortunately, directly questioning a child who has just returned from school or who has shifted gears and is thinking about other things often garners no response. It is more helpful to share events that happened during your day that might interest the child—for example, what you saw in the street, what the dog was doing, or what happened at work. This will help the child think of something that happened at school during the day and may motivate the child to talk about it.

The morning hours can be stressful. Getting everyone up on time, fed, and dressed, getting lunches made, and getting everyone out the door is truly a major accomplishment. Watching morning television further complicates the time before leaving for school. A friendly hug and cheerful goodbye is a positive base on which to start the day. Tears and power struggles, by contrast, deprive the child of the emotional energy necessary for school. Angry conflicts over what to wear and bickering over the breakfast table often are taken to school where they interfere with concentration, focus, and positive social interactions.

Decisions about clothes can be made the night before; laying them out ahead of time will make the morning easier. Some morning arguments about dressing or eating may be a result of the child's worries about the school day and separating from the parents. For the child, it may be easier to refuse to wear a particular shirt than to express anxieties about something at school or concerns about the parent's whereabouts.

When we are upset and angry, we can work off the negative energy by sweeping the floor, washing the dishes, weeding the garden, or mowing the lawn. But it is very hard to read a book or newspaper and know what we have read. Our minds tend to be full of the feelings and the issues that caused the worry and anger. In the same way, children who go to school burdened with a stormy send off or an ongoing difficult situation at home have a harder time listening to the teacher and concentrating on their school work.

To immerse oneself in the flow of learning requires the mind to be free to take in, absorb, and integrate knowledge undistracted by upsets, worries, anger, and tension. You can contribute to your children's learning by providing a secure base from which they can sally forth. Toddlers and younger children don't engage in exploration if they are anxious and worried about the whereabouts of the parent. The school-age child has many new worries, but the same inhibitions to explore and learn may occur.

Parents often underestimate the role of feelings and emotions in successful school functioning. Parents also may underestimate their own role in supporting the child in school and in the learning process. Try to find the middle ground—neither an absence of support and interest in the child's school career, nor too much intrusion and pressure, depriving the child of coping with and managing the school experience. This balance is not easy to find, especially for parents whose own parents ignored school, nagged and pressured them, or overvalued success and grades.

For children to function successfully in school, the following must occur:

- The child needs to get along with the teacher.
- The child needs to feel comfortable with other children.
- The child needs to come to school reasonably free of worry and stress.
- The child needs to be assigned to a group compatible with his or her ability and emotional maturity.
- The child should not be struggling with perceptual or learning difficulties without appropriate extra help, either in school or after school.

Homework

"Did you do your homework?" is a common refrain from parents of school-age children. How easy it is for the child to say *"yes"* and to *"shine"* the parents on! *"I did it at school"* and *"I don't have any today"* may be common answers from a child who is having difficulty being accountable and who may want to play or watch TV. These irritating dialogues may begin in the elementary school years and may continue well into high school, causing frustration to all. Agree on a special block of time with each child for homework, whether it be in the afternoon or evening, and provide the child with a wristwatch or clock. *"This is your homework time. Would you like some company to help you get started?"* may work better than that nagging question, *"Did you do your homework?"*

The whole family needs to respect this time. Perhaps there should be no television running in the home to disrupt the child's concentration. If the child finishes the homework before the homework period ends, he or she should read, build, draw, or play until the end of the period is reached. This may discourage the child from rushing through the homework to begin to watch TV or a videotape, which the child may perceive as dessert at the end of a meal. It also may help to encourage TV watching before homework begins rather than after, so that the schoolwork is not shortchanged or rushed. In this way, you are making it clear that school work is a truly important part of your child's world.

Take care not to play the part of the teacher in relation to your child's schoolwork. Parents at times mistakenly cross over, intrude, and attempt to take over the teacher's job. Unfortunately, when the child makes mistakes, the disappointed parent tends to react more emotionally and intensely then would the teacher, who has a more objective relationship with the child. Also, the child may be confused by the parent's way of teaching, which differs from the teacher's, or may wail, *"You don't know what my teacher wants!"* It is your job to provide support, interest, and warmth. This is much more important than attempting to teach the child actively or correcting homework. Parents own competitive feelings may get mixed up with the child's school success. They may want their child to excel so that they themselves can feel gratified and rewarded.

Most children want to perform successfully for the parent. If the child does not and the parent attempts to take on the teacher's job of evaluating and judging, it complicates both the child's learning as well as the parent-child relationship. This is not to say that parents should never engage in reading with the child, playing word and number games, or reviewing spelling lists, but these activities should be separate from correcting or teaching formal schoolwork.

Teachers use children's homework to discover what the children really understand and have learned. If parents become too actively involved in doing the homework, the teacher will not know where the child needs help and what the child hasn't mastered. In other words, the child should be accountable to the teacher, not the parent, for schoolwork. Unfortunately, teachers sometimes assign projects and reports that are too difficult for children to do independently. It may be hard for parents to see their children floundering because they are frustrated and don't know how to proceed. When this happens, parents can lend a hand, make a trip to the library, or offer some suggestions to get the project started.

Report Cards and Grades

Report cards are a link between the school and the parents. They are like a small window into the child's school day. The problem with report cards and grades is that they often do not give the parents a complete picture of the child's experience in school, but instead focus largely on performance.

It is a good idea to ask your children how they feel about their report cards before you comment on them: *"Would you have given yourself these grades if you had the chance?"* This will give the children an opportunity to express their feelings about their school experience. It is important for children's school experiences to be their own. They are not in school only to please you; they are there to enjoy and participate in the process of learning, much of which may not be graded.

It is not advisable to reward high grades with money or gifts. They make it more difficult for children to look at school as providing its own intrinsic satisfaction. Children need to find pleasure in new ideas, new skills, and a sense of mastery. A good grade should be pleasure enough.

A poor grade is a disappointment, a negative communication from the teacher, and it may be painful as well. Punishing children by grounding them or depriving them because of low grades is not fair. Disappointments at school should be handled there. Home should be a restorative and supportive place, where the goal is to help children improve and feel better, not to make them feel more angry or inadequate.

Sometimes report cards or parent conferences reveal that a child who may be doing well academically is creating disturbances in the classroom and treating other children badly. When children act out in an aggressive way, teachers may feel that they are losing control of the class. Often teachers end up disliking difficult children.

The reasons for disruptive behavior may be numerous. Some may be attributed to the lack of skill of the teacher in providing an interesting and stimulating environment for the children. However, you need to explore what events are occurring at home that may stimulate this negative behavior. Are you too strict and demanding so that the expression of feelings has no outlet at home? Do you respond aggressively and meanly to each other and to the child? Is the child dealing with a special anxiety due to stress from a sibling, absence of a parent, or too much television?

If a teacher complains about your child's behavior, you may want to punish and ground the child. Unfortunately, this often increases the underlying angry feelings with which the child must deal. Of course, you are angry, the child has disappointed you and caused you embarrassment or humiliation. But, as with academic problems, it is the teacher's responsibility to deal with the difficult behavior in the classroom. You need to be supportive of the teacher by truly looking into the causes of stress at home. For example, Jane's report card reflects the fact that she is pulling hair, hitting others on the playground, and using "bad" language. Jane's parents frequently express tension and angry feelings at home. It might help if mom or dad can talk to Jane about what is happening to their marriage and ask her what else she feels upset about. The parent may say, *"It must scare you when we get so mad that we end up calling each other names. We will try to work on controlling our behavior, and maybe you can do the same on the playground with your friends."*

It is important not to punish the child or add to the stress, but rather to suggest ways that both you and your child can calm the situation. This is not always the easiest thing to do when you are angry with the child and want to blame and punish him or her for difficult behavior. Nonetheless, it is crucial for the child to see that you are taking some responsibility for changing the environment and listening to his or her concerns. Hopefully, the child will have increased motivation to work on behavior at school.

Home Schooling

An increasing number of parents are deciding to home school their children. Parents who take on this task are adding the role of teacher to the roles of mom and dad. They need to understand what curriculum their children are expected to master as they grow, and they need to learn how to communicate concepts at age-appropriate levels. Time for teaching and study must be allocated during the day when other household responsibilities must be met.

Parents are usually more emotionally involved than teachers, and they may communicate anger and frustration to their children who experience difficulties in learning. Children may be more aware of how to irritate, tease, and be oppositional with a parent. Yet some children may also be concerned about disappointing mother or father by not dealing appropriately with the learning material presented. Nevertheless, schooling at home can provide many learning experiences without many of the stresses of formal education.

- Math problems arise in cooking and shopping;
- physical science concepts can be explored in terms of heating, electricity, water, air, and light.
- Gardening projects and the nurturing of animals can be useful in teaching biology, responsibility, and empathy.
- Short trips into the community can stimulate interests in society's needs and history.

Not only do children who are schooled at home benefit from increased personal attention, but they can engage in a variety of projects not offered in traditional schools to stimulate their interests. However, a great deal depends on the creativity and dedication of the parents. To increase social experiences, some parents who home school their children share their teaching skills and curriculums with other families.

Home schooling can work. As the child grows and develops, more traditional school experiences may be provided in later years.

Sports and Skills

Schoolwork is important, but there is much to learn that is not academic. Children aged five to eleven increasingly feel good about themselves as they conquer their fears and anxieties and learn to swim and dive, ride a bike or horse, roller skate, ice skate, ski, play ball, and camp in the wilds. Children often feel frightened during the process of learning these skills, and parents can easily underestimate the effect of fear on their mastery. Children may worry about deep water and drowning. They may worry about falling off of bikes, skates, skis, horses, or skateboards. They may be anxious about being hit by a ball or colliding with a big kid when playing soccer. They may feel tense and embarrassed when standing up alone at the plate when it is their turn to bat.

Provide warmth and understanding and help your children persevere so that they can obtain the ego benefits of becoming a participant. Many of these skills will stay with them for their lifetimes and will provide pleasure and relaxation into old age. The child who was never taught to swim or ride a bike may be isolated from many teenage activities as their friends swim off to the raft or ride their bikes to a nearby store.

Parents are often not the best people to teach their children sports and skills. As with academic subjects, the child may be afraid to disappoint the parents, and is also much more likely to fall apart, throw a tantrum, or become uncooperative and oppositional. Parents can help the child practice or play, and this can be a pleasurable time for both. But if the parents act as the primary teacher of a sport, their expectations may be too high, and tension may escalate. With a relative stranger, children may tend to try harder and not give up.

Some teachers may also expect too much, causing the child to become frightened, withdrawn, and inattentive. If the child wants to give up, the problem may be the quality of the teaching. If feasible, a change of teachers may be considered. No matter who the teacher is, it is important to recognize that there can be anxiety and fear for the child who is learning. Reassure the child: *"Many children are frightened when they start to learn to ride a bike, but after a while the fear gets less and goes away."* Of course, it is important, when children are first learning, that no or few painful mishaps occur to increase terror. For example, when you are helping a child learn to ride a bike, a firm grip on the child with belting or a rope will help stabilize the child and prevent a bad spill. It is also helpful to find a quiet, safe area with little or no traffic; an empty parking lot is ideal. Children do better when learning on a small bike rather than one with large wheels that place the child farther from the ground. Swimming should be taught in a quiet pool or lake far from the chaos of splashing children. Skating rinks that are overcrowded with terrifying speeders do not provide the best environment in which to learn ice skating or roller-skating.

Once children begin to develop skills, they can use the expression *"I can."* What a good feeling that is for a child! The childhood classic *The Little Engine That Could* shows that even a little person with motivation and perseverance can succeed! This is certainly true for the school-age children who persevere and learn "how-to-do it".

The sense of competence and the good feeling mastery brings allows the child to more easily tolerate disappointments. The child can then focus on the rules of playing. Wins, losses, high scores, low scores, and appreciation of the abilities of others all come into play once the child achieves the basic skills. Cheating becomes less of a problem. Children will experience joy because they have learned their sport and have also learned that losses and disappointments are part of the game.

Private Lessons

Scheduling is essential for school-age children, not only because there must be a time for homework, but also because there must be a time to practice piano, tennis, singing etc. Children select activities in order to master an instrument or other skill. But they often have little understanding of commitment and of how much time is needed to get pleasure from an instrument or sport. Because lessons cost money, it is easy to become irritated and resentful when a child fails to practice.

It's helpful for parent and child to decide on a realistic time to practice. Here again, the child needs to be accountable to the teacher rather than to the parent. The parent can remind the child to check the schedule and perhaps keep the child company while he or she gets started. If practicing time becomes fraught with difficulties, it may be that the child does not want to continue. Not every child has the talent or the perseverance to continue with something they thought might be interesting and appealing.

Since children do not have to play the piano or take ballet or tennis lessons, they can be more involved in decision of whether to continue. For this reason, it is probably wise not to invest in an expensive instrument (these can be rented) until it is known that the child is truly interested in the experience. When there is continuing difficulty finding time to practice, suggest that the child can take a vacation from the lessons for a while, and perhaps wait for the child to be more mature and more motivated to practice before resuming. Children may also want to stop taking lessons because of a poor relationship with a teacher, because the pace of learning is too fast and frustrating, or because they experience too much anxiety over performances, recitals, or competitions.

Parents must be aware that they themselves have expectations for the child's achievements. Perhaps they long to have the child do something that they themselves were denied, and they wish to glean satisfaction from the child's performance and competence. Step back and allow your child to learn new skills for their own pleasure and to be responsible for their own commitments. Parents often communicate feelings of profound disappointment and anger when their children fail to continue with lessons. As a result, the children may end up experiencing some guilt as well as feeling they have failed or regretting their decision to give up an instrument or sport. Encourage children to stay with an activity for a limited amount of time to see if their negative feelings continue.

Parent's Contributions to the School Experience

Even though it is important to respect the teacher-child

relationship and not cross the boundary or try to take over the school's job of teaching the curriculum, you can be vitally involved in your child's school experience. A variety of enriching family outings gives children things to talk, read, write, and think about that may increase understanding of school work. Trips to museums, zoos, parks, beaches, and historical sites can be enormously enriching, although they may not seem as immediately gratifying as a trip to an amusement park or neighborhood fun fair. Children often act bored and restless. Nevertheless, they are nourished with some images and information that they can draw on later. Repeated trips allow them to re-experience places as they mature. In addition, outings and events create a shared body of family lore.

Children are constantly learning by listening to adults' conversations. They learn how their parents express themselves, what they feel is important and interesting, and what is happening in the outside world. It is during weekend outings, mealtimes, and when the parents have friends visiting, that children begin to learn about the adult world. They also see the parents modeling participation in the larger community as they notice what problems the parents encounter, how they deal with issues, and the vocabulary around these activities. Parents do not realize how much children learn by simply "hanging around".

It is during the school-age years that children are most receptive to learning from and identifying with their parents. This is a precious time. After children turn eleven, there is a natural developmental shift away from spending time at home to spending time with the adolescent peer group. Therefore, it is during these school-age years, before the upheavals of adolescence, that you can best share your values, interests, hobbies, and skills with your children. Whether you collect rocks, play chess or baseball, sew, work on cars, cook, go camping, work with wood, play music, or create art, involving your children gives them information and experiences, and is a window into a world they ordinarily do not see. Perhaps your love of camping and nature may inspire your child's later interest in botany and biology.

Additionally, find books that you and your child can read and enjoy together. Stories can be read, a chapter or two at a time, all through the school-age years and into adolescence. Characters, events, and emotions can stimulate discussion that goes beyond the usual daily communications. Reading an adventure book, a historical novel, or your favorite childhood book brings shared pleasure and a lot to talk about.

Simply telling a child, *"School is important"* and *"We want you to get good grades"* does not provide support and the sense that you value school. You need to do more:

- Create regular routines.
- Respect time commitments.
- Read aloud to your child, even when the child can read, rather than just watching television together.
- Listen to you child express ideas and feelings; plan private times to allow this to happen.
- Create an atmosphere of warmth and fun at home or on outings.

These are a few of the things that help support the child's school experience. Remember that you are responsible for providing the atmosphere and structure within the home from which the child can go forth and learn.

CHAPTER 5

DEALING WITH SEXUAL ISSUES

School-age children ponder many questions related to sexuality:

"Where did I come from?"

"When will I look like a grown up?"

"What are those special things in mommy's bathroom?"

"What does gay mean?"

"Why is the bedroom door sometimes locked?"

"Why do you get upset when I use certain words?"

"Would my parents get mad if I told them about what happened with Uncle Bill when they were away?"

How adults feel about their bodies, respond to their erotic and sexual sensations, and to whom they relate in an intimate and loving way often depends on their early sexual experiences and how sexual information was explained to them. This information begins to be introduced and communicated during the toddler and preschool years. Sexual understanding continues to expand well into adulthood.

This information is probably more useful in determining the quality of adult life than math, history, and geography. It helps determine how we feel about our bodies, respond to our feelings, and relate emotionally and sexually to others. Attitudes about childbirth, nursing, and enjoying sexual expression grow out of this early learning.

Today many parents seem to take a more active role in communicating sexual information. However, others are still embarrassed and uncomfortable talking about sexual intercourse, menstruation, and related topics. A parent who is uncomfortable talking about these matters should at least provide some books or ask another adult to explain sexual concepts to the child. That way, the child will feel that the parent respects his or her need to know and is not neglecting this part of the child's education.

Here, as with any complicated information, it is important not to give too much too soon. The child should be able to understand and become interested in what is being taught. Ideally, information should come from the parent and perhaps be reinforced by discussions in school before it is giggled about with friends. Often the reverse occurs. Children tell each other about sex, and some of the explanations may be distorted and inaccurate. Similarly, children who observe animals in sexual situations may assume that what they do is what adult humans do.

Preparation for Menstruation

School-age children (8–11) should be prepared for the biological changes that occur during adolescence. No event can be more dramatic for the female child than the onset of menstruation. It is extremely helpful for both boys and girls to be aware of and to understand this biological rite of passage.

Many women have reported, with a mixture of anger and sadness, that their mothers and other women in their lives never took the time to explain what was happening to them at their first menstruation. Oh, how they wished that they had had some warning! Because they did not know what to expect, they were frightened by the sight of the menstrual blood, and they feared that they were injured or ill. At the time, there was no one to turn to for reassurance or even an explanation, and with great fear and embarrassment, they tried to hide the evidence of this normal event. For a girl who does not know what to expect, menstruation may cause feelings of shame and embarrassment associated with the lack of control of bodily functions. In preschool years, children learned to control these function and not soil their clothes. Menstruation cannot be controlled in the same way, so it may produce the same sense of shame as having an "accident" because of inability to control sphincters.

Preparation for this event may occur any time during the school-age years when the girl is intellectually and emotionally ready. It is important to select a time when you and your child are private and relaxed. The communicating adult can be mother, father, an older sibling, or a friend of the family. Don't feel that this is a one-time communication. It is important to set the stage for later questions, when the girl may need further or repeated explanations. The goal is for the girl to feel comfortable and be prepared for important and normal changes in her life.

Explain what the girl can expect on reaching puberty. Begin by saying:

> *"When you are as old as Jennifer (13), your body will begin to change. Your breasts will grow larger, and hair will appear under your arms and in the pubic area that is between your legs. About a year after the pubic hair appears, most young girls begin to menstruate. Menstruation usually occurs once every month. Two or three teaspoons of fluid will slowly come out of your vagina every day. This is a special opening in your body. It is between the one where your BM's come out and the place your urine comes out. Menstruation is a normal event that happens to all girls each month. It is not bleeding. It does have some blood cells in it. It is colored red and looks like blood. Special napkins or absorbent tampons are used to keep your clothes from becoming discolored. Each period lasts about four to six days and then stops until the next month. For many girls, periods occur irregularly and can come early or late. Menstruation is an important occurrence in your life because it means that you are growing up. It tells you that in the future your body will be able to have a baby, when you are ready and decide to become pregnant."*

The goal is to be factual and not too detailed or complex and to avoid creating negative images. School-age children do not need to know the physiological concepts dealing with ovulation, conception, and pregnancy, but some may be interested in more details. They do need to be prepared and know what to expect, and to be assured that they will not be in pain or be ill because of the appearance of blood. It also helps to mention that what comes out is a relatively small amount and that there are simple ways of dealing with the flow. Collect feminine supplies in the months preceding the onset of menses for the child to have on hand. Offer to discuss this subject again when they are older, or any time they have more questions.

It is important to be aware of your own child's physical development. Early growth of pubic hair and breast development may alert the parent to focus on this issue earlier than ordinarily expected.

When you start to talk about this subject, the child may act embarrassed and try to sidestep the discussion, telling you, "I know all about it." But you should persist. In the long run, the child will be grateful that you supplied this information.

Preparations for Other Body Changes

Before puberty, some time between ages 9 and 11, both sexes should also be prepared for the fact that, during adolescence, hair will appear on their bodies, their skin may get oily and pimples may appear, and their bodies may begin to have a special odor and perspire. Boys should be prepared for the fact that when they reach puberty certain changes will occur (male puberty has been defined as one year after the pubic hair curls). They can be told that, "at night, when you dream, sometimes a teaspoon or so of a fluid called semen will come out of your penis and wet your pajamas or sheets." Boys can also be told that erotic dreams ("wet" dreams) stimulate sexual feelings and that it is normal for the body to react this way.

Other sexual information should not be discussed until later. For example, early adolescence is time enough to discuss birth control methods and protection, including abortion, venereal disease, and AIDS. School-age children may still be "grossed out" by sexual intercourse, and you don't need to complicate their thinking with these more emotionally loaded and fear-laden concepts. Age-appropriate discussions about sex will be a foundation for learning more complex information later as the child matures.

It is important to communicate easy-to-understand information so that the child can develop positive attitudes about the body and body changes. It is also important to have a foundation to build on, so that the child can continue to learn more complex sexual concepts from books and health classes in school. The child will then be able to contradict a friend's sexual fantasies or explanations if and when sexual material is discussed.

Sexual Intercourse

Most preschool children have some understanding of where babies come from. The general concept is usually explained in the preschool years. Most school-age children are ready for more information dealing with conception and how a baby actually gets started. They can be told:

> *"For a baby to be started, a female cell and a male cell must meet. The female cell lives in the women's body, inside the womb, and is as small as a dot on a page. The male cells live inside a special place behind the penis, inside the scrotum, which is a sac behind the penis. Inside the scrotum are two round balls called testicles, and inside the testicles live many tiny male cells.*
>
> *When a man and a woman decide to make a baby, the man places his penis inside the special opening called the vagina, and a little bit of a special type of fluid comes out of the penis. In this fluid there are many, many male cells called sperm. They move into the womb and try to meet the female cell. The first one to get there is the one that starts the baby. The man removes his penis after the fluid comes out".*

It is helpful to state the amount—a teaspoon or two. This will help the child understand that the male does not urinate inside the woman, since this is what they know comes out of the penis.

This explanation avoids any discussion of the pleasure of sexual intercourse. Initially, children are mainly interested in the process of how it happens. Many children who are told about this activity may find it difficult to imagine and not particularly appealing. You can accept the fact and add that *"when you were a baby you enjoyed nursing, which is something you probably would not like to do now that you are eight years old. When you are older it might be easier for you to understand and accept the private and personal act of sexual intercourse as well."*

Children may start to giggle when this kind of information is expressed. You can encourage the laughter and say *"this information does make children laugh a lot, and if you feel like laughing and giggling it's okay."*

It is probably not a good idea to explain the process of sexual intercourse by pointing out how animals do it. One father decided to teach sexual intercourse to his child by pointing to cats that were copulating on a fence outside. The father explained what was taking place. Later the child questioned, *"I understand what the cats were doing, but how do parents get up so high on the fence?"* Also, occasionally, dogs and other animals may appear to be in pain while copulating, especially if there is a problem separating.

The goal is to create positive, understandable images, free of embarrassment and pain, to become the foundation for later enjoyment of the sexual act. Sexual intercourse is best explained in the third person. Not relating what the mother and father do personally may make it easier to talk about.

Protection of Sexual Privacy

Adults need to be vigilant about their own privacy while engaging in any form of sexual intimacy. Listening to or witnessing such acts can upset school-age children. What they see and hear may be hard for them to translate into a loving and pleasurable experience. Lock the door to slow down the intruding child and give yourselves a chance to regroup.

On the other hand, it is a good idea to show warmth, tenderness, and consideration to each other in front of the child so as to provide the best model for future enjoyment of sex. If parents engage in continual sniping, bickering, and fighting without affection, children are likely to be more wary about closeness with the opposite sex. It is also important for both mothers and fathers act in a loving, responsive, and protective manner with your child of the opposite sex to ensure future positive feelings.

Masturbation

Not all school-age children masturbate, but many give themselves pleasure by touching or rubbing their genitals. This usually takes place in their own rooms or in the bath. For those few children who have not learned to be private about masturbating, a reminder about what is acceptable is in order: *"Giving pleasure to yourself is something you do that is private and personal. It's best to masturbate in your own room or in the bath."*

Some children appear to have no way to sooth themselves or relax other than masturbating, and they seem to engage more actively and compulsively in the activity. A gentle reminder about when and where to do it is usually all that is needed. Further discussion of masturbation can occur in adolescence, when there may be a resurgence of interest in the process and often anxiety about it.

Homosexuality

In the past, most children were unaware of homosexuality. They often used words like "fag" and "queer" in a hostile way, but they seldom had any real understanding of what the words meant. That is no longer the case. As a result of the AIDS epidemic and the development of the gay rights movement, homosexuality is more openly discussed and is often a topic in the news and entertainment media, so children are much more likely to have some awareness of it.

As children begin to identify homosexuals as people who develop affectionate ties with members of the same sex, they also begin to feel that homosexuality is strange, different, and wrong. The idea of homosexuality may cause the school-age child some anxiety because it is natural and normal for their closest friends to be of the same sex. Children from ages five to eleven are seldom ready to be involved in intimate heterosexual relationships.

Their close friendships, which are extremely important to them, are usually monosexual. They enjoy the companionship and conversation of their same-sex friends. There may even be some natural frolicking, physical tussling, or hugging and kissing, and perhaps some mutual body exploration. This is part of the normal scheme of things, and neither the child nor the parent should be made to feel anxious about the intensity of these friendships.

Parents may worry if their daughters seem to enjoy sports or hang out with a group of energetic boys. Girls may refuse to wear dresses and may strut around like a "good teammate." Boys may occasionally put tennis balls in their t-shirts and prance around in high heels to feel what it's like to be a girl. Parents may be worried about their children developing into homosexuals and may, unfortunately, encourage early dating and premature boy–girl activities so as to reassure themselves that their child is "normal." However, the wise parent will not get upset about such conduct. It is normal, and it will stop.

One way to explain homosexuality to your child is to say:

"When a baby is born, the first strong attachments that he or she makes is to the mother and father. Moms and dads are the ones who babies, toddlers, and preschool children really love and feel close to. As children start elementary school, their best friends of the same sex can become very important to them. When children get even older and become teenagers, they usually find someone of the opposite sex exciting and interesting and then they may feel they are in love with that person. This usually doesn't happen until adolescence. When people reach adulthood, they can feel so close to someone and so loving that they decide to share their life with each other, get married, and raise a family. Some people decide not to pick someone of the opposite sex but feel more close to their own sex. They may even live together like married people, but not biologically produce children together. These people are called gays, lesbians, or homosexuals."

During the school-age years, it is not necessary to explain to children how homosexuals engage in sexual activity. This information can be delayed until increased maturity, towards early or middle adolescence.

The goal is to communicate a developmental approach to sexual choice. This allows the child to feel that a close relationship with peers of the same sex is normal. The child will not have to rush into heterosexual activity before he or she is ready so as to feel sexually normal. It also gives children a way of thinking about the names they hear and banter about.

It is recognized that there are many complicated genetic, biological, developmental, and psychological explanations for homosexuality. Most school-age children can more easily understand that homosexuality as something an adult decides, not a condition that a school-age child needs to worry about. Parents need to be alert and open to any communications in which the child expresses anxiety and concerns about sexual identity.

Rape and Molestation

School-age children do not need to know about rape and the possibility of molestation. What they do need to know is that their bodies are very important, belong to them, and should be kept private. Parents should refrain from talking about their own negative sexual experiences. They should also consciously avoid exposing children to upsetting information presented by the media.

Unfortunately, children do need to be more adequately supervised today than in the past. The casual freedom once allowed school-age children is no longer the best option, especially in the larger cities. Adults should accompany children to public bathrooms, for example. Such supervision should be handled in a matter-of-fact manner. Don't go into gory explanations of what could happen when the child is alone. This is especially important in the case of girls. Because men are more often the perpetrators of rape, kidnapping, and molestation, communicating the details may cause girls to develop negative and frightening images about men.

It is also important to be alert if a child attempts to report a sexual experience. Dismissing or negating the child's statements may preclude important and necessary communication about molestation. Remember that the most frequent molester is a family member, close friend, or a relative. If they become discouraged or afraid, many children will never again bring up the subject. Parents may be the last to know about the child's encounters. This is especially true if they were not responsive or overreacted to initial attempts by the child to discuss the personal experience.

Chapter 6

Dealing with Upsets

Moms and dads who provide for their children the comfort of co-sleeping in the family bed, may help to ease the intensity of their night time fears. Or if the family does not co-sleep, a parent may come into the childrens' room to reassure them at night that they are safe. By eight or nine, most children opt to sleep in their own bed, even though they have co-slept with their parents since infancy.

While preschoolers directly express their feelings and thoughts, what the school-age child is feeling tends to be more of a puzzle to parents. By this age, children have learned which emotions are safe to reveal and which may bring shame, ridicule, criticism, and anger. School-age children are often ashamed that they are still experiencing many of the scary feelings they associate with their earlier years.

Separation Issues

School-age children still worry about separating from one or both parents. Loss of a mother or father is their strongest and most common worry. With mothers as well as fathers pursuing careers, school-age children may not have a parent available when they need them. They may worry, "*Who will pick me up from school? What will happen after school? Who will take care of me and protect me? Where are Mom and Dad when I'm not with them? When will I see them? Will they be late?*" All of these preoccupations add to the tensions, fears, and angers experienced by school-age children, but adults may not be aware of the children's concerns about separations and abandonments.

Children from dual-custody families experience many of these issues more intensely, having to cope with two sets of routines as well as recurring separation from one of the parents. This is not easy. Even though school-age children may appear, on the surface, to handle these breaks in routines, the disruptions are stressful.

Another source of tension and worry may be the presence of marital difficulties and fighting. Children often misinterpret what they see and hear. If parents express intense anger, the child may feel that the parents are headed for divorce. Parents often are not aware of how ferocious they become and how it provokes anxiety and concerns for children.

Often, children experience separation anxiety the first time they sleep over at a friend's house. It may also occur on the first days at a new school, a trip to stay with grandparents, or at the start of summer camp. It may be helpful to discuss the upcoming experiences and impending separation with your child. A visit to the new school or pictures of the camp facility or the grandparents' home can help relieve some anxieties. Going to a new school, camp, or after-school activity is easier if a friend is also attending the new program.

Tensions around separations can be reduced if time commitments are spelled out—when they are leaving and when and how they will return. Children need to be told who will be responsible for their well-being, meals, bedtime, and protection. Special expectations of behavior or special responsibilities should be clarified. Children also need to know how to contact their parents if they become upset or concerned. Make sure they have phone numbers and/or a pager number.

Sibling Rivalry and Teasing

Sibling rivalry, teasing, and aggressive responses are aggravating and irritating for parents and also create stress for the children. The school-age child has gained physical strength and has become more sophisticated about tormenting, teasing, and name-calling. Any meal, ride in the car, or evening in front of the television can turn into a battlefield when a child feels deprived or demands control. The issues may seem absurd and petty: *"He looked at me!" "She got the best spoon!" "He got the biggest piece of pie!"*

These skirmishes tap into intense feelings and doubts. Children are really worrying that their parents love the sibling more, that the sibling is better or smarter and gets all the attention. They are afraid that they may never get what they want and that they are not lovable. They may also crave warmth and appreciation from an older sibling. Getting the biggest piece of cake or picking the program becomes a symbol of how much they are loved and appreciated. Getting their way or winning means that they are loved the most and helps them deal with uncomfortable feelings of self-doubt. Children don't know how to ask for a smile, a hug, or a cheerful and heartfelt word of appreciation, but they do know how to fight and bicker over what is tangible in their world.

The children's attacks arouse anger in parents as well. Frustrated parents may increase the problem by name-calling, hitting, blaming, taking sides, punishing or comparing one child to the other. It is hard to step back, especially when the noise is escalating. But adding parental anger to the hot mix of feelings does not model constructive ways for the children to restore good feelings.

Parental presence is often needed to suspend the action and restore equilibrium so that solutions can be tried out. Start by acknowledging the strong feelings that are involved and by discovering what is upsetting each child. The next step could be to see if each child can state what the other wants or what is angering their sibling. Usually children end up expressing or defending their own positions and not appreciating other points of view. At some point, it is appropriate to step back and see if the children can find their own solutions. By doing this, you can avoid taking sides, being pulled into the conflict, or escalating the stress with your own rage and upset.

Parents are often unaware that each child has his or her own place in the family system. The oldest or only child often experiences more pressure from parents to achieve and perform.

Parents seem to communicate more anxiety to their first child. The firstborn may feel more rage at an intruding sibling than does a child born later, and may also experience more anxiety about taking new developmental steps, such as going off to camp, playing on a team, or starting a new class or activity. Such events may generate surprising amounts or tension and stress for the oldest school-age child.

School-age children often experience both depression and anger around a new baby or adorable toddler. The normal aggressive responses available to younger children—hitting, biting, pinching—are not age-appropriate for the older child, who often seems to have no easy outlet for this volcano of feelings. The jealous school-age child may seem irritable, demanding, moody, tearful, and bossy. A sympathetic statement may help, such as *"It is hard to be around such a cute baby. Everyone makes such a fuss over him."*

The younger child in the family may fear he or she cannot catch up with the older siblings and will never be able to do things as well or be as competent. The fact that the younger child has a model and a guide to follow and a clearer road ahead is a bigger support than the child is likely to realize at the time. The younger child may also be subject to hostility and brutality from older siblings. Conversely, some younger children spend a good deal of time and energy setting the scene to get older siblings into trouble with the parents.

One child can immobilize the whole family, depriving the others of time, attention, resources, and nurturing. Such children can create a tempest over nothing. The focus is always on them. In such cases, the other children are always seen as the good children, which creates its own heavy burden.

> Alice's brother was constantly generating trouble and had to be placed in a special school. The tuition drained the family's resources, and Alice was not able to have the clothes and other things her friends had. This added to her tensions at school and increased her anger at her brother and parents. She felt deprived and devalued even though she knew her socially acceptable behavior was appreciated.

Friends and Peers

Friends and peers are centrally important to school-age children. They are a source not only of pleasure, but also of stress and tension. It can be painful to lose a friend who moves away, to be rejected by a pal, left out of events, or teased by a bully, or to be jealous over close friendships. Parents often dismiss their children's intense and excruciating feelings about these social interactions, denying their force and the resulting stresses, rage, hurt, sadness, and depression.

It is necessary for parents to keep a casual eye on what is going on. Children victimize, bully, tease, and torment each other when adequate supervision is not supplied. When an alert adult is on the scene or in the background, it is easier for children to be accountable for their behavior.

Don't add to the tensions by being critical of your own child's behavior, constantly taking the visitor's side, and unwittingly depriving your child of acceptance and support. Talk over alternative techniques for getting along to help lessen peer tensions and to let your child know that you are interested and concerned.

Peer and neighborhood tensions are sometimes played out in the home, with other siblings being the victim of these tensions. Pets may also be on the receiving end. Much trouble can be avoided if you are alert to the social stresses your school-age children may be experiencing.

It is important not to overreact, but to be there and listen attentively. When seven-year-old John complained that no one wanted to sit with him on the school bus, his father strongly identified with the pain of rejection because he himself was once a victim. If John's father becomes too emotional, John may feel he has to calm and comfort his father. In the end, John may not receive the support he needs. Instead, John's father should say: *"Everyone likes to have a friend with whom to sit. If things do not improve next week, maybe we can arrange for someone to keep you company. In the meantime, try to think of a few things that you can do to encourage a friend to sit with you. One thing is certain; feelings do change, so in a few days your friends might want to ride the bus with you again."*

Neighborhood parks and other resources may provide alternative play and social activities. Perhaps the child can have experiences in another environment that balance out the negative ones at school.

Sometimes children can easily complain about their friends' rejections when the issue may be that they yearn for more parental involvement. It's hard for school-age children to say, "I wish my dad or mom was interested in my games and would spend more time with me." It may be easier to say, "No one calls me to play or come over to visit" than to ask for a loving. involved relationship with a parent.

Fear of Death and Disasters

Five- to eleven-year-olds worry about death—their own or the death of those close to them. Violence and death seem pervasive when the media revel in kidnappings, shootings, mass killings, rapes, plane crashes, earthquakes, floods, and fires. Parents unwittingly communicate danger in everyday conversations, not realizing that they are frightening their children. Bars on the windows and home burglar alarms reinforce the idea that home is not invincible or impregnable—and not completely safe. It can be difficult to give children appropriate information about realistic dangers in the world without burdening them with excessive worry, anxiety, and distrust.

When children become excessively frightened or worried, we may first notice that they are not as carefree, exploratory, or independent as they once were. Children as old as eleven may require someone to be with them even on simple expeditions, such as going upstairs, to the bathroom, or into the garage. Some children seem immobilized by these worries, yet tell no one what is bothering them. You may notice an increase in anxious or aggressive behavior, withdrawal, or depression without associating these behaviors with an unexpressed fear or worry. Children will often refuse to participate in a program, be reluctant to do a chore alone, or be unwilling to visit a friend, yet be unable to express their true concern or fear underlying their resistance.

A group of second-grade students reported that they feared the following:

- Getting lost; not being able to find their way home.
- Falling off bikes when they are learning to ride.
- Diving off different places; swimming across the deep end of the pool.
- Trying new things like water skiing, riding a horse.
- Kidnappers
- The dark
- Sleeping overnight at camp.

Children are sometimes frightened when they are away from their parents and their own home. Parents may never realize that the child's emotional upsets may be connected to these simple fears. Even at home school age children can experience night terrors. Comforting your child by snuggling close to them in bed can allow them to feel protected and help to lessen their bad feelings. When children cry out, a parent can either go to their room or invite them into their own bed until their fears are calmed.

Loss of a Pet

Children become very attached to their pets, and the loss of a pet is usually felt intensely. Even though the child may not be conscientious about tending to the pet's needs, there is often an intense emotional bond between the child and animal. If the pet dies or disappears or if the pet is given away, the child will generally feel this loss profoundly.

The death of a pet may be the school-age child's first experience with loss. The child not only misses a beloved creature that at times absorbed both loving and angry feelings, but the child additionally experiences shock. Children may feel responsible and guilty for the disappearance or death of their pet or that they are being punished for something they did, said, or failed to do.

Most importantly, the loss of a pet brings up anxieties about other feared separations, losses, and death. Separation anxiety may be dramatically heightened. Children may become more clingy, fearful, tearful, and resistant. Play and healthy exploration may decrease, and they may act withdrawn and experience sadness.

Children from single-parent families may worry about the safety of their sole parent. Often, these children are concerned about who will take care of them if something should happen to their only parent. Many children are fortunate to have grandparents who can play an important part in extending attachment relationships beyond the one-parent household. It may be helpful if your child can learn to know and develop a secure feeling with another adult or family member who could provide protection and nurturing in an emergency.

Parents need to tell a coherent story about the death of a pet and create some closure. Placing a marker in the backyard, writing a poem or story, drawing a picture, or displaying a photo may help with accepting the loss. Disposing of a dead pet by placing it in the trash may evoke frightening images concerning what happens to people when they die.

Bedwetting

Most parents and children are concerned about bedwetting during the elementary-school years. Not only does the release of urine at night cause extra laundry for the parent, but it also signals that an important developmental step associated with the preschool years has not been mastered.

When bedwetting continues, sometimes into adolescence, the child experiences a mixture of feelings, including shame and erotic pleasure, anger, and perhaps the need to feel like a much younger child. Bedwetting may be the only way a well-behaved child has of expressing rage, disappointment, or tension. Such children cannot verbalize their concerns, but at night they can let it all flow out. The child may feel the warmth of the urine as pleasurable and tension-reducing. The child who wets the bed is also more reluctant to sleep overnight at the homes of friends or relatives or leave home for camp. Bedwetting may be a way of staying close to the safe attachment figures and not risking separation.

Name-calling, humiliation, spanking, and scolding are seldom effective. Rewards are equally ineffective if the underlying stress or pleasure is not addressed. Children need to be told to talk about their angers and worries before they go to sleep.

Children may subconsciously feel that the only time they were loved and cared for was when they were diapered and could "go" whenever they experienced the urge. This may be the case when there has been death, divorce, or a new baby and the child is under new tension and stress. It is important to explore with the child the changes and stress that the family is going through. Ten minutes of talking before bedtime can preclude aggravation and hours of laundering linens. It may also help to awaken the child to empty his or her bladder before you go to sleep and once during the middle of the night.

School Pressures, After-School Commitments, and the Overscheduled Child

Living up to unrealistic parental expectations or difficult academic commitments can feel like a heavy burden to a school-age child. Homework can pile up and become overwhelming. Children may not feel good about themselves or valued unless they bring home top grades. Even in the best of schools, a child may feel disappointed or inadequate, experience a conflict with a teacher, or fail to obtain a much-desired part in a play, a position of leadership, or a place on the team. Parents may never realize that the child's emotional upset are connected to these daily school frustrations.

Tensions also may be generated during after-school activities. Parents usually assume that what children do after school is relaxing, fun, and tension free, not stress-producing. However, many after-school activities involve competitive, cooperative, and competent behavior. Baseball, scouting, dance, gymnastics, religious instruction, and music lessons can be complicated. There are wins and losses, evaluations, and the stresses and strains of performances. For example, eight-year-old Andrew was mad all week because he sat on the bench during an important soccer game. William worried a lot because he didn't practice the piano as much as he was supposed to, and he was afraid that his teacher would scold him.

It is important to step back and look at whether your child has enough stimulation and scheduling after school, or if there is too much structure, with not enough free time. Most children need free time to help restore equilibrium. They need to play and interact without formal structure. They must have adequate time to solve interpersonal problems on their own and to play or perform well or badly without an adult keeping score or watching. One child commented, *"My Mom and Dad are grouchy when I don't get a hit at Little League."* Unwittingly, a parent may add pressure. forgetting that this should be a time for the child to play, enjoy, relax, and unwind. Today, too many children are pressured into participating in a myriad of after school programs. Parents may well ask themselves: *"Have I unwittingly-overscheduled and stressed my child?*

The Underscheduled Child

At the other end of the spectrum, many children are not involved in any formal after-school activities. For these children, television and video may be a seductive and addictive alternative to active play and competence-building, robbing them of the time to play with other children and to tap into their own resources for pleasure and amusement.

The school years are a fertile time of practice and mastery in which children learn to pursue and organize projects, collections, and hobbies; develop physical skills and coordination; and explore books, music, and instruments. If all after-school hours are spent in front of the television or computer screen, important developmental tasks are not mastered.

Children who spend much of their free time passively watching aggressive and violent behavior, observing chasing, fighting, killing, shooting, swearing, and anger, may build up a reservoir of tension and hostility. Unexpressed in active play, the tension may erupt later in home and school behavior. There may be increased fighting among siblings, talking back rudely, or problems going to sleep. It is a difficult but a vital parental task to balance the child's need for stimulation, exercise, mastery, and competence against the need to relax, unwind, daydream, and restore equilibrium.

The Aggressive or Shy Child

Children who are either extremely aggressive or shy and withdrawn are usually dealing with many of the upsets, concerns, and anxieties that have just been discussed. Often children are aggressive in their own homes, but behave in a controlled way at school or in neighborhood play. Some children are outgoing or even aggressive at home, but shy and withdrawn in social situations. The extremely aggressive child is not usually liked, and peers also often reject the extremely shy child as well. Both kinds of behavior may be of concern to parents and teachers.

Shyness and aggression may be outcomes of problems within the family home. It is important to determine how much hitting and physical punishment is taking place in the home and whether the child is seeing physical fighting and abuse between the parents. Such children may be struggling with fears of separation and abandonment. They may be unable to express their worries, but by acting aggressively, they discharge the tension and obtain a response from the adults around them. Or they may get attention from adults by acting timid, clingy, and fearful. Even though the response from adults may be negative, the child does not feel alone or abandoned.

At a point when children are acting appropriately and when there is good rapport, explore the reasons for the extremes in behavior. Help children acknowledge that negative feelings may be causing their aggressive or shy behavior. Perhaps they are jealous of siblings or friends, feel unloved and neglected, worry that they are not learning to read or function adequately at school, sad that their grandfather died, mad that they are always picked last when teams are formed, or disappointed that a vacation was cancelled because of lack of funds.

It is important to help children describe these worries. They need to acknowledge anger, disappointment, jealousy, envy, inadequacy, and fear. They need to know that it is acceptable to feel these feelings, but that it is not acceptable to express them in inappropriate ways. These children also need to be reassured that nothing bad will happen to them when they express their emotions at an appropriate time and place. Usually a shy child is so afraid of their anger at the parent that they need to stay close to see that their angry feelings will not cause something dreadful to happen. Some shy and withdrawn children are as angry as are belligerent, aggressive children.

Suggesting constructive ways of expressing their feelings and suggesting alternative behaviors may help children learn new scripts and behave more appropriately. Children may be encouraged to talk about whom they would like to slug, fantasize about disasters befalling their enemies. or draw pictures expressing their hostile feelings. Children can even construct targets of the troublesome people in their lives and throw balls or darts at them.

Set up times to practice some new behaviors. Help your child practice some sentences to facilitate social interaction, including words to use when someone says hello and how to ask a friend to play. Also, address the problems of inadequacy experienced by the child. For example, if your child is concerned about difficulty in reading or sports, address those problems with tutors or extra practice.

Chapter 7

Dealing with Discipline

The preschool and early school-age years are critical in determining whether children will grow up to be responsible adults. Investing the time and energy necessary for teaching them disciplined behavior is like saving for the rainy day of adolescence. Parents have less control over their adolescents than over their school age children, who still need, respect and at times even enjoy their parents' companionship.

Parents seldom think about discipline when children are functioning well, handling their responsibilities, and getting along with friends, siblings, and adults. Discipline mostly comes to mind when the children are fighting or refusing to study, brush their teeth, take a shower, or do homework—and when unattended bicycles are stolen, rooms resemble the aftermath of earthquakes, or children utter curses and invectives, embarrassing the family. It is hard to step back and calmly and objectively assess such conduct. Instead, most parents discharge their anger and respond punitively and impulsively.

There are better ways to handle such situations. One alternative is to remove children who are misbehaving from the scene for a five or ten minutes by sending them to their rooms to settle down. Be careful not to make idle threats. Design effective consequences for undisciplined behavior. And make sure that your responses are really effective. Such common punishments as spankings, depriving children of treats, "grounding" them, and even sending them to their rooms do not always work as expected.

Think about possible underlying causes of children's behavior. Are the children dealing with underlying stress? Do they know clearly and specifically what you expect of them? Explore the part each parent plays in modeling negative behavior for the children. Have you been late, neglected your own chores, or bickered with your spouse? Do you respond in a verbally abusive manner, with name-calling, branding, and so on?

The key to creating harmony and discipline is to plan the time and save the emotional energy to address these issue. The goal is to treat negative behavior as a problem to be analyzed and solutions to be explored and addressed. Then make the children accountable for the behavior you expect.

It is difficult to separate this process of positive teaching from the immediate irritation caused by the offending behavior. It is as difficult to control an explosive reaction as it is to plan quiet time to talk about what is upsetting you. When children are out of control and misbehaving, the most effective approach is to say little and, when possible, to shift away from the social environment and help them collect and restore themselves.

- Remove the child to a neutral location, such as the child's room or another part of the house.
- If the difficulty arises outside of the home, send the child back into the house.
- If the misbehavior occurs at a restaurant or on an outing, take the child to the car or, in extreme cases, drive home quietly and grimly, which can communicate to the child that the behavior is not acceptable and that alternative behavior must be looked into.

Usually, separating an out-of-control child from the social situation allows the child the opportunity to restore and regulate himself or herself.

Although scheduling time to discuss the behavior calmly may take effort and creative planning, in the long run it saves future expenditures of emotional energy and time. When you create an atmosphere characterized by rapport, harmony, and loving feelings, your children will hear what you are saying and will feel that you are listening to them.

Teaching does not end with the initial discussion of the

problem. Give the child an opportunity to succeed or fail, and then evaluate the child's progress at a later time. This is similar to what goes on in school, where children are expected to learn age-appropriate ideas, concepts, and skills, are given an opportunity to practice them, and are later tested to see how much they have learned.

It would be wonderful if you could find the perfect threat, punishment, or magic spell to change behavior. Sometimes punitive methods do work and changes do result. However, in the process the child may develop more anger, stress, and tension, which later may be discharged in negative behaviors. The parent is also modeling punitive ways of dealing with irritation, which in turn teaches the child to respond in an aggressive way as well.

Expect age-appropriate behavior from children. Let children know what changes in behavior you expect.

"Next time you are out riding your bike, you need to check your watch to make sure that you arrive home when expected."

"Tomorrow you can start your homework before dinner time, instead of later, when you are tired. After two weeks, let's see if this works better for you."

"Saturday night, when we have company, you can talk to the guests when they first arrive, but we expect you to read or play in your room after the adults sit down for dinner."

Acknowledge that you will try to improve the situation as well.

"It might make it easier if I stayed in your room while you start your homework or begin your chores."

"I am going to try not to scream so much, and maybe you can try not to pester and tease your baby sister and to stop when she doesn't like it any more."

"Maybe we can trade off chores next week. I can do some of yours, and you can do some of mine."

"I don't mind your complaining. Even I complain. But we all must do the things that are expected of us."

When parents focus only on what annoys or enrages them, children may feel that they have failed their parents and are incompetent and inadequate. By providing second chances and focusing on the future, you make it possible for them to imagine pleasing you and successfully achieving acceptable behavior. In other words, stressing what children can do, rather than what they haven't done, may be an important key to establishing discipline with self-esteem.

Threats

How easy it is to make a threat!

"If you don't get your clothes on, I'm leaving without you!"

"If you don't pick up your toys, you won't get a birthday present."

"If you don't stop bothering your baby sister, you'll have to stay in your room the rest of the day."

What makes threatening so difficult is the necessity of following through with the threat. The need to follow through makes it feel like the parent is the one being disciplined. If you do not follow through, the child learns that you say things you don't mean. The child's trust in you is weakened. The child may feel less certain about the outcome.

A major problem with idle threats is that children become concerned with what will happen to them rather than on focusing on the expected behavior. It also suggests that they can chose to obey or chance the threatened consequences. It is dangerous to leave a young child alone in the house. It is difficult to withhold presents on Christmas morning or to supervise children so that they stay in their rooms for hours.

Instead of making threats, tell the child what is expected and what the consequences of not obeying will be.

"It's time to put your clothes on. If you're not done by the time we leave, you can finish dressing in the car."

"It's pick up time. When your games and equipment are on the shelf and clothes are in the closet, you'll be ready to play outside."

"You and your brother are having a hard time right now. If you continue to fight, I've decided that you should play separately for about ten minutes, and after that you can try to play together again."

Consequences should occur immediately and be limited in duration; ten minutes alone in a room is usually sufficient to make the point. A longer time may generate additional anger, which adds to the child's resistance and rebelliousness. Threatening punishment at a distant time—e.g., Christmas or birthday—is of limited value because it necessitate following through at a time that has no connection to the event at hand.

Parents under stress and tension often threaten in ways that leave lasting emotional effects and scars:

"I can't take this anymore – I'm leaving for good."

"You're driving me crazy—I'll end up in a hospital."

"You're impossible. You'll have to go to a foster home."

Needless to say, these spontaneous expressions of anger, impotence, and abandonment are better unexpressed. They may cause vulnerable children to experience anxiety for many years, never really knowing when the axe will fall and the parent will follow through and leave or send them away.

Designing Effective Consequences

Designing effective consequences is a difficult as well as challenging aspect of being a parent. When consequences are successfully designed and executed, parents and children are satisfied, the air is cleared, and self-esteem is strengthened. For example, separating children whose play has gotten out of hand will enable the children to restore themselves. Children who have spilled milk can be actively involved in the cleanup process, helping you bring things back to normal. When a window is broken, the child can go with you to the hardware store and watch you make the repairs. If a book is torn, the child can help tape or repair it.

A creative consequence tends to be an effective learning

experience. A trip to the store to replace a damaged item, for example, teaches accountability. Sometimes a clear expression of anger, exasperation, or disappointment can be enough of a consequence to change future behavior. *"When you do that to the dog, it makes me angry! I want you to treat her more gently."*

Rewards

Ultimately, children who learn appropriate behavior and who function effectively in a disciplined way feel a sense of well-being, pleasure, and pride. Children do not necessarily need either punishment or rewards to learn what is expected of them. Parental pleasure, shown in moderation, helps a child's growing self-confidence. Accomplishing developmentally appropriate tasks also creates ego satisfaction. Unrelated external rewards in the form of bribes may not be necessary and may lead to manipulative behavior: *"I'll obey you only if you give me..."*

When rewards are given, children may focus mainly on the rewards, diminishing the intrinsic satisfaction of appropriate behavior. Your smiling presence quietly acknowledges the child's accomplishment. *"I'll bet you feel good about that."* is a responsive comment, and it is a better response than routinely handing the child a reward in the form of money, a present, or food. When a child is frequently rewarded with presents, stars, or privileges, there is a danger that the reward, not the change in behavior, will become the focus.

However, it is appropriate to give a child an occasional treat or special present. Doing so can be nurturing for all concerned. It is also appropriate to say, *"If it will help you get started cleaning up your room, let's begin by fixing something good to eat."*

Punishments

When children bombard us with negative and inappropriate behavior, we tend to get angry and frustrated. Our immediate response may be to punish—to deliver pain to—them. Both revenge and retribution may be involved. This may especially true for parents who were punished and given pain by their own parents; people tend to "repeat the script."

Depriving children of favorite objects, food, television, or outings makes the parent feel better temporally, but it tends to build up angry feelings in the child. These in turn inspire further negative and oppositional reactions. Negative behavior that stems from punishment by the parents evokes further punishment, so that a minor infraction can quickly spiral into a major event.

> Janet was teasing her younger brother. He was screaming because he wanted a bigger piece of clay. Janet's mother stormed into the room and told Janet to go to bed early. Janet threw her clay, and it hit her mother in the neck. Further enraged, the mother sent Janet to her room and shouted, *"No dinner for you!"* Once in her room, Janet threw her books around, and soon her room was a disaster. Her mother then told her she couldn't watch television for a week. A minor disciplinary problem had escalated into a major felony.

Many adults recall their parents' anger and punishments with fear and resentment. These are sometimes the only clear memories of childhood that adults have. If you can imagine being struck and screamed at by a twenty-foot giant who has complete power over your life, you can begin to understand how it is for a child to be confronted by an enraged parent who is meting out punishment. Angry parents get translated into wild animals, giants, ogres, and scary monsters in children's dreams. A child may be unable to acknowledge being terrified by mother and father, but he or she can easily state the fear of a monster or fantasy character.

Punishment may help a parent reduce his or her own angry feelings and frustrations. However, the biggest disadvantage in using punishment to change behavior is that it leads to an increase in the child's angry feelings, which fuels more oppositional and aggressive behavior.

Spanking and Corporeal Punishment

Most children are spanked once in a while. Spanking

communicates that the parent is upset and angry and is resorting to superior size and strength to influence the child's behavior. Unfortunately, spanking teaches children that hitting another person is acceptable. The ultimate irony is that children are often hit as punishment for such aggressive behavior as hitting, kicking, biting, and spitting.

In our culture, there are mixed and contradictory messages about violence and corporeal punishment. "Spare the rod, spoil the child" is a well-known maxim that justifies spanking. Parents may feel that they are discharging their duty by intervening in this way.

When the parent hurts the child and then says, *"This hurts me more than it hurts you,"* the child receives a confusing message. It is impossible for the child to understand that the parent feels pain when the child is being spanked. It would be more honest and more believable for the parent to say, *"I am furious and angry with you, and I am going to hurt you to teach you a lesson. I don't know what else to do."* Unfortunately, the lesson the child learns is that it's okay to hit a smaller person. It often helps for the parent to acknowledge his or her loss of control and to tell the child, *"I regret my behavior and will try to handle my anger differently."*

Parents who do not spank their children regularly may feel that spanking is justifiable when a child runs into the street. It's hard for a parent not to respond impulsively. However, this is not the best way to teach safety. The idea is not for the child to remember the anger and fear associated with a spanking, but rather to learn the rules of crossing the street. At a neutral time, tell the child, *"You need to look both ways and always walk. Never run. Drivers of cars can see you more easily when you walk slowly and do not ever run. Also you can watch for cars approaching if you are walking."* Learning about street safety requires many repetitions and much practice. It is an important part of the parent's responsibility.

Parents sometimes report that spanking appears to work and that the child is subdued and behaves in a more acceptable fashion. Of course, the same is true when parents threaten the child with fearful images—police, bogeyman, witches.

There is no doubt that every parent can be driven wild with irritation and rage at times. But there are many reasons to develop alternatives to spanking and hitting. Parents who become child abusers were themselves beaten and abused as children. Most people who commit violent crimes were disciplined as children with abusive physical punishment.

Rather than punish, anticipate the problem, verbally communicate alternative behaviors, allow the child a practice run, and give the child on-the-spot feedback about what needs further practice. Then compliment or praise what the child did well.

Patience

"I try to be patient, but sometimes I just explode," a mother complained. Good parents are often described as being patient. However, there is a distinction between the patience involved in giving a child sufficient time and space to function at an age-appropriate pace, and the patience involved in allowing the child to continue to act contrary to what is appropriate or acceptable.

In the latter case, allowing the child to operate in opposition to clearly expressed expectations creates growing tensions for both adult and child. Aware that he or she is pushing the limit, the child does not relax and enjoy the activity. The child has one eye on the parent and one hand into mischief—hardly a stress-free situation. The mother also has one eye on the child, wondering what to do and when. *"If I am patient, maybe he'll stop."*

By not intervening immediately, the parent communicates a double message. When the parent does react, pent up anger is expressed. Unfortunately, responding promptly to mischief often means interrupting your own activity. But prompt intervention defines the child's limits clearly and respectfully. When you act promptly, both you and the child can remain in better control.

Power Struggles

"You will!" "I won't!"

"You must." "You can't make me."

"You can't do that." "I'm doing it anyway."

As children's sense of themselves grow and their power develops, they are more likely to take strong positions. They are more likely to respond with a firm *"No!"* and persistent opposition. It may be a sign of children's health and strength that they are able to verbalize what they want and what they believe.

These signs of individuality and conviction need to be respected and appreciated. Generally, when parents want children to respond quickly and efficiently, it is usually to satisfy themselves. Often they are caught up in their own pressing needs and are confident of their own wisdom. They do not pay attention to the child's agenda. By allowing children to participate, you are helping build their self-esteem.

Finding creative techniques to resolve power struggles is very important. Face-saving delays may help: *"I see it is too hard right now for you to do this. In ten minutes, it will be easier for you."* Or, *"I see you want to wear your new party dress to school. The rule about party clothes is that they are for parties and special times. But let's say you can wear it to school, and once you are there, change into some other, more comfortable clothes."*

Sometimes, power struggles have less to do with the issue at hand, and more to do with underlying fatigue, frustration, and tension. For example, a nine-year-old is feeling abandoned by his mother because she is overwhelmed and preoccupied with a new job. This child may create power struggles to capture his mother's time and energy. If a child does not receive sufficient warm and caring attention, the danger is that the child will settle for an angry interchange or a fight rather than no contact at all.

At times it is important for the child's growing self-esteem and self-worth to negotiate, to listen to what he or she has to say, and to allow the child appropriate expression of feelings. Listening and negotiation will help create a win-win situation for both you and child. You have a great deal of control in these situations, defining the limits and creating ways the child can gain a point and "win."

> Willie, age eight, did not want to take a much-needed bath. He screamed, *"I won't. I won't."* He wanted to continue playing his computer game. His father said, *"Willie, I see that you don't want to take your bath now. In a few minutes, I will bring you a wash cloth and a towel so you can clean yourself and get ready for dinner. Meanwhile, you can play with your game some more today. However, tomorrow, remember to take an early bath and remember that there will be no protesting."* The next day, Willie took his bath without a fuss.

This solution allows both child and parent to win. Of course, Willie's father could have lifted him bodily and plunked him, kicking and screaming, into the tub. However, this consumes much more negative physical and emotional energy from both parent and child. Creating compromises teaches flexibility.

When power struggles are a result of underlying distress, winning will not bring satisfaction to the child. For example:

> Sarah's mother is preoccupied with a sick infant and has little time for Sarah. In response, Sarah refuses to eat, resulting in mealtime power struggles. Sarah's mother can say, *"Sarah, I know how hard it is for you when I am always with your baby brother who is sick. So from now on we are going to schedule some special time together."*

In this case, finding time to be with her child to play cards, talk, walk, take a trip to the mall, read a story, or just quietly watch television was effective in diminishing the frequency and intensity of family wars.

Part II
Special Situations

Chapter 8

When Both Parents Work

It has become common for mothers as well as fathers to be employed outside the home. There are many reasons women join the workforce. The high cost of living often demands a second income. Divorce catapults women into supporting single-parent homes. Women who are trained and skilled want to utilize their training and keep up with their professional and business roles. Some women yearn for increased stimulation outside the household arena. Some volunteer in hospitals, schools, and other organizations, which may absorb time and energy similar to regular paying jobs.

School-age children may be pleased that their mothers are working and may benefit from their work experience. Children may enjoy some of the economic benefits of a second income. They may live in a larger home and in a safer neighborhood. Mothers who work model commitment to something enjoyable or useful. They bring ideas, information, and stimulation to discussions at home. They may not be dependent on their children's success in school and after-school activities for their only satisfactions. Mothers who work may not be as intrusive as those who stay home. Their identities as women are more than just Mom. And they may be happier and less depressed; even though they are tired at the end of the day, they are glad to be with their children.

The implications of having both parents work outside of the home are perhaps not as profound for school-age children as for infants, toddlers, or preschoolers. The absence of parents during the day deprives the very young child of important contact with the primary caregiver. As children grow older and develop a sense of time, they are able to predict and understand a regular routine of coming and going. For the school-age child, it is somewhat less stressful for the parents to be away at work.

After-School Child Care

School-age children need to feel cared for and protected, valued and respected. They need parents to be there for them. It is true that they do not need their mothers to stay at home during the school day, but they may need an adult to supervise and care for them when they return from school. The four to six hours from school dismissal to the time parents return are a large percentage of a child's day. It is the parent's responsibility to provide a secure, protected, and stimulating environment during the after-school hours.

> Jeremy, age eight, returns home from school, to an empty house. His parents are divorced, and his mother usually returns from work at 7 p.m. Dinner is not ready until almost 8 o'clock, and there is still homework to do. Mom walks in asking Jeremy what he has done around the house. She is tired and frazzled, and she becomes enraged when she thinks all he has done is watch television. Jeremy is both upset at having to wait so long for his mother and mad at her for expecting him to do what he thinks she should do. He doesn't feel important or like a child. He calls himself *"a lonely slave."*

> Jane, age nine, on the other hand, goes to a community center where she can play outside and participate in crafts. As times she wishes she could fool around at home, but basically she feels cared for and has play

experience appropriate for a nine-year-old. She is glad to see her parents when they pick her up at 6:30.

Ten-year-old Steven's mother has arranged for him to go to a neighbor's house after school. Steven checks in with Mrs. Gardner, has a snack, plays a little out front, or watches television. He watches Mrs. Gardner's preschool child while she makes dinner. He wishes his mother was home, but he also feels that his mother cares enough about him to pay for these arrangements.

John, age ten, is picked up from school each day by Michael, a high-school student, who drives him home. They sometimes stop at a fast-food restaurant or play ball in the park. Other times, they come directly home. John is glad there is somebody in the house with him because he worries a lot about burglars and criminals. There are few neighbors or other children at home in his quiet neighborhood, and he is glad to have Michael's companionship.

Many more preschools are providing after-school care. Slowly, elementary schools, neighborhood centers, and religious organizations are recognizing that children need adult supervision during these after-school hours. More schools and community centers are making their facilities available to children of working parents.

Not all after-school programs are ideal. Some hire inadequate adult helpers who are mean, negligent, or abusive. The programs may be overcrowded or have inadequate equipment and facilities. They may function without the watchful eye of a concerned working parent or supervisory personnel.

Fortunately, school-age children have the ability to communicate their complaints and distress. It is important to respectfully listen to children's reports, to not discount their complaints, and to address the problems they bring up. This may feel like an added burden to a parent who is having a hard enough time working and running a home. However, because abuses can take place after school, children need to feel that their parents will respond and look into the after-school care situation. Often, abuses occur because the adults in the program (or the baby sitter) know that the parents are trapped at work and won't drop in casually to observe what is going on. Basically, your children are the best judge of what kind of after-school care functions well for them, so it is important to take their complaints seriously and then respond.

Sick Children and Working Parents

Conflict also arises when children become ill. It may be easier to send them to school than to take time off work to take care of them. It is important to provide care for a sick child. When a child is very sick, parental presence is most comforting. As the child convalesces, other custodial care can be provided.

When the child feels vulnerable and the parent is not there for comfort, the child may feel devalued, unimportant, and upset. He or she may feel anger at the parent. At such times, having a parent present is experienced as an act of love. Telling the child that you love him or her, then leaving for work sends a mixed message, and the child may feel that the parent is more interested in working than in the child's feelings or well being.

It is important to give children attention and affection at times other than when they are ill. Children who receive their parents' attention only during an illness or accident may get sick in order to feel that they are cared for and loved. The secondary satisfaction from parental presence and contact may be far greater than the discomfort of the illness itself.

Working Parents and the Development of Moral Values

Working parents are at a disadvantage when it comes to helping children with their developing consciences and value systems. Because children are away from the parents such a large part of their day, there is less opportunity for parents to confront children if they are lying, stealing, or acting in an abusive and antisocial way. Children need adult concern and response to help them differentiate right from wrong and acceptable behavior from unacceptable behavior. It takes an adult who is motivated to create a responsible person. Such motivation is rarely found in hired help or in the casual custodial person often acting as baby sitter to the school-age child.

Many parents may not understand or feel the need to supervise the development of their children's behavior, values of honesty, truthfulness, accountability and responsibility. But, socially acceptable versions of these values may be essential for children to feel good about themselves and to be productive in their community. Parents who fail to do this wonder why their children are misbehaving or getting into trouble. The answer may be directly related to the parents' lack of contact, concern, and relationship with their children.

During the school-age years, parents must assume the responsibility for teaching, supervising, and communicating expected social behavior and the need for accountability. Children cannot be relied on to learn civility, good manners, honesty, generosity, fairness, or good work habits from the air, from casual caregivers, or from parents who are not there. Nor are such essential values inherited; there is no morality "gene". These values come from parental teaching as well as from the child's unconscious identification with the parent's behavior. If neither parent is physically or verbally present for most of the day, the child is deprived of the opportunity to receive the parental teachings and transmission of moral values.

In the past, children learned these things from their mothers, since working fathers were often away from the family for a good part of the day. Today many mothers are also removed from the child's world. When a mother returns from work, she is often tired, irritable, and rushed. She doesn't relate to the child in a relaxed, warm, and carefree way—the way in which the best teaching and learning take place. When parents are tired and irritable, children often respond in an oppositional, negative way and are deaf to lectures about social behavior and responsibilities. Furthermore, when both parents work outside the home, they are absent a significant part of the child's life. It is no small wonder that there is little time to inculcate values.

It may take creative planning to find a time when tempers are calm and the child seems receptive to the discussion of values and socially acceptable behavior. It may also require revision of family financial priorities so that one parent can be at home with the children. This is not to say that every child can have a parent at home after school. Some parents do not have a choice. Many single and married women must work a forty-hour week to be able to put food on the table. The welfare system now expects women to bring home a paycheck, rather than accept a stipend from the government.

If it is not possible for a parent to be at home with the children, the next best thing is to provide some form of adult supervision. Older school-age children may declare that they need no one to look after them and that they don't want to be treated like babies. However, when parents insist and arrange for companionship in spite of their protests, the children often feel more valued. Children may feel freer to study and concentrate on homework when they do not have to be responsible for themselves and an empty house.

The telephone can also serve as a way of maintaining contact as and showing care and concern to the child. Having the child check in with the working parent regularly or having the parent call home communicates the parent's interest and involvement.

Allowing children to pay visits to the job site helps them have a clearer understanding of what their parents are doing while at work. Meeting parents' coworkers also increases children's ability to imagine their parents' working environments. This will allow children to understand more about their parents' lives and feel more a part of them. It will keep children from fantasizing that their parents are out having a great time while they are bored and lonely waiting for their parents to return home.

Work Alternatives

More and more working men and women are exploring alternatives to working full time outside of the home. Working from the home and working part time can relieve the stress of commuting and the expense of transportation and a more costly wardrobe. Having a parent working at home decreases the anxiety the child may experience when separated from the mother or father. It may also model, in a more direct way, the parent's commitment to work. It may facilitate the teaching and transmission of basic moral values. It allows parents to be more flexible in the after-school hours when the child needs supervision. Parents are more available when the child becomes ill. Of course, there may be some frustrations and difficulty using the home as a work place, but it may provide an emotionally healthier and more flexible environment for both parent and child during the crucial years of child rearing.

The computer, fax machine, and telephone can be important aids in using the home as a workplace. Initially, it may be difficult to work at home. Starting a new business or professional practice is stressful, especially if income is uncertain. It helps to have one parent earning a regular outside income to tide the family over during the initial phases of building a home-based business or profession.

Job sharing can also be an alternative. If the mother works in the morning and another person works the afternoon, the mother will be able to spend time with her children after school.

Parents can work six-hour days instead of the usual eight-hour days. Nurses and hospital personnel can work a shift that ends at three, coinciding with children's return from school. Some hospital personnel and nurses work a twelve-hour day, freeing them up for four days of the week to be home with their families. Parents can explore the use of work shifts to provide adequate adult supervision and contact with their children during the crucial after-school hours.

More fathers are opting to act as primary caregivers and work at home, while their wives have jobs that provide insurance coverage and other benefits. There are approximately two million stay-at-home fathers in the United States. Fathers can provide excellent supervision and can take over many household responsibilities effectively. Children can benefit from more intimate daily contact with not just their mothers but also their fathers as well.

In any case, creative planning by working parents can allow them to be more available to their children. One parent may be able to arrange to be home with the children during the important after-school hours. A parental presence may be important to create an atmosphere of security and affection as well as to facilitate the child's involvement in the arts, music, or sports.

Chapter 9

Adoption

Adoption allows parents who are unable to produce their own biological baby to raise a child born from another woman. There are many different reasons to adopt. The process is varied as well. A family may work with a traditional adoption agency or travel to a foreign country to bring a baby into their life. A lawyer can arrange an individual adoption between a pregnant woman and someone who longs to raise a child.

In some cases, no information about the parents is available for the adoptive parent. In contrast, open adoptions provide a freer exchange of information about the infant's biological, genetic, and social background, and the adoptive parent may actually participate in the child's birth.

Some babies enter their new family hours after they are born; some arrive months later; and some years later. Some childless couples adopt more than one infant, and some adopted children become part of families with one or more siblings who may also be adopted or biologically related. More and more older single women are adopting babies, and gay couples are reaching out to create families.

The process is complicated, and it is not without problems. But it has the potential to be a rewarding and wonderful life experience for parents and children.

Talking to Your Child about Adoption

Even though the adoption process may have taken place before your child was born, it is during the years from five to eleven that the developing child most easily understands the concept of adoption. You can begin to use the word *adoption* when your child is between three and five years of age. While holding your young child in a relaxed, loving manner, show the preschooler pictures that were taken when you first laid eyes on him or her. Talk about your delight at your first meeting, and explain where the baby slept, what he or she drank or ate, and how he or she was soothed. Also include a story about a trip to your family's home, or about the special blanket or stuffed animal you carried.

In some cases, the young child may actually know the birth mother or know the birth mother's name and has a picture or her. However, the idea that a child is born from another mother is hard for a three- or four-year-old to understand. The concept of adoption may be better communicated after the child feels well-bonded to you and has worked through the intense separation issues that are normal in the first three to four years.

You may not be able to control how and when your child first hears the word *adoption*. You may want to communicate the idea of adoption in the most understandable and positive way before an older child, friend, or neighbor uses the word in an unpredictable context. You need to keep in mind how easy it is for a preschooler to misunderstand what you are saying. When you tell your young child that he or she was "chosen" or "selected," the child may take your words to mean that he or she was "stolen from" or "thrown away by" the real mother or was found somewhere by the new parents.

A preschool child does not understand or appreciate economic pressures, immaturity, or the lack of an intact family as reasons for giving a baby up for adoption. Most young children—whether adopted or biological—fear that their mother and father may disappear or may not return to them. Telling a young child about adoption in great detail can increase this worry and dramatically reinforce the painful notion that mothers and their babies can be permanently separated.

You may have brought up the subject of adoption early because of your own anxiety to get the truth out and feel reassured that your child will continue to love you. In such a case, it is best to delay discussion of the reasons and meaning of *adoption* until the child is older. Instead, use the word adoption in a matter-of-fact way, providing a simple explanation: "Many children are adopted, and many are not. We are your parents because we take care of you, we protect you, we teach you, and we have fun together."

One of the values of waiting until children are in the school-age years to explore the concept of adoption more fully is that children will be better able to understand the legal process involved. The school-age child does understand something about rules and laws in everyday life. The idea that a baby is legally adopted may give the child a feeling of permanence. The question often arises, "Can my biological parents take me back?" Explaining that the adoptive parents went through a court procedure and have been officially declared the legal parents may help diffuse some of the worry. All of the legalities may not be completely appreciated until the child reaches adolescence.

Some adopted children may be curious about their biological parents, and other may not be able to or want to talk about it at all. If the child asks and you have information about the birth parents, tell your child in a matter-of-fact way. However, children will create their own fantasies about their biological parents, and it is extremely important to listen to these fantasies. One child fantasized that his adoptive mother's counselor was his "real" mother because his mother so often explained that Dr. Ellen helped her raise him so well. He reasoned that if she was so interested in helping his mother be a good parent, maybe she was the one who gave birth to him.

Parents are often worried that children will want to leave and move back with their biological parents. At times, children may even threaten to do so. However, most children feel a strong attachment to the parents who raised them and are basically terrified of any kind of drastic change. Even biological children will threaten to run away to live with "a good mother and father" during stressful moments. Even birth parents sometimes wish that their child would "vanish or go live in another household." These flashes of rejection may produce guilt. But the impulse to "get out of my life" seldom lasts.

Because of their own negative feelings, parents may worry that their adopted child wants to leave home and move back with the biological parents. It is important for parents to face up to their own ambivalent feelings and accept the fact that children also have these feelings. A child is likely to be less inhibited than the parent about expressing mixed feelings, resulting in the escalation of tension with the adoptive family.

When children are angry and threaten to move back with their "real" parents, adoptive parents can respond, *"I feel you are really mad at me right now and going to another home might seem like a good idea. When your angry feelings leave, maybe we can talk about how to make life better for you here."* Don't give in to the tendency to say *"Go already! I'll help you pack your bags!"* This would make the child feel less wanted and more alone with his or her anger. Fortunately, angry feelings usually do not last very long.

Parents of adopted children should be prepared for stormier times during adolescence. Many adolescent adopted children become interested in their biological and genetic beginnings. They are curious about the people who look like them. They are also increasingly involved with sexual feelings and affectionate relationships. It is common for some adopted children to believe that their biological parents were irresponsible, sexually and in other ways: *"Why else was I conceived. and why else weren't they in a position to take care of me if they were really responsible?"* The adopted child is often in conflict during adolescence, identifying with the more socially acceptable adopted family they live with, and the fantasy parents they may think were in "plenty of trouble" or were "just having a ball when they were young teenagers." So the adoptive parents need to develop a positive, loving relationship in the early school-age years in order to have a solid foundation for the stormy years ahead.

Some adopted children act irresponsibly as a way to punish parents who are not nurturing toward them.

Jennifer a, thirteen-year-old said, *"I started drinking so I could feel free to confront my mom who was constantly putting pressure on me. I thought my 'real mom' was so brave to carry me inside her, to go through labor and give birth to me. She was a heroic person in my eyes."*

Both adoptive parents and adopted children need to face the sadness of not having a biological connection with one another. Even though parents feel fortunate in adopting a child, and the adopted child is fortunate to be placed in a caring family, the underlying emotions about the loss of the biological connection are profound. The tendency is to try to make an adopted child feel lucky and special, thereby hoping to deflect the disappointment that the child is not living with his or her biological mother. However, it is important not to deny the child the experience of sadness, anger, or disappointment. Sad feelings must be faced and talked about before the child can work through the stress and mourn the loss of his or her biological beginnings.

It is important for parents to tell the child about their longing to have a baby and their disappointment that they couldn't start one or carry one to term. The mother can further communicate that she wished the adopted child had grown inside of her and had been born from her. Parents can further add that not only were they sad when they couldn't have their own baby, but the biological parents were also upset that they couldn't keep their child. They loved their baby and wanted to see that the child had a good life. It was a difficult time for the biological parents; they were still in school, or the father was not home, but they wanted the child they loved to be taken care of by both a mother and father and treated well. They were truly sad that they could not do it themselves.

Eventually the child will adjust and make peace, but it is easier when both the positive and negative aspects of adoption are talked about. The parent must also come to grips with the lack of fertility, biological continuity, and confirmation of sexual identity. This may be one of life's disappointments, but compared to experiencing death, divorce, or other disabilities, it may not be the hardest thing to face. It does need to be discussed however.

If children want to know why they weren't told many details about their adoption sooner, parents can reply, *"When you were a younger child, you needed to feel that you were a part of our family and were safe and secure within our home. Now that you are older and can understand more about other families, we feel you are ready to hear about where you were before you became a part of our lives and how you came to be our child."*

During the school-age year, even children who are not adopted may at one time or another fantasize that they were adopted, maybe out of yearning for a "decent mom and dad." This fantasy may especially occur after they have gotten into trouble or have been treated "meanly" by the parents. Children tend to create idealized images of their parents, and when their parents fail them by being unreasonable or too strict or by expecting too much of them, they may imagine a more understanding mom and dad.

Children love classic fairy tales because even though there is a witch, ogre, or cruel stepmother, there is also fairy princess, godmother, or a handsome prince to come to the rescue. Forces of good always win over the forces of cruelty, evil, and abuse. Similarly, some adopted children imagine they come from royalty, and others feel they were rescued from a wicked witch. Still others feel they were conceived in passion, then neglected.

For some adopted children, the need to fantasize about biological parents may be intense. This may be less true in an open adoption when the child has contact with the biological mother. It is easy to imagine a "good" set of parents and a "bad" set of parents, especially if the adoptive parents are not showing love, acceptance, and support.

Parents' Psychological Issues

Parents must face the fact that the adopted child is not a biological child and that the child's characteristics may be a result of inheritance and prenatal influences. When the child is misbehaving, it is easy for parents to attribute characteristics to the biological parents: *"Nobody in our family has such a temper." "Did we get a bad apple?" "I wonder if there is insanity in Jennifer's family.*" It may be easier to place the blame on inherited characteristics than take responsibility for how you are treating your child.

It is important to explore the underlying reasons for wanting to adopt. Acknowledging that some reasons may be less than mature may be an important part of the process.

> Jane's sister had a boy, and Jane didn't have any children. Jane felt that her sister was always getting a better deal in the family, and having a child was another way of getting more attention from her parents. Jane primarily wanted a baby to catch up with her sister and gain a more equal position in the family.
>
> Mary desperately wanted a baby girl. After having three boys, she adopted a girl to fill this ache. She had had a difficult relationship with her own brothers and father, and she felt that a little girl would be a soul-mate and an ally. She felt indifferent toward her own three boys.
>
> Jennifer's marriage was under siege, and the fertility tests weren't making it easier. Her husband was sure that once Jennifer had a baby in her arms, her disposition and sexual responsiveness would improve. Alas, he was wrong!

Unfortunately, when parents go through the process of adoption, they have trouble facing these underlying issues because they are so anxious about being judged acceptable as parents by the visiting social worker. To admit these underlying motivations or expectations, even to themselves, may be too threatening. As a result, many of these reasons, anxieties, and fantasies are buried. Later, they may erupt in the form of disappointment and anger toward the innocent adopted child, whose entrance into the family may not alter the ongoing problems it was meant to solve.

During the stressful first year, when all infants are demanding and require a consistent, loving relationship, adoptive parents are on trial. Legal adoption usually takes place after one year. Parents may worry about losing their child until the time the court gives them their adoption papers. Acknowledging the ambivalent feelings that are natural for all new parents may be too frightening. As a result, the feelings never get addressed. Also, it may be hard to fully love or totally commit to a child who may be taken away during this trying first year, even though the possibility is slight.

Adopted infants may experience biological disruption after their birth, although it is rare when the adoptive parents take over immediately. For children who spend weeks or months in foster care or in a hospital setting, separation from both the caretakers and the environment increases stress. It may be hard for adoptive parents to form a loving bond with a stressed-out baby. The attachment process may be more difficult for the adoptive parents and the baby when there is a separation from both the biological mother and the first caretakers.

The process is more difficult when older children are adopted because of the many traumas over loss of the attachment figures with whom the child has had relationships. A child who is adopted in the preschool or school-age years may express anger over the losses by acting withdrawn and depressed, by being hostile and aggressive, or by exhibiting behaviors of a much younger child. All these responses make parenting more difficult, especially in the absence of the affection that develops when a parent bonds to a helpless, captivating infant and participates in its growth. It may take a good deal of active support, education, and preparation to adopt an older child. Parents need to address multiple psychological and emotional problems when adopting an older child.

Single parents who adopt may not appreciate the fact that they will be separated from the new baby. Usually, single parents are the sole supporters and have to leave the child to return to work. Finding stable childcare is difficult and will further separate parent and child. It takes not only time but also continuity of care for a child to develop trust in the adopting parent. This is complicated when the child has to form attachments to new caregivers as well. It is not an easy task for an infant, toddler, or young child.

One of Us is Adopted

Very often, couples who go through the process of adopting suddenly find themselves expecting a biological child. Or parents with biological children may want to increase their family and adopt a child. Some parents are so eager to have a child of a particular sex that they will adopt only a male or female. That child may come into a family of boys or girls.

These families then have a combination of biological and adopted children. The combination may pose different problems for both the children and the adults. Adopted children may feel they are not as loved as the biological children. Parents may not love the adopted child as much as the biological child, or they may love the adopted child more, depending on the particular family dynamics. Parents love different children differently in every household.

However, parents of an adopted child are often less able to acknowledge their negative feelings and may feel extremely guilty if they feel closer to the biological child. As a result, they may overindulge the adopted child. It is important for parents to acknowledge sentiments that are not socially acceptable. However, it is their responsibility to provide a positive environment for all the children, one that is respectful, basically fair, caring, and nurturing. Favoritism, partiality, or scapegoating of one child creates hostility, guilt, and disharmony in the family.

It is also important for parents to refrain from comparing and branding children and to spend some special alone time with each child—adopted and biological. Adopted children may sense that their parents feel closer to their biological child than to themselves. However, if they are treated and raised in a warm, respectful environment, they will grow to feel secure. As children become older, satisfactions can come from other relationships. Feelings of academic, artistic, or physical competence are ways all children can feel valued, even though they may not be the actual "favorites" in their families.

Stepfathers often want to adopt the child or children of their wives. For children who are just starting elementary school, being able to use the same name as their parents may be easier.

> Julie Jackson was uncomfortable introducing her mother as Mrs. Williams. She was relieved when her stepfather changed her name. Being adopted by her stepfather made her feel that she was really a part of her mother's new family. She now had the same last name as her baby brother. Her "real" father had moved far away, and she didn't see him any more. Now that she is legally adopted, she feels better and less embarrassed.
>
> On the other hand, Elizabeth was in a state of terror for months when her family was talking about adopting her. From the six-year-old's point of view, adoption meant that she was to be given away. She was depressed and terrified imagining that her family didn't want her. She did not know who would take her. She was enormously relieved when her aunt took the time to explain that soon she would adopted officially by her own stepfather. And she would permanently and legally be part of their whole family. This conversation took place after Elizabeth shared her worries with her aunt.

It is important to truly explain the words you use as well as take the time to listen to your child's special concerns.

Adoption can be an extremely rewarding experience for families. However, it is important to face the many feelings that are related to this process and to recognize that adoption does create some difficulties for both the children and the parents. As in rearing any child, parents need to establish a close attachment and bond. They must provide the continuity of loving care as well as age-appropriate life experiences.

Chapter 10

Divorce and Remarriage

Divorce and parental separation are a major upset in a school-age child's life. In some ways, these events are less stressful for the school-age child than they would be for a preschooler or toddler. School-age children can more easily deal with the fact that someone they care about has left the home and is living apart from the family. They have a better understanding of distances and a better sense of time as well as the ability to make contact on the telephone or in letters or e-mail.

Tension and strife before parents separate may prepare children for the eventual break. But children from five to eleven are mainly involved with their own concerns, and they may be completely unaware that the marriage is in crisis. When those children are told of the break, the news may be an enormous shock, an earthquake that rocks their stable and predictable home. They have many concerns:

"Where and with whom will I live?"

"Don't they know I have enough to worry about at school and at Little League? Now I have to worry about them. too."

"When do I get to see my mom or dad?"

"Did my getting into trouble cause all of this?"

"Why is this happening to my family?"

"Will they still remember my birthday? Will they both come to the party, or will I have two celebrations?"

"Why don't they care enough about me to stay married?"

"When mom starts screaming at me, I can see why she bugs my dad."

"My dad always comes home late and never keeps his promises, that's why my mom and I get mad at him."

"Will I still see my grandparents as often?"

"If my mom and dad get mad and stop loving each other, will they leave me when they get mad at me?"

"Am I going to live with my dad and will my sisters live with my mom, or will we all live with one of our parents?"

Some children may be relieved that the parents are finally going to separate and live apart. They may feel that their lives will be safer and more predictable, especially if alcohol, drugs, physical abuse, or violence has been a part of the scene. Children may anticipate the time when they will be free of tension and stress caused by the disturbed parent.

For most children, separation means making new adjustments. Unfortunately, families are under greater financial strain when there are two households. Mothers may need to go to work or work longer hours to help pay the bills. The family home may have to be sold to divide the property as a joint asset. The child may need to attend a different school and make new friends, adding to the many other adjustments the child has to make. The child must learn to know new caregivers and babysitters. In each home, there will be new rules, expectations, and routines.

Often, the separation is not permanent. Parents may attempt reconciliation and raise everyone's hopes that the family will return to normal. Conversely, the parents may begin to date and spend time with other adults in and away from home.

Children are often sucked into a morass of negative emotions when parents are going through separation and divorce. They must deal with the anger, sadness, jealousy, and despair of one or both parents. Parents have little time and energy for laughter, loving words, relaxed and mellow outings, and joyful celebrations at home.

Parents may expect a school-age child to fill the emotional void created by divorce, separation, or death. This is a burden for a young child. Often, a boy is expected to be the "man of the house" and a girl to be "mom's little helper," which places too much responsibility on the young child. Of course, age-appropriate expectations are important to sustain. But depriving children of a carefree childhood and expecting more from them than they can provide is somewhat exploitative.

Children who are expected to protect the family often yearn for a new father to take over the protective duties. Young girls may hope for a stepmother to help run the household. Children of divorce and separation are often left home alone for long periods of time. Both parents may be committed to a demanding work schedule to deal with financial needs. They also may be pursuing their own adult social lives. Dating and going to meetings, parties, or other social events may intrude on the precious time they could be sharing their children.

Sharing a Bed

Regularly sharing a bed with a divorced parent may be convenient and comforting for both parent and school-age child. But it may communicate that the child is not safe sleeping alone in his or her own bed. It may also make it much more difficult when another adult moves in and takes that spot, excluding the child.

A respectful and gradual transition to the child's own bed should be arranged. That is not to say that some cuddling or reading cannot take place in the parental bed or that adult and child cannot occasionally share a bed. Even parents who are not divorced encourage their children to sleep with them when the spouse is away. Parents often miss the warmth and feelings of closeness associated with a body on the empty side of the bed.

Children about ten years and older who are allowed to take over the absent parent's place in the conjugal bed may expect to act as spouse in all other ways. They may have sexual fantasies, which may be arousing to them. For children approaching puberty, sleeping with parents can be sexually stimulating. These sexual fantasies are usually repressed or put out of mind, since children have no acceptable way to act on them. Children may also have some expectations that they can be the parent's companion at other times and stay up late to socialize and communicate.

Custody and Visitation

Probably the hardest thing for children to deal with is parents' anger over custody and visitation arrangements. It is so easy to battle over the amount of time and the particular days that the child spends with each parent. It is easier for parents to dwell on these issues than to face their own feelings of rejection, disappointment, fear, and guilt.

Joint legal custody and joint physical custody may communicate to children that both parents care about them and want to be involved in their lives. For most children, that is a positive feeling. However, joint custody demands a good working alliance between the divorced or separated parents, something that may have been absent during the marriage itself. A divorced parent often expects the former spouse to respond in a sensitive, reliable, and caring way. Often this is not realistic; if the spouse had that capacity, the couple probably wouldn't be getting divorced or separated in the first place.

Children need to become accustomed to the visitation arrangements and to be able to trust the schedule. It is important for their lives to be predictable. Frequent, capricious change erodes a child's sense of trust. This in turn may lay the foundation for problems in the child's own social relationships and future marriage, causing difficulties in achieving intimacy.

School-age children are at a stage in their development where they begin to analyze and evaluate people around them. It is during these years that they begin to identify the reasons for the divorce or separation, as well as the personal strengths and problems that are associated with each parent. If parents refrain from badmouthing the other spouse and allow the child the freedom to experience each parent independently, the child will learn to make sense out of the altered state of the marriage. The child will also feel less internal conflict with his or her own male and female components. The child will feel less under siege and more in harmony.

Parents may find it difficult to give their child the freedom and privacy to experience the other parent. They often want to know what has happened during the visitation with the other parent. Their own perceptions of the former spouse's personality need to be validated and confirmed, and they need to release their own tensions and angers. Even though it may be difficult, divorced and separated parents must control these impulses to intrude on the child's personal experience with the other parent.

A child who is free to develop a relationship with each parent will more likely form a positive identification with the parent of the same sex and have less conflict over his or her own sexual identity.

> Kenny's father was an athletic, fun-loving, aggressive, explosive, and unreliable man. At an early age, Kenny wanted to be like his father, but because his mother so openly condemned his father's character, Kenny felt conflicted about what to admire in this man. It was safer to identify with his mother's point of view, but he was left with no acceptable male role model. He felt guilty at wanting to be with his Dad.

We must assume that neither the mother nor the father is abusive and that the environment is safe for the visiting child. If drugs, alcohol, or physical abuse is involved, it is important to limit the conditions of the visitation, perhaps by increasing supervision. Also, if the child is left unsupervised or in danger, visitation and custody must be evaluated and altered so that the child is safe.

In most situations, each parent needs to be responsible for the time he or she is together with the child. Constructive, age-appropriate activities should be provided. The visits should be infused with some pleasure. Parents who obsess over what has happened in the other household waste an enormous amount of emotional energy. A parent has very little control over what happens in the other parent's home. Providing a positive experience for your child in your own home will make it easier for the child to handle visits with the other parent. In other words, worry about the things you can control, and try to stop worrying about what you cannot control in the home of your ex-spouse.

The Weekend Parent

It is easy for a weekend parent, who is most likely to be the father, to be more indulgent. Fun-filled experiences and more toys may be part of the child's visit with a weekend parent. The responsibilities of getting ready for school, practicing piano, and homework are mostly absent during the weekends.

When one parent is a weekend parent, both parents may feel deprived. A father who misses out on seeing his children cope with their daily commitments has no idea what stress the other parent is under to get the child through the day. The weekend parent is often amazed at accounts of emotional storms and power struggles. The weekend father has no idea how tired and cranky the child is after Saturday and Sunday and doesn't understand why the mother say, *"It takes two days to get them back to normal."*

The primary-care parent is often "blessed" with the child's explosions and emotional outbursts, while the parent who has weekend visitation sees the child's best behavior. People fall apart in the environment where they feel safest. Since it is usually the father who moves out, the children may be more careful about how they behave in front of him. They may be afraid that negative behavior will push him farther away. So it is usually the mother who has to deal with the children's exhaustion from weekend events and their reaction to having to be "good" for a two-day stretch.

This same situation occurs in households where there is no divorce. When children stay overnight with a friend or relative, they are often basket-cases when they return home. Sleeping in a different bed, having an altered eating schedule, and being exposed to exciting or scary movies or tapes can cause children to be wiped out when they return home. It may take children a day or two to recover from long car rides and tiring outings, even in the most stable household. Yet the tendency in divorce or separation is to feel that the weekend parent is causing all the trouble.

It is hard for children not to press sensitive buttons by demanding the possessions, privileges, or altered routines they experience in each household: *"Mommy always lets me"* or *"Daddy always gets me."* This can threaten even the most secure adults who think they know what they are doing. Each parent wants to be loved more than the other. Children's demands often throw parents into a state of defensive irritation. Coming back from a weekend Santa Claus Dad to a hard-working, penny-pinching Mom may be difficult for all concerned.

Children who regularly move from one household to another may be deprived of experiencing outcomes and resolutions to problems or events. To the child, it may feel like reading every other chapter in a novel or missing every other segment in a television series.

> Lindsey sometimes left her father's house during a fight between her stepmother and father. When she returned five days later, she expected them to still be angry with each other. She didn't experience the resolution of the disagreement or feel the affection that followed.

If children miss a party or outing, they feel left out when it is reminisced over and laughed about. They also may not be able to share their own positive or negative experiences with their other parent. They may be afraid to stir up jealous or angry feelings. As a result, they may feel a sense of isolation and alienation from one or both parents much of the time.

It is important for the children to be the focus of attention during visitation and not to be regularly relegated to babysitters or grandparents. If emergencies arise, childcare arrangements will need to be made, but it is best if this does not happen too often. If it does, children may feel that their company is not valued and their presence is an intrusion.

However, some children feel that they are getting to know their weekend parent better than they did when the family was living together. The father was often away and never took the time to relate individually to the children.

Dating

One or both parents may start to openly date following the separation or divorce. Dating may be stressful for the children, who are still dealing with stress from the changes they have experienced. Dating may mean new things to worry about:

"When will mom return from the date?"

"Will he be my new stepfather?"

"Am I going to have to have that sitter again, or will I be sent over to Aunt Jean's house?"

"Why does she need to go out, anyway?"

"Why are they always locking the door and making noises?"

"How can my parents get back together again if they keep spending time with these other people?"

"Maybe if I am mean and obnoxious to him, he won't bother with my mom. After all, I broke up my parents' marriage by misbehaving. I can do the same thing again."

"It is hard enough to like my parents all the time, how can I ever like these strangers?"

"These dates try to be so nice to me, but I can see through them. Wait till they really know what I'm like, then I bet they won't be so friendly."

"I don't get enough attention from my own parents. And now they bring someone else in with their own children, and my father acts so nice to them and let her kids get away with murder! Why, if I behaved like that, my parents would kill me. But he's trying so hard to please her, he lets her kids do anything!"

"My mom and dad don't care about me anymore. All they talk about is this new person."

"My mom spends all her time on the phone to her friends, and all they talk about is her dates."

"How will I know who will become my stepparents? There are so many my parents are dating."

"Do you think my mom or dad will care if I like this person?

They will probably get married anyway without asking me!"

"I don't mind the woman my Dad is dating, but her pesky four-year-old drives me wild, and her snobby teenager just ignores me!"

A parent who is mourning the loss of the marriage may find dating a distraction and a stressful experience. The loss of the "marriage hat" may be harder than the loss of the spouse. Putting on the "singles hat" may be difficult. It is no easy matter to act as like a teenager again, worrying about attracting the opposite sex and trying to feel poised and comfortable. The divorced parent may suddenly become more interested in his or her physical appearance, clothes, makeup, and body weight. Sexual urges that may have been dormant in the marriage are reawakened. Parents who had difficulty forming relationships when they were teenagers and young adults may be even more anxious about having to begin dating again.

It is hard to deal with mundane issues of what to wear, what to talk about, and finding a sitter. The parent wonders, *"Can I mention my ex-spouse?" "How much should I talk about my kids?" "Can I pry into my date's life?" "Would this person make a good parent?" "It seemed so simple when we were young."* Parents caught up in the dating process may feel more sensitive and upset over possible rejections, especially if they still feel insecure about the previous marriage.

Francine worried that Jeffrey dated her only during the week. She felt that perhaps she wasn't good enough for a weekend date. She really obsessed over this, but couldn't get herself to talk about it with him.

Sarah felt that Alec liked her a lot, but he wasn't very intelligent. She enjoyed his company and sweet nature, but she knew she was going to have to eventually break it off. She worried and was anxious about hurting his feelings.

Children have no idea that parents have these intense concerns. They might not understand why their parent seems so "spacey" and "doesn't really listen."

Kevin complained that it was bad enough when his

parents were fighting and bickering when they were married, but now that they are divorced and dating, they seem out of it, preoccupied, and even less available.

The parents may feel that finding a new mate is more important to their sanity and future than spending time with their children. Children may be considered a real intrusion into the process of dating and establishing a new, intimate relationship.

School-age children are more aware of what people do on dates and how they share their affectionate and sexual feelings. Parents often assume that when children are asleep, they can not hear, but sleep may not be continuous and the child may be unwittingly exposed to much more stimulation than he or she can handle comfortably. Many children report that the most difficult experience they remember is hearing a parent "fooling around" in bed with a new person.

Casual sexual interactions are probably best kept away from home, especially when the child is present. Allowing another person to share the parent's bed is sending an important message to children. The message is, *"I care about this person, I expect that we will spend time together and eventually make a commitment."* Most parents want to communicate to their children that sexual intimacy does not take place capriciously, casually, and irresponsibly. If parents don't model this for their children, they should not expect their teenagers to be sexually responsible and to avoid acting in a promiscuous manner.

Considering Remarriage

At some point in the dating relationship, the question may arise, *"Is this a person I might marry?"* There are many more concerns and emotional issues to deal with in remarriage than when couples without children decide to take the plunge.

"Will the same problems arise in this marriage?"

"Will I fail at this relationship as well?"

"How will my new spouse parent my children?"

"How will I parent my new stepchildren?"

"Will there be enough money for two families?"

"How will my former spouse relate to my new one?"

"How will we handle holidays and celebrations?"

"Will we ever have a chance to have a honeymoon or any romance with all these children around?"

"What if my children don't like my new spouse or don't get along with their stepsiblings?"

"Do I know enough about this new person, the family, and their history?"

"Am I getting married for the wrong reasons? To beat my ex to the punch? Because I am lonely? So I won't be the only one responsible for these difficult children? To have someone to help pay the bills? To do the housework? Or to sleep with?"

It may be difficult to answer these questions and truly address the implications of these issues. Talking to a good friend or a professional may help. Focusing on these concerns may be an investment in the next marriage.

It is important to prepare for difficult times ahead and create realistic expectations. Wanting to be a perfect mother or father and expecting well-behaved children all the time are unrealistic goals. When they are not met, everyone feels anger and disappointment. The mother who shops, cooks, cleans, and launders to impress a new mate often feels unappreciated. The father who is providing his hard-earned money for food, schooling, and lessons can't understand why the children hate him. Talking about these possibilities ahead of time can help when embarking on a new marriage and the blending of families.

The Wedding Ceremony

Plans and arrangements for the wedding ceremony must consider all of the children. It is important to include the children in discussions of the plans at least some weeks before the actual event. Dropping the bomb just before the wedding takes place is not respectful to their feelings. It does not give them time to adjust to the news, continue to mourn the end of their primary family, and become ready to participate in and enjoy the coming event.

There are several options available: eloping and arranging for childcare; excluding the children from the ceremony, or having a formal wedding in which the children are part of the procedures. The children can be ring bearers, flower girls, or bridesmaids or groomsmen.

Since most weddings are filled with excitement and tension and the focus is on the bride and groom, parents are unprepared to deal with the children's reactions and immediate needs. Preparation is the key to a smooth event. Playing out everyone's role with toy people or a formal rehearsal can help immensely. Assigning some adults to be in charge of the school-age children can also be helpful, since the bride and groom will have other things on their minds and may not be available to respond to their own children.

Preparations for the honeymoon and childcare arrangements need to be made and explained. Specifics of where the parents are going, where the children will stay, who will supervise them, and how long the parents will be away need to be communicated. Phone numbers can be made available and times for phone calls can be set.

It is easy for children to feel rejected, ignored, and devalued during this period. Adults are preoccupied with a multitude of details, out-of-town guests, and clothes. They don't have the time or energy to attend to children's whims and ego needs. For young children, the wedding itself may not be so stressful, but the honeymoon period is—everyone disappears, the excitement is over, and the child worries whether and when the parents will return. One preschool child assumed, after four days of the honeymoon, that the parents had died and were never coming back.

After the honeymoon is over and the family is reunited, the children may begin to act up and try to find their place in the new family. All the anger and irritation that they controlled throughout the stress of the prenuptial, wedding, and honeymoon begins to ooze out. Moves to a new home often occur before the wedding, but sometimes they occur afterwards, and there are problems of adjustment.

The children may also find it hard to deal with the stress and anger of the other parent who has not yet remarried. This parent may feel anger, jealousy, and frustration at the seeming happiness the ex-spouse is achieving. The unmarried parent may be a basket-case the week of the big event and may provide little support for children who may need attention and stability. Even worse, the children may be getting little emotional support from the parent who is getting remarried.

Stepparenting

Once the marriage and honeymoon are over, parents are confronted with the longer-term issues of stepparenting. There may be a let down in everyone's good behavior now that the marriage contract has been signed. Lovers may seem to become wicked stepmothers and cruel stepfathers. An amorous intended spouse is exhausted. A considerate and thoughtful husband becomes demanding and insatiable. Visiting siblings who were cooperative suddenly start fighting and teasing. A parent may feel that the money is hemorrhaging in all directions, especially to "people I don't even care about."

> *"How different this marriage is from our first! We had no children. We could play together as husband and wife before we had children. We didn't have so many obligations to school events, Little League games, recitals... Money wasn't flowing out to an ex-spouse. We were both biologically connected to our new baby, and grew bonded to our infant. We didn't worry about the marriage failing. We're now so much more conscious of wanting to have a lasting relationship."*

As difficult as a second marriage might be, and it is certainly made more stressful when each parent brings along a set of children, there can be many positive benefits for all concerned.

Children's Reactions to the New Family

Children may be pleased about once again being part of a family. They may feel protected and supported by the presence of two adults. They also may be delighted to have an older sibling or a younger one. Each stepsibling can help dilute the intensity of the child's role in the family as well as provide the opportunity to play out different roles. The youngest can play the part of the older bossy child to a younger stepsibling in the new family, or the oldest child can look up to and learn from an even older stepsister or stepbrother. Relating to new brothers and sisters can be an important experience for the children.

Children can also learn from the different talents, strengths, and passions of the stepparent, and can experience their parent relating in a more loving way to someone of the opposite sex. Children may indeed be fortunate to have someone new to relate to, who is able to teach them and model a different approach to life.

Forming a relationship with a stepparent is very different from the process of forming a relationship with a parent, which started in infancy and developed through the toddler and preschool years. The child literally "steps" into the role of "stepchild" before any attachment is created. The child's opinion is usually not a major consideration in the selection process—the child is not the one who fell in love with the new parent. The child usually already has a father or a mother. Children may feel disloyal to their own biological parent when they develop close and loving feelings for the stepparent. They may feel that they can't love two mothers or two fathers freely.

Children may also feel that they dislike and are irritated with their stepparent, but they are afraid to let their biological parent know of these feelings. In other words, they may be unable to share feelings that are positive and loving and feelings that are hateful and rejecting. They may be repressing a heavy load of emotions. Eruptions may occur any time and often seem inexplicable, since they are related to ambivalent feelings about the stepparent. It is important for an adult to actively listen to and explore these complicated feelings.

Ideally, if the biological parent can give the child permission to develop a warm and loving relationship with the new stepparent, conflict over these feelings will lessen. This may be difficult for the biological parent to do, since their former mate's new spouse may have become the enemy. The parent may be secretly delighted that the child is not forming a positive attachment to the new stepparent. The parent may also fear that the child will like the stepparent better and that the biological parent will ultimately be rejected and abandoned. Sometimes the battle over what the stepparent is called symbolizes this conflict: *"Do I call my stepfather 'Dad' or my stepmother 'Mom'? Do I use their first names? And how do my 'real' parents feel about that?"*

> Jennifer wanted to call her stepfather "dad," but her real father refused to let her, saying, *"I am your only real dad."* This was upsetting to the child, who wanted to feel a part of the new family especially now that there was new baby who was beginning to say "da-da."

Last names also can be a problem. When a child does not have the same last name as the mother because of remarriage, the child may feel that he or she is not really a part of the new family. It may be difficult for the child to introduce the mother to friends or teachers using her new married name.

Children are often upset when they see the stepparent behaving in a more loving, sensitive, and caring way to their biological children. The reality may be that this stepparent does feel differently about his or her own children and that a sensitive stepchild can perceive this difference. The stepchild may never feel loved or accepted by the stepparent. Often, the parents will defend their own children in sibling conflicts. It may be reassuring for the child to have the biological parent as an active ally, but it is also guilt-provoking, especially when the child imagines that these conflicts will break apart the new marriage. It may be further complicated when there is only one stepchild in the family and the rest are the biological children of both parents.

The advent of a new baby may be extremely stressful for school-age children. Not only are they going through the same jealous feelings as all children when a new baby is born, but they may also feel as if they are truly outsiders to the new biological unit formed as a result of the new baby. School-age children may be too old to express their primitive aggressive feelings towards the baby, even though they are sitting on a volcano of emotions. They may have trouble at school or act depressed or oppositional.

On the other hand, they may be delighted to have a sibling, even though it may be a half-brother or sister. They may have yearned for many years for a sibling and may be truly pleased to have their family extended.

Stepfathers' Conflicts

The stepfather is more likely than the stepmother to feel intense guilt feelings in the parenting process. He often spends most of his time with his stepchildren and perhaps every other weekend with his own children. Some fathers try to provide a holiday atmosphere on the weekend visits of biological children and may exclude the stepchildren from these activities. The father may also be conflicted about the amount of money he has to spend on his stepchildren as compared with the child support he gives his former wife. Further complications arise when the blending of all the children results in fighting, bickering, and tantrums. The father often yearns to have his own children present during special outings and family activities with his new family. He may often resent providing a more fun-filled and secure life for the stepchildren than he can for his own children.

Some fathers may feel that they have failed with their own children and may be disappointed with the way they seem to be turning out. These same fathers may turn to their stepchildren with greater intensity and interest, trying to create more successful children than they did the first time around. Basically, such a father is trying to repair his image of himself as father.

> Harry was a hard-working accountant. He was never home or available to his wife and three children. Childhood years flew by, and the marriage disintegrated. When he married Shirley, Harry began to feel what it was like to be a participating dad. He attended outings with his stepchildren and shared his presence and skills with them. His own children grew up deprived of this kind of participating father.

As children grow older, their financial needs grow as well. Families are stressed by high tuition payments or needs for transportation. Adolescents may not require as much physical contact with their parents, but they may need more money for clothes, equipment, travel, or tuition. The stepfather may feel the pinch trying to support these growing children.

Conflict also arises when a parent does not fulfill the other parent's expectations of how to parent. A parent may be annoyed at the permissiveness or the hostility shown to the children. Conflicts can arise over the lack of structure or the severity of punishments.

> Jane was disappointed that her new husband, Jeff, whom she loved dearly, showed no enthusiasm toward her son Tom. Jeff virtually ignored Tom. Sometimes, when Tom wouldn't listen to his mother or was sassy to her, Jeff would bark, *"Why don't you do what your mother says?"* Jeff himself had an annoying younger brother whom he disliked. He had a cold and distant father who taught him little about how to be a nurturing, involved parent. In fact, Jeff saw himself as a good father who provided Tom with a comfortable, secure home. Jane had longed for a mate who would delight in her child's appealing manner, and she was disappointed that Jeff couldn't fulfill her expectation. She eventually accepted Jeff's inability to be an involved father and was glad other aspects of the marriage were so good. Tom never developed a close bond with his stepfather, but continued a positive relationship with his mother.

Stepmothers' Conflicts

A stepmother has her own concerns. She is often overwhelmed by extra household duties. She may feel isolated and deprived of her husband's company and affection when his children are present. She may say she wants her husband to spend time with his own offspring, but she resent his closeness and contact when he does so.

Some stepmothers who have not had their own children may find parenting new and difficult. Often, such a woman initially tries to be the good super-mother. However, not being involved from birth in the development of a relationship with these children complicates her feelings, especially when the children are irritable, hostile, and demanding. The "good" mother feels like she is turning into the "wicked witch" or the mean stepmother. She may be amazed by her own negative feelings and may be unable to share them with her husband. Hating his children may be frightening to her, even if the feelings come and go.

A stepmother can resent the closeness, humor, and reminiscences between the husband and his children. She may be disappointed in the changes that she sees in herself. She wants to show what a good mother she can be, and she doesn't want to be the hateful, annoyed, overburdened, and exploited person she feels she is.

A stepmother who is not much older than her teenage stepchildren may find it difficult to set limits and control the stepchildren's behavior. As a young person not many years from her teens, she may strongly identify with what these teenagers are up to and find it hard to play the part of the wise and authoritative mother. The children sense this and may push to the limit, in essence saying, *"You can't tell me what to do. You're too young to be my mother."*

The husband's former wife may also contribute to the problem by communicating a negative attitude about the new wife. Her message is, *"If it weren't for this evil woman, your dad and I would still be married. She's no mother. She's not much older than you."* Most children want to feel that their parents are correct in their evaluations. The children may therefore provoke the new stepmother until she indeed turns into the mean witch their mother described.

Stepmothers who have their own children are also confronted with problems of discipline when the stepchildren are present. It may be easier for the stepmother to protect and defend her own children's actions and feel that the stepchildren are the cause of all the upset. The husband, on the other hand, may be critical of the wife's attitude, feeling that she is too harsh and that she expects too high a standard of behavior from his children. Conflicts escalate into two warring camps. It may be hard to accept the fact that "my spouse does not love my children" the way he or she loves his or her own.

It may also happen that stepparents let the stepchildren behave in ways they would never tolerate in their own children. However, the adult does not wish to make demands or to anger the stepchildren, so he or she may never take action to make the children accountable for unacceptable behavior.

It is best if each parent can learn to treat all the children in the family respectfully and fairly. Parents can be careful not to become the judge, evaluating the guilt of any child. They can work toward resolving conflict in a positive and growth-producing manner. This in turn will strengthen the marriage.

What Stepparents Can Do

Probably the most therapeutic and important act that a stepparent can take is to establish a relationship with the stepchildren. Plan some regular special time alone together. When the stepparent requests the child's companionship, how special that child will feel!

Children need to learn about their stepparents and experience them in a private, uncomplicated way. To always compete for attention with their biological parent or other siblings makes it difficult to establish a relationship with this relative stranger. By attending school functions, games, and other events, the stepparent communicates a special interest in the child.

Some parents feel enormous conflict when they participate in the lives of their stepchildren. They feel guilty about their separation from their own children, with whom they feel they should be spending time. These and other problems concerning stepchildren require careful and extended discussion about

- Where the visiting stepchildren sleep. Do they have their own rooms? A place to keep clothes and toys?
- How to schedule the week and provide special time for each child and stepchild.
- How to provide time for the couple to nurture their marriage.

- How holidays and birthdays will be celebrated.
- How the children's responsibilities will be handled. Will stepchildren have any special chores or tasks when they're visiting?
- Whether the biological parent or the stepparent will make all the demands and decide on how the children are accountable.
- What role the stepparent will play in discipline.
- How parents will back each other up and avoid being sucked into battles over discipline and expectations. Often, one parent has more realistic understandings of what is age appropriate than the other. Problems arise when either too much or too little is expected of the children.

Money issues need to be discussed. Stepparents often have to support their stepchildren if the biological parent is absent or refuses to participate. Paying for lessons, tuition, and medical bills may make a stepparent feel used or exploited. Fighting sometimes arises over equipment, toys, and clothes that remain at each home. Sometimes, it is easier to fight about money than to address the other issues in the relationship.

When both parents have full-time employment, there is increased stress over parenting and household responsibilities. More effort must be made to accommodate the needs of every family member in the few hours left at the end of the day. Time must be more carefully regulated, and fatigue levels must be respected.

Feelings of jealousy, envy, abandonment ,and isolation must be addressed more energetically in stepfamilies. All of these feelings are present in the most stable of households, but they may grow in intensity and magnitude when the parents remarry and try to blend two families. New stepsiblings, step-grandparents, aunts, and uncles, plus changes in routines, all bring about stress.

Open communication is essential. Children and parents

need to be listened to in a neutral and affectionate environment. Each person's worries and anxieties need to be taken seriously. Often this is accomplished by providing special time, when parents can listen to the children and respond to each other in a relaxed atmosphere. If family discussions take place during conflicts, it is difficult to listen to what the other person is really saying.

Finding special times may take creative planning, but every person needs to be listened to in a private, respectful way. Acknowledging discomforts, unfairness, and anger is often all that is needed to diminish upsets and tension. Sometimes the simple fact of scheduling special times can be of great value, since each child knows that he or she will soon have a turn. In large families, the special times may not occur as frequently, but they are nonetheless essential. Spending twenty minutes alone communicates that every child is important. It provides a time and place for upsets and feelings to be shared. It provides an opportunity for parents to acknowledge the value of each child.

Chapter 11

Death and Loss

Unfortunately, some school-age children experience the death of a parent, grandparent, sibling, or other significant person. The death can occur suddenly, with no warning or preparation, because of an accident or illness. Or it can take place after many months of pain, disability, and hospitalization.

The death of an important person may be one of the most significant and profound events in a child's life. A child who is deprived of a parent during the school-age years experiences intense feelings of sadness, anger, and fear. Such children may grieve in ways adults find hard to identify. They may be ashamed that they no longer have a mother or father and are often not able to communicate their loss to anyone. They feel that they are jinxed and unlucky. They may worry excessively about the health and well-being of the remaining parent.

Child may also wish the parent who is now alive could trade places with the dead parent. There may be moments when the child secretly feels glad that the parent died, especially if that parent was difficult and abused them. Children may experience guilt feelings, and they may wonder if their behavior or lack of loving feelings brought about the death.

Children may also have been frightened and repelled by being close to the dying person, or they may feel that they were unable to give the dying parent the affection and warmth that was expected of them. They may worry that their feelings are not appropriate, and they may be angry at the other adults who are ignoring them. Children—as well as the adults—may wish that the sick person would hurry up and die so things can return to normal.

School-age children are still very self-centered and self-involved. They worry about who is going to protect and support them. Will they have to move, and how will their life change? They may be extremely angry that their mother or father died and left them. They may be angry at the doctors and nurses who did not keep their parent alive.

A child may feel ill and have stomach pains or develop symptoms similar to the illness that caused the loss of the parent. A child may have fantasies that the parent is just away on a trip. The child may dream about the dead parent.

Children go through much the same process of grief and mourning as adults do. However, they may be more able to shift their intense feelings and at times be distracted and act as if nothing significant has happened to them.

The Terminally Ill Parent

Adults find it extremely difficult to talk to children about the anticipated death of a parent. It is easier to deny the intense feelings associated with loss and to exclude the children from the process. But children need to know what illness or sickness the parent has, what is being done for the parent, and what the surviving parent is worrying about. School-age children can more easily understand why the healthy parent is irritable, sad, and preoccupied if they are told about the condition of the dying parent. When children are kept uninformed or the seriousness of the condition is denied, they may feel excluded and neglected. On the other hand, sharing age-appropriate information can help children feel valued and a part of the family. It may also help them with the eventual loss and to prepare for the mourning process.

Children who are continually ignored may begin to misbehave, create messes, get sick, or have accidents, desperately trying to obtain attention. It is important for adults to acknowledge that this is a hard time for everyone: *"We are all feeling sad and angry that this is happening."*

Children should be allowed to visit a sick parent but they

should be prepared for the observable changes as well as for the medical apparatus surrounding the patient. A child who sees a parent's deteriorating condition can more readily make sense out of the eventual death. However, it might be inadvisable for a child to see a parent who is hallucinating or is connected to many machines. Adults need to use their best judgment in deciding when a child makes a last visit, and the dying parent should know as well.

Sometimes, a parent will die before the child has been allowed a final visit to say goodbye. This happens either because the adults feel that the child cannot deal with the experience or because they are so preoccupied that they forget to include the children. Children who are denied this last visit may feel intense resentment. These feelings may last through their lifetime. They may continue to yearn for a last goodbye, which would have brought closure to the relationship.

> John's father was dying of cancer upstairs. He was sick for a long time, but the end was near. John and his younger brother were ignored and left downstairs to play. His sister and older brother were with their mother and father the last hour of their father's life. They were able to say goodbye. But John is still angry and resentful that he was not allowed to be with his father at the end. He feels that his mother was insensitive to his feelings, even though he intellectually understands that she was distraught and preoccupied.

When a Parent Dies Suddenly

It is hard to imagine anything more traumatic for a child than the sudden death of one or both parents. The shock is profound, especially because there is no preparation. The sudden loss of a mother or father is most children's primal fear come true. It is an all-consuming trauma.

The child's primary concerns are deep and personal.

"Who will take care of me?"

"Who will support me?"

"Who will help me with my schoolwork?"

"Who will comfort me and put me to bed?"

"Who will play with me?"

The remaining parent may be equally traumatized and overwhelmed with feelings of shock and loss and may be unable to focus on the needs of the children.

Children want to know what happened to cause the death. They should be told a story that they can comprehend. They need to be included in the funeral procedures and participate with the rituals of mourning. They may feel profoundly unlucky: *"What did I do to bring this pain on myself?"* They may conjure up numerous explanations and reasons for this event. They often have fantasies related to feelings of guilt and superstition. They may feel that their anger and occasional death wish actually caused the death. Many children hate their parents at times and may feel or even say, *"I wish you were dead!"* They may feel that these transient feelings of anger and hate brought about the death.

Children may develop aversions to wearing certain clothes or participating in certain activities immediately associated with the traumatic event. They may be afraid to leave home and go to school, especially if the death occurred while they were at school.

> Billy, age seven, came home from school one day to find his house filled with people. He was told that his dad had been killed in a traffic accident. From that time onward, his schoolwork suffered; he was no longer the good student he had been. He appeared to be preoccupied, distant, and anxious. He dreaded coming home from school. He created excuses to hang around school or to visit friends. He associated coming home with the painful loss.

Children may need a sympathetic adult with whom they can talk about the death and make sense out of their feelings. Of course, this is true for anyone who suffers a sudden loss. They need to be encouraged to express their feelings of sadness, fear, anger, and concerns. But many children refuse to talk, and it may take months before the subject of their loss can be addressed.

It can be therapeutic for children to listen to adults talk about the death, even though they are not actually participating in the discussion. Often, it is hard for children to express their emotions appropriately, but they do need the presence of a caring, nurturing person to help them through the process of grief and mourning. It may be hard for the surviving parent to be a good listener; adults too are struggling with their own issues and may be needy themselves. The child may also be reluctant to bring up their own questions not wanting to upset an already grieving parent and bring on more tears.

Sudden death of a parent is experienced differently than when the parent has been ill for a long time. During the time the parent is dying, the survivors anticipate the death and may begin to mourn. When the person finally dies, relief that the suffering and ordeal are over may be mixed with the sadness of the event. This is not the case with sudden death. Instead, the world seems unpredictable and frightening. The child cannot trust that things will proceed in an orderly way. The child feels out of balance and afraid, and that he has lost control over life events.

Children may develop phobic reactions after sudden death. Some may unable to leave home. They may be unable to go to school or participate in certain activities. Sleep disturbances may also be common. Children may worry about going off to bed alone and about having intense dreams or nightmares. They may experience stomach aches, headaches, or asthmatic attacks. They may wet their bed and begin to have problems with bowel and bladder control. They may experience increased anxiety over almost any kind of separation. An example of this could occur if the remaining parent was required to leave the family home and the child is sent to unfamiliar surroundings.

> Eileen's father was suddenly killed in an accident in a distant state. Her mother flew there to make arrangements for transport of the body and funeral plans. Eileen was sent to temporarily stay with an aunt that she hardly

knew. These two separations made her father's death even more traumatic.

Helping the Grieving Child

Familiar grandparents, aunts, and uncles who are not as directly related to the loss can serve as important supports to the child. As shown by the previous example of Eileen, the tendency is to send children away to stay with relatives. However, it may be more comforting for children to remain at home and have the adults come to them. Children should not have to deal with too many changes all at once. They should not have to be separated from their remaining parent, home, neighborhood, and friends at the same time they are struggling with loss.

Children need reassurance that the tragedy is not going to continue and that people are "there for them." They need to talk about the positive aspects of the person but not overlook the real characteristics of the deceased. Confirming that the decreased parent was no saint may be very important, since children's actual experiences with a parent may have been infused with ambivalence and negative interactions. Children may have specific memories of irritability, anger, loss of control, and negligence. This is especially true when relationships just prior to death were less than satisfactory.

Adults need to make the events leading up to the sudden death as clear as possible to the child, and to explain what happened immediately afterwards. For school-age children up to about nine or ten years old, using play people and toy cars to reenact a car accident may help them conceptualize what happened and create a clearer picture. The child may need the story retold many times. A child may also benefit from having immediate future plans explained, so as not to feel isolated and alone, ignorant of what will happen next.

Children will be able to more easily move ahead and work through the grieving process if they are able to face the realities and are not dealing with secrets. Secrets absorb energy within a family, both on the part of the keeper of the secret as well as the person trying to discover it. It may be difficult for adults to present the truth in an age-appropriate way.

> Elaine's father was decapitated in a construction accident. Her mother told her that his head was badly injured by a moving beam, but did not graphically describe the mutilation of the body. Elaine's mother felt that this image would be too upsetting to a child of eight. She was more comfortable communicating the truth in this less upsetting way.

Suicide as a cause of death is often withheld from the school-age child. This secret is hard to keep. Children's ears are attuned to quiet communications on the phone and the hushed whispers of conversations between friends and relatives. It is true that suicide is a complicated and intensely charged event. Not only did the parent die, but the parent chose to die. There is probably no more hostile act than taking one's own life. The remaining family members may experience remorse and guilt as well as sadness and rage. It may be difficult for surviving adults to create a plausible scenario for the child, but it is important that it be done.

When a Sibling Dies

The death of a child can be one of the most tragic events a parent has to face, and it has profound implications for the surviving children. Even children who are born into the family after the death of a child can be affected by the loss. Children are not supposed to die before their parents, especially in a nation with low infant mortality. However, fatal accidents do occur, and children occasionally succumb to terminal illness.

The surviving children not only have to deal with their own sense of loss and guilt, but also with their parents' intense emotions. Most children have ambivalent feelings about siblings. Some children feel like they are the favorite, and others feel like outcasts or scapegoats. Many feel a combination of pleasure and envy when thinking about their brothers or sisters. As children grow older, they usually take greater pleasure in each other, and they can share events, feelings, play, and good times. This may be especially true of siblings of the same sex, but brothers and sisters also enjoy each other during the school-age years.

Losing a sibling is losing a special connection with one's childhood. Siblings live life in ways that are close to a child's experience. Siblings laugh together differently than children laugh with their parents or persons in the outside world. As they grow into teenage years and beyond, siblings find comfort in each other's perceptions of the parents. They can be strong allies against the "that impossible" or "old-fashioned" mom or dad.

After the death of a sibling, children may fantasize that their lives will be much better. Their parents won't have to spend time and money on or pay attention to that irritating member of the family. The thought may be, *"I will get more attention and lots of things now that my brother is dead."* What children don't understand is that the parents will usually be so overwhelmed by sorrow and so preoccupied by the events surrounding the death that the surviving child receives very little attention. This may be especially true if the sibling has been ill for a long time.

It is hard for children to deal with depressed parents who are inattentive, preoccupied, and irritable. They may receive little support and be truly disappointed that more is not coming to them. They may feel devalued, angry, and annoyed at the parents. They may even wish that that they had died so the parents could mourn over them. They may become ill or commit dangerous acts, tempting the fates to bring about increased concern and interest from their parents. They may feel guilty about wishing for their sibling's death. They may feel anger that their life is so altered and sad. *"There is no fun left in our family,"* one child moaned.

Parents also deal with a complicated set of feelings. They may wish that a different child had died, *"Why did it have to be my favorite?"* Or they may be relieved that the child was the one who was most troublesome. Feeling relief may bring about intense guilt feelings. Part of their future has been cut off; they have lost their immortality or their security in old age. Parents may mourn the loss of all the time, effort, teaching, and car pooling that went into raising this child and mourn the loss of graduations, marriages, and grandchildren now denied to them.

The remaining child may suddenly become an only child or be thrown into the adult world more intensely. Parents may suddenly become overprotective of remaining children, curtailing independent activities. Children may feel that the parents do care about them, but they may be enraged when their independence is curtailed.

It is important for parents to talk to the remaining children and share their feelings, the events surrounding the death, and plans for the future, just as in the case of the death of a parent or any close attachment figure. The more the children feel understood and loved, the easier it will be for them to work through the loss of their sibling. It also helps for the children to understand and be prepared for their parent's long-lasting depression and grief. Shared insights may increase the understanding and expectations in the family even though it will not remove the pain.

Some parents are pathologically obsessed with their loss and can discuss nothing else in the years to come. Nevertheless, it is important for people to continue to talk and reminisce about the dead child and to explore and share remembered experiences. Adults need to be attuned to the more serous concerns and worries of the surviving children and can express a variety of feelings surrounding this important event.

Children may refrain from bringing up reminiscences or concerns for fear of upsetting the parent. The response from the mother or father could be, *"Tears come to my eyes when I think of your sister, but I am still glad to talk to you about her. Thank you for sharing your thoughts with me. Don't worry about my tears."*

Part III
Adolescence

Chapter 12

Transition to Adolescence

Adolescence is the stage of life before adulthood. There are few parents who do not have some anxiety about surviving their child's adolescence. Many parents consciously worry about this period more than any other.

Until recently, adolescence spanned a relatively short number of years. It was not that long ago that young people were considered adults by the end of their teens. They often married and began their life's work before their twenty-first birthday. Children waited until junior high school for the more formalized rites of passage into adolescence. In junior high, they wore special clothes and makeup, participated in special activities and sports, and were allowed greater freedom and adventures. There were extremes of teenage behavior that created concern for parents. But each generation of teenagers seems to find its own way of individuating, creating another burden for mom and dad.

Today, even elementary school children seem to behave like adolescents. This may be the result of the media, which expose children to the behavior, clothes, interests, music, and dance of adolescence before they are physiologically there. Some children are developing earlier, with the onset of puberty often beginning at about age ten. At the other end of adolescence, we find young people still in college and graduate school and dependent on their parents. Often, they are not in a position to make adult commitments to marriage and child-rearing until they are well into their twenties and early thirties.

Since developmental changes take place over so many years, it is helpful to divide adolescence into three stages: early (eleven to fifteen years of age), middle (fifteen to eighteen years of age) and late adolescence (eighteen to twenty-two years). Not every child fits into a specific chronological classification. But for purposes of discussion, these three periods have different developmental tasks and normal stresses.

You may feel that your child's adolescence is your last chance to be parental. You may see this as the most important time to exert your presence. This period of physical, emotional, and social change in your child may coincide with your midlife issues. Many parents in their forties are going through an identity crisis and dealing with the physical changes of menopause. This may complicate the interactions between parent and child. Mothers and fathers of adolescents may also be coping with aging parents who may be increasingly dependent and needy. The needs of the older generation and the demands of the unpredictable adolescents can be a challenge.

The adolescent period may be a time when many of the difficulties that the child experienced as a preschooler are played out again, often with increased intensity. Teens' anger, tears, and depression can be just as stressful for parents as they were when the three-year-old was oppositional, demanding, difficult, irritable, and moody. The difference is that the three-year-old can be picked up, held, and put into bed.

Teenagers are intensely focused on themselves and their friends. They are not interested in their parents. They are usually not as involved with their family as they once were. Their idols may be older teenagers, teachers, or performers. Parents are often low on the totem pole.

Many of the techniques parents used to interact with their child no longer work. Just looking at a teenager or mildly making a suggestion can cause a volcanic eruption. A simple request may seem like an enormous intrusion to a teenager.

Children mature physically, socially, and emotionally at different rates. Parents are confronted with the immense task of understanding their teenager. There is no other group of children or parents experiencing the same constellation of behaviors at the same time. Support, validation, and reassurance are hard to find when each family is confronted with individual stress and change in their teenager.

It appears that parents who enjoyed their own adolescence and who sailed through the stormy waters comfortably will be more relaxed as they respond to their teenager. Parents who experienced unusual stress, trauma, or deprivation as adolescents may find parenting teenagers much more difficult. For example, Holocaust survivors could not tolerate the carefree, self-centered behaviors their teenagers displayed. They had no basis for identifying with their children's adolescent experience. All they could remember was their own need to survive in a cruel world. Similarly, parents who lived in poverty and had to work to help their family provide enough food to eat have little patience with teenage materialism and self-centeredness. On the other hand, some mothers and fathers may indulge their adolescents in order to repair their own deprived years. *"I didn't have these luxuries, but now I can provide them for my kids to enjoy."*

Parents also react to the changing appearances of their children. The emerging sexuality stimulates many memories and fantasies associated with the parent's own budding teenage sexuality. Parents may find themselves attracted to their children and become very frightened by their feelings. For many mothers and fathers, it was certainly easier when their adolescents looked and acted like children.

Developmental Tasks of Adolescence

There are three major groups of developmental tasks that the adolescent must accomplish during this period of life. It helps if parents can understand that much of the strange and difficult behavior is an attempt to deal with biological, social, and emotional tasks and challenges.

1. The biological tasks of adolescence relate to physical and sexual maturation. The adolescent must learn to understand and control sexual impulses, relate to new bodily sensations, and deal with pubescent changes. These biological events in adolescence equip their bodies to be sexual and to reproduce. Adolescents must also learn to make peace with new physical body contours and facial appearance. They must learn to accept the size of their breasts, the curve of their noses, the length of their legs, and the texture of their hair.
2. Socially, adolescents must decide on and prepare for future occupations. They must select adult roles as doctors, pilots, lawyers, salespeople, engineers, teachers, chefs, and the like. They must also search for and find a mate, competing for someone to love and to be loved by. And they must learn to live within the morality of their culture and take on responsible social roles in their community.
3. Emotionally, teenagers must prepare themselves to live independent lives without undue emotional dependence on other family members. They must learn to live in their own homes separately from their family. They must also find intimacy with a partner and be able to receive and give affection spontaneously and freely.

When parents understand the difficulty and complexity of these tasks and challenges, they can more easily enjoy their teenager and respect this period filled with change, stress, and expectation.

When Teenagers Misbehave

When parents are confronted with a teenager who misbehaves or has broken the house rules, they feel rage, frustration, and at times despair. No longer is the home a well-ordered, calm environment; it has become a war zone, and the rebels seem to have the upper hand. Parents desperately look for punishments to inflict pain on the offending teenager. This pain is in direct response to the parents own state of fury.

> Nora returned home more than an hour late, and she brought a friend with her. She had not called to let her mother know she would be late. Nora and her friend immediately went into the kitchen and began noisily preparing a snack. Nora's mother stormed in the kitchen saying that Nora was grounded for two weeks. Nora called her mother a "fool," and her mother escalated the punishment to a month. That's when Nora threw a glass of milk on the floor. The glass shattered. The grounding was increased until late in the twenty-first century.

This often happens when parents respond to their anger explosively. It is difficult not to react violently. It is hard to step back and figure out the most appropriate time and place to explore what has just happened. Nora's mother could have said, *"I worried about your not coming home on time, and I waited for you to call. Now I am angry about the whole thing. Tomorrow we will discuss the matter, after I have calmed down a little."* This would tell the teenager how he or she aggravated the parent and that there is a better time to discuss the situation.

Later, when the subject is discussed in a calmer way, the parent can give the teenager another opportunity to respect the parent's concerns and the agreed-on rules. The mother can also apologize for screaming at Nora in front of her friend and promise to work on her explosive reactions (justified as they may be). It is also important to stay with the issue of "coming home on time" or "calling to explain the delay." Discussing the fact that Nora called her mother a "fool" or broke the glass clouds the picture because Nora was responding to her mother's reaction as well as to her own tension and guilt. It's better to focus on the original sin than to dilute the issue you want to stress.

If a teenager who has been given a second chance fails to come home on time or call, he or she can be expected to forgo visiting friends the next weekend. Depriving the teenager of socializing is directly related to the problem of acting irresponsibly when away from home. Taking away the teenager's allowance or television privilege does not relate to the issue at hand.

It is important that the consequences are not so severe, or

that they last over a long period of time. Otherwise, the parent cannot enforce the consequences or the young person responds with increased anger that may be discharged in other unacceptable ways. This situation may be similar to the preschooler who is misbehaving and needs to be removed from the situation for a short time to regroup and restore equilibrium. The teenager may need to stay home, but only for a short time so that the punishment does not create its own problems.

Re-discuss the rules with the early adolescent and formulate new rules dealing with allowance, coming and going with friends (curfew), school responsibility, household chores, telephone use, meal attendance, television watching, and video viewing. The teenager and parents must feel comfortable with the altered rules and expectations. These new rules must consider the neighborhood standards. One child's rules cannot be enormously out of sync with the community's expectations. Each family has the right to different approaches in setting limits for their teenager. Nevertheless, an attempt should be made to set up rules that are compatible with other families in the community.

When teenagers challenge the rules, neglect their responsibilities, and act in a destructive manner, they need to be held accountable for their behavior. Parents may find this difficult because it means seeing that the teenager follows through. If teenagers break or destroy property, they need to help restore it. For example, if a teenager breaks a window, paints graffiti on a wall, or vandalizes a car, he or she needs to restore it, clean it, paint it, buy new glass, and/or help pay the costs to return it to its original state. This demands follow-through with time, effort, and money on the part of the parent, but it is an important part of teaching responsible behavior. It may be easier to ground teenagers or yell at them than to see that they are accountable for the mess they created.

Parents need to listen to the young person's explanations, excuses, and reasons, but still hold the teenager accountable. Most teenagers spin great yarns about *"Why it wasn't my fault."* Sometimes they may have a partial defense, but they should be held responsible.

If certain behaviors continue, it may be necessary to explore the underlying family problems or school pressures with which the young person may be dealing. You as a parent can acknowledge your own part in the problems and talk about what you will work on and change so as not to add to the stress. For example, parents can stop nagging, name-calling, or being explosive. They can practice not reacting in a hostile, provocative, and uncontrolled way.

Preparing a young person for anticipated difficult times and what behaviors are expected is important. For example, if you know that you will be unable to come home at the usual hour because of work commitments or extended family obligations, make sure your teenager knows what he or she is responsible for while you are away. Making a deal ahead of time is both respectful and fair. Teenagers do respond to fairness and are exquisitely sensitive to exploitation.

Give your teenager a second chance to change his or her behavior. This helps create a supportive environment for obeying the rules. Praising and acknowledging the teenager's changes may be all a young person needs to continue to act in a more responsible manner. Some families feel that offering money, clothes, or gifts will increase motivation to obey the family rules. However, if the rules are fair and responsive to the teenagers' growing maturity, bribes should not be necessary.

Even though young people misbehave, they still need an allowance, clothes, and some form of enjoyment. Depriving them may increase the tension and the interpersonal anger. Such punishments should be used sparingly so as not to escalate the negative feelings within the home, thus creating more stress.

Stay rule oriented and focus on the unacceptable behavior. Name-calling, branding, and prophesizing disaster often leave a young person with negative feelings and help consolidate oppositional feelings. Also be careful not to spiral the punishment as Nora's mother did. The issue was coming home late, not abusive language. At another time, the use of foul language may be the problem, but that issue should be addressed separately.

Be thoughtful in the way you carry out discipline. When

things are rough at home, young people often imagine that they can leave their family and survive on their own, free of physical and psychological abuse. If the home environment is stressful, rejecting, fearful, and disrespectful, teenagers may leave home with no safe place to go. Of course, down deep, the young person wants to be run after by mom or dad and brought back to a more nurturing environment where they will feel loved and respected.

A good approach is to:

- Treat a teenager as you would an out-of-town guest or your best friend.
- Carefully communicate with a teenager.
- Not intrude into the teenager's private business.
- Not demand certain behavior from a teenager in an authoritarian way.

You will be on safer grounds when you are considerate and fair and take responsibility for your own negative actions. This may help create an atmosphere where you are treated more respectfully and the rules are less frequently broken or challenged.

Chapter 13

The Early Adolescent

Children aged eleven to fifteen are in their early adolescent years. Many parents find that their early adolescent children irritate them from the moment they walk in the house, slam the door, shuffle their feet, strew their possessions behind them, and collapse in a chair and start twirling their hair. Almost anything the teenager says or does seems to provoke the parents. Often, adults who try to play it cool and not overreact find themselves sucked into controversy that erupts into hostile feelings before a minute goes by.

Many of the suggestions and positive statements that opened up easy communication during childhood are responded to with a shrug, *"You don't know what you're talking about," "What's this, twenty questions?"* or another statement equally abusive, rejecting, and sarcastic. An hour later, this negative creature can be reasonable and delightful. But seldom does it last.

Biological Changes

The most striking characteristic of early adolescence seems to be the teenager's change in appearance. There is a growth in height and weight. There is a heavier cast to their bones and a spurt in muscular development. This gives rise to awkwardness of movement. Hair begins to crop up in the pubic area and under the arms. Sweat glands produce perspiration that has an odor more characteristic of an adult. Their skin becomes thicker. Pimples and blemishes dot the face and body. In time, girls must deal with menstruation and boys experience nocturnal emissions. Their bodies are strange and mystifying.

These changes are especially difficult for teenagers to handle. While there is a certain amount of stress in every change and developmental step, there are many things that make adolescent changes particularly stressful. No two teenagers develop in exactly the same way or at the same time. A teenager's best friend may suddenly be a head taller and interested in the opposite sex. It is hard for teenagers to understand that they are not the only one who is going through these changes. Their nose may be growing. Their breasts may not be growing. They may be sweating much of the time. They may find themselves tearful and irritated one minute, hysterically laughing the next, brooding alone or eagerly and responsively talking on the phone with friends. The chaotic growth pattern and wide emotional swings leave the young adolescent perplexed, anxious, and often exhausted.

The Self-Centered, Introspective Teenager

One of the complaints of parents is that their children spend inordinate amounts of time in the bathroom with the door closed. In fact, they spend a great deal of time behind closed doors in general. How different from the toddler who couldn't bear to be separated from the parents even when the parents wanted some privacy.

Young adolescents spend much of their time looking at themselves, using any mirror that is close at hand. They are inspecting for new hairs, blemishes, and changes in their profile. She is examining the fullness of her breasts; he is checking out the size of his penis. They are extremely self-conscious about these changes. They may not see the same changes in any of their peers.

Teenagers need this time of privacy to become accustomed to their new bodies. They certainly do not look like anything they expected. They are different from their old bodies, yet do not have the look of an adult. Young adolescents often feel embarrassed and critical of these physical changes because the changes are happening before they think they should or do not appear to be happening at all. Young adolescents often wear tent-like clothing or huge shirts to cover their alien bodies. Some teenagers even swim in T-shirts or cover up their bodies in the hottest weather so that no one will know what changes may or may not be taking place. Wearing a bra is embarrassing to some girls, and others wish they needed one. Some girls buy a padded bra or stuff tissue into a regular one to keep up with a friend's breast development.

Some boys feel they will never grow and can't understand why so many girls in their class are so tall. Some young adolescents don't understand why they are always stumbling and dropping things. Their elongating arms and legs are certainly not in control any more! One boy worried that one nipple was growing larger and the other was not. Many teenagers can't stand the way they perspire and smell, and they spend hours in the shower and use tanks of hot water to cleanse their offending bodies. Hair may also become a problem. It becomes an oily, stringy mess in six hours! Where shampooing was a nightmare for the toddler, it becomes an obsession with the teenager. Teenagers love to stand in front of a mirror for hours, grooming, combing, brushing, and blow-drying. All the while, they are trying to make sense of this state of disequilibrium and change.

Not only do physical changes seem chaotic; the teenager's emotional reactions are also unpredictable. The early adolescent often has no idea what caused a tearful response or a flare up of temper. It used to be that certain things made them mad, sad, happy, or fearful. Now they respond with an intense emotional outburst, often for no reason, which is anxiety-producing. Parents, too, have a hard time getting a handle on the emotional roller-coaster they have on their hands.

Early adolescents are not only concerned about what is happening to them in the present, but at times they are depressed about their "lost" childhood. They are still not worried about the future. They have lost their familiar bodies and the pleasure of playing simple games. They have also lost a comfortable place within the family. They now have many worries, real and imaginary. Early adolescents are intensely critical of their younger siblings, who are still enjoying predictable childhood. They call their siblings "stupid" or "baby," covering up their yearning to be back in a safe, developmental stage.

It's as if they know very well where they have been, but they aren't sure what is happening to them now and can identify with little in terms of the future. The grief for their lost childhood comes and goes, but it may account for some of the irritability, depression, tears, and rude responses. Parents may also be wishing that their children would return to a simpler stage in life, where they were more cooperative and responsible and respected their parents.

Clothes

Early adolescents use clothes, shoes, and other possessions as a defense against feeling isolated and different: *"If I can wear a shirt with a popular logo or the right shoes, I will be more like my friends and not feel so alien."* This may place a great burden on the family budget. When teenagers moan in distress that they have "nothing to wear," they really mean that they feel the need to have something acceptable to their immediate peer group. They often feel defined by what they wear. The "right" clothes are much more important during this vulnerable time than later on in life.

Shopping becomes a nightmare for some parents and their children. Early adolescents are so intense in their likes and dislikes, so sure the parents have no taste at all. They want to wear something their friends will admire and yet not copy exactly. Teenagers may begin to actively crave certain makeup, underwear, boots, and sports equipment. When parents don't provide an opportunity for children to satisfy these materialistic longings, children may begin to shoplift to obtain them. Parents lament, *"You don't need this"* or *"I already bought one for you."* They are exasperated by their formerly sensible child who has suddenly become materialistic and wasteful. They may panic that their child will end up an irresponsible spender who does not appreciate the value of a dollar.

Social Cliques and Peer Groups

The early teenager switches from trying to privately explore what is going on with his or her body to rushing out to be with friends. Teenagers try to distract themselves from feelings that are alien to them. Merging with their peer group, conforming by wearing the right clothes and hairdos, developing a stylized manner of walking, using unique speech patterns, and focusing on special interests, bands, and movies helps early adolescents escape from their personal concerns and not feel so isolated, anxious, and different.

Early adolescents swing from being totally involved with their peers and social cliques to being isolated and self-centered. They need to feel that their friends like them and accept them. These friends are usually of the same sex. Interest in the opposite sex may be just starting, and there is lots of talk. However, interest in the opposite sex is more a reflection of what young teenagers are expected to be involved in rather than an indication of any real ability to sustain a relationship.

Of course, there is an enormous variety in this kind of development. At age eleven to fifteen, it is important for a child to feel that peers of the same sex accept him or her. A best friend may be the first intimate relationship, other than with the family, that the young person has made. It is with peers that children begin to redefine their values: what to like, what to hate, how to behave, and what words to use.

A great deal of this learning takes place on the telephone. Early adolescents talk endlessly on the phone. Even though they may be with their friends all day at school, they rush to the phone as soon as they get home to rehash their day and debrief. They talk about how other kids look, what they did, what music is the rage, what they are going to wear, and what they are going to do on the weekend. They talk about who they like, who is popular, who is a nerd, and who is stuck up. All this talk helps them learn about themselves, how to behave, and in what to believe.

The phone is one of the most important pieces of equipment for the early adolescent. It helps for parents to see the phone not as a diluter of energy and waster of time and money, but as a way for teenagers to develop important social skills and an acceptance of who they are. Even adults use the phone after a social evening to confirm their perceptions and to reminisce about the good, bad, or embarrassing aspects of a party.

E-mail, instant messaging, and computer chat rooms can bring several children together. This type of communication may be less personal than the phone, but it serves as a way of staying in contact with peers. As computer technology continues to develop, parents can be sure that more advanced types of communication will become available.

Testing Rules and Values

During the early adolescent years, young people start to break rules. Their chores are often neglected. They fail to return home at expected times. They may experiment with cigarettes, alcohol, or drugs. They may not do their homework. They may shoplift. They often stop practicing one instrument and start learning another. They may give up a favorite hobby entirely or become passionately interested in a new fad. Their oppositional, negative, and unpredictable behavior is truly difficult. Parents are often ready to tear their hair out. They feel exasperated and are in a panic about losing control when rules and values are questioned and disregarded.

Parents' Role in Early Adolescence

Early adolescence is reminiscent of the three- to five-year-old age group. The emotional struggle is similar to that of the preschooler who is establishing a sense of self, autonomy, the ability to say no, and close feelings to the parent of the opposite sex. Early feelings of attachment and attraction may be intense, but the child is basically presexual, and the feelings are not acted on.

With the normal arousal of sexual feelings in the teenage years comes a renewed attraction to the parent of the opposite sex. However, the teenager feels that these erotic feelings are unacceptable and may push that parent away with sarcasm, rudeness, and rejection. At times, dad and mom can do nothing right when it comes to their teenage daughter or son. Although young teenagers consciously reject their parents, they are still sensitive to both parents' values and certainly need the parental presence for a sense of well-being.

The consistency, affection, and sound value system you gave your children as they were developing will help them during these stormy adolescent years. Your investment in time and energy is a buffer and a reserve to be drawn on.

Many parenting skills that worked with infants, preschoolers, and school-age children no longer work with adolescents. Teenagers need increased independence in taking care of their bodily needs, in selecting what to eat, and in deciding when to sleep, how often to bathe, and with whom to associate. These issues are truly the early adolescent's business. Unless the teen asks you a question about these matters, it is best to step back and avoid involvement. This may be one of the most difficult tasks for parents who have been used to controlling and intruding into their children's bodily needs and care. By keeping their children clean, well-fed, and rested, parents felt that they were being responsible and nurturing. They now must look away and allow the adolescent greater freedom and control of his or her changing body.

It is important not to comment about adolescents' pimples, weight, or odor in either a positive or negative way. *"Stop looking at me!"* a teenager protests. Teenagers are looking at themselves more than enough, forever examining and smelling themselves. A teenager perceives any comment about this changing body as an invasion and often responds with anger and irritation. Leaving some deodorant in the adolescent's bedroom or bathroom may be the easiest way to handle this delicate issue.

Respecting Privacy

Respect teenagers' privacy and their closed doors. Try not to question them about telephone conversations you overheard or personal notes, letters, or diaries that you might have seen. If you do happen to hear something or the diary just happened to fall open and you are overcome with insatiable curiosity, never confront the teenager with what was essentially private business. If what you have learned is serious, of course, the problem needs to be dealt with, but not by revealing the fact that you snooped.

Supporting Friendships

It is important for teenagers to make friends and join clubs, teams, and cliques. It is helpful not to criticize or disparage their choices of friends. Any judgmental remark about teenagers' selections of friends may be interpreted as a direct criticism of them. They may become immediately defensive and reject your position. It is more helpful to comment on some aspect of a friend's behavior and ask the adolescent about the reason for the behavior.

> June's friend Sally was always picking on June's younger brother. Sally also displayed other assorted annoying traits when visiting. There was always tension when she came over. At a private time, June's mother asked June what went on at Sally's house that might cause Sally to pick on Jimmy. Together, they analyzed the problem, and June did not feel that her mother was attacking her choice of friends.

It is important not to brag about your teenagers or take their side against their friends. They do not like to be evaluated, even when the comments are positive. They often feel so vulnerable that any attention feels intolerable and embarrassing. Criticism of friends is often taken personally.

Drive Me, Mom

Driving early adolescents to group activities is one of the biggest supports that parents can provide. It is truly an act of love. It facilitates their social experiences. Social events and work experiences are vital distractions from the teenager's self-involved preoccupations. They are socially stimulating, or adventuresome, or otherwise satisfying. These activities are necessary to the social and emotional-well being of adolescents.

Parents who cheerfully drive their teenagers and pick them up on time are also modeling responsibility and support. This is not easy when the teenager's social schedule conflicts with that of the adult. However, providing transportation may ensure the safety of your teenager. The teenager will be less inclined to hitch rides or ride a bike at unsafe times or in unsafe places. It might be possible to find other parents willing to share this task, but if it is not possible, each adult in the family can take a turn. Paying for transportation by a responsible driver may be another alternative. One of the positive byproducts of driving is that you may hear what is happening and may develop insights into the personalities with whom your adolescent is associating. In other words, you have a special window into the teenager's world that might not be otherwise available.

Do's and Don'ts for Parents

It is easy for parents to ruin this early adolescent period. It is the parent's responsibility to shift attitudes and techniques when dealing with these young people.

- Don't remind them that when you were a child, you worked hard and were responsible.
- Don't question them about telephone conversations or private communications you may overhear.
- Don't interfere with their business; don't tell them what to wear, when to bathe, etc.
- Don't criticize or disparage their clubs or friends.
- Don't brag about them or take sides against their friends.
- Don't provide them with too much money or deprive them of spending money.
- Don't talk to them only about the state of their room.

- Don't talk about their weight, their complexion, or their hair unless an opinion is requested.
- Do respect their privacy.
- Do give them increased independence in spending nights out and going to camp or shopping malls.
- Do respect their need to make friends. It takes time and effort to develop these relationships.
- Do provide them with the use of a telephone. If funds are available, consider a private phone just for the adolescent!
- Do allow them to follow the fashions.
- Do provide them with the freedom to belong and participate in team, club, clique, and work activities.
- Do drive them.
- Do anticipate that the adolescent will break some old rules and question some assumed values.
- Do expect that they will have some secrets that cannot be shared with their parents.
- Try not to overeact to an upsurge of profanity.

It's Not Easy for Parents

It may be hard for you to step back from the usual responsibilities and involvement. Often parents are afraid that they are losing control of their child and that their authority within the home is threatened. They may also be frightened of their own intense feelings toward teenagers who are becoming more sexual. They may be jealous of their child's new attachments. Parents may feel threatened by maturing teenagers and want to keep them children, not allowing them to experience more independence and closer relationships with those outside the family. Parents may also be concerned about whether their child will be heterosexual. They may unwittingly encourage premature boy-girl dating as a way to reassure themselves that their teenager is "normal."

Chores and family responsibilities may have to be redefined and changes negotiated. The teenager's room is a source of conflict. It is as chaotic as the teen's own state of being, strewn with clothes, papers, food, and sentimental objects. If possible, this room should be considered the adolescent's sanctuary. Asking if the teenager needs some help with the cleanup or organization may communicate that something should be done about the chaos and filth. Mutually agreeing on a future date to clean the room may help. But falling into a pattern of daily nagging is not productive and adds to family conflicts.

It may be important to look into your own adolescent experience if you find you are overreacting to your teenager much of the time. It is hard to provide supervision, parental presence, and security for your adolescent and at the same time provide increased independence and time for adventure. The goal here is to let out plenty of line, but to keep the adolescent on the hook and to still hold on to the rod.

Chapter 14

Sexuality and the Early Adolescent

Although there is great variation, most formal dating doesn't usually begin until mid- adolescence. However, younger adolescents meet in groups in or out of school and often find someone of the opposite sex whom they enjoy. Experiences between boys and girls are then shared and giggled about with same-sex friends. A relationship often serves as a status symbol. To be going with someone or to be considered an item is valued. The early adolescent usually does not have the maturity to sustain an intimate relationship, but having a boyfriend or girlfriend is something to talk about with peers.

Some teenagers-of either sex-may temporarily lose interest in their school commitments because they become intensely involved in "crushes" or passionate feelings that can easily absorb most or all of their emotional energy. Usually, parents have little influence over these relationships-whether real or fantasy. Perhaps the wisest course is to do little and "wait it out." It will pass!

In the past, traditional dating began when a boy or girl could go someplace without a parent. Young adolescents often need their parents to drive them. This is especially the case in suburban communities. Driving boys and girls to movies, school dances, or parties may allow boy-girl friendships to develop appropriately without creating a premature seductive situation.

It is very important for an adult to be present at parties and when young teenagers of the opposite sex spend time at home together. An adult presence may prevent boy-girl intimacies from being acted on.

The emerging sexuality of adolescents has always been a concern for parents. Parents worry that the adolescent is maturing too fast and is precociously involved with the opposite sex, or they worry that the adolescent is not developing fast enough and seems out of sync with peers. Some parents may worry that the child is not developing heterosexually, although this is seldom openly discussed.

Today, many children seem precociously sexual. There are a number of single family households where the parents are dating and modeling different aspects of courting behavior and seduction. Adolescents may watch their mother or father get ready for a date, listen to their telephone conversations, watch them hug and kiss their friends, or even observe other, more intimate, sexual behavior. Similarly, the media show young people many explicit images of how people make love. Children are exposed to scenes of seduction and lovemaking on television and in movies.

Adolescents are increasingly left unsupervised during much of their day. As a defense against painful feelings of loneliness, young people look to friends for companionship. With long periods of unsupervised time together, sexual experimentation and more intimate contact may develop. Adolescents who are having trouble in school, not finding success on the playing field, and not involved in music or art may act out sexually in order to feel more mature and grown-up. When good feelings are not obtained from success and competence, positive feelings of acceptance and affection can be sought in early sexual contact.

There has been more peer pressure for teenagers to participate in sex since the sexual revolution began in the 1960s. Old values stressing the importance of virginity until marriage are seldom verbalized. In the 1970s and 1980s, few adolescents were proud of holding to the traditional values of abstinence from sexual intercourse. With the advent of the AIDS virus, values began changing. However, many teenagers feel invincible, and the AIDS virus may have little significant effect on their sexual conduct.

With better nutrition, there seems to be an earlier onset of puberty. Sexual feelings may also be experienced sooner. This surge of erotic sensation is hard for the early adolescent to understand and control. Sexual impulses and concerns conflict with and drain energy from other activities and experiences that help the adolescent develop self-esteem and feelings of competence. Preoccupation with sexual urges may get in the way of studying, performing, or the general ability to function productively.

Many children have not learned how to delay gratification of their wishes. Often, middle- and upper-class children experience and receive too much too soon. They have not had the opportunity to long for something that is important to them. It is hard for adolescents to imagine controlling or delaying gratification of their sexual urges if other wishes have always been promptly gratified. As well, when today's adolescents were children, they became involved in activities that once were reserved for teenagers. Having already experienced team sports, travel, special clothes, parties, and the like, they may be jaded by the time they begin junior high school. Having tried almost everything else by the time they are eleven, sex may be the one experience that is left.

Parents may add to their children's sexual interest by setting up seductive situations. Some parents allow children to have boy-girl sleepovers or unsupervised parties during the early adolescent years. However, boy-girl sleepovers with parental presence and supervision, can sometimes provide positive experiences. But, these activities may also stimulate premature sexual experimentation. Also, parents may (unconsciously) want to feel that they have a "normal kid" and may be relieved, especially if their male child is acting like a "real boy." Traditionally, parents do not worry as much about the early sexual encounters of their male children as compared to their female children. In fact, in the past, some fathers arranged for their sons' first sexual experience with prostitutes, often when the boy turned fifteen. With the prevalence of AIDS and other sexually communicated diseases, this is certainly not advised. There are other negative psychological ramifications when a young boy has this kind of first experience.

Parents' Role in Teaching Sexual Behavior

It is important for parents to develop and model a positive attitude about sex and marriage. Witnessing a happy marriage in which both partners are respectful and affectionate is perhaps the best communicator of the value of marriage. Most good marriages include a joyful sex life, although the more intimate aspects of sexual behavior should be kept private.

Infants, toddlers, and young children receive great benefits from being held, rocked, cuddled, and hugged. This type of nurturing by both parents is an investment in the attitudes and behavior of the adolescent. Depriving a child of physical warmth in the early years may unfortunately catapult them into premature sexual experiences because they yearn for the body contact of which they were deprived of when they were very young. Some teenagers are comfortable receiving physical affection from their mom or dad. But others reject such conduct and squirm away from parental hugs and kisses.

When parents talk about their sexual values, it may be helpful not to talk personally. To discuss personal details of your sexual life may be embarrassing for the adolescent. Questioning a teenager about their sexual behavior is intrusive and often nonproductive. Young people can easily lie when asked directly about their behavior. In fact, most teenagers have secrets that they keep from their parents well into their adult years.

Although some adolescents may openly discuss their sexual experience, it may be unrealistic to expect your adolescent to confide in you about behavior that may be intimate or guilt-producing. When they are with their peers, teenagers can more accurately describe their behavior, laugh about incidents, and make jokes about their sexual experiences. Parents are of another generation, and the teenager sees them as being judgmental and old-fashioned. Remember how little you shared with your own parents during the time of sexual exploration, and do not expect that your teenager to be much different.

Communication of sexual attitudes and values can take place when young people hear you or other adults discuss problems of neighbors and friends or read newspaper articles and watch television specials dealing with sexual issues. These allow young people to listen to and participate in discussions without feeling personally lectured or shamed.

You should take an active role in communicating specific and practical information dealing with menstruation, sexual intercourse, birth control, nocturnal emissions, and masturbation. Do not confuse these issues with discussions about venereal disease and AIDS. On the one hand, parents want teenagers to feel positive about their bodies, to delay gratification, and to eventually enjoy the sexual act. At the same time, parents want them to be safe. The dangerous and the negative aspects of sexual behavior should be explained at a different time, when other health problems are the focus of the discussion.

The more the teenagers are frightened, the more they may try to test their sexual vulnerability. For the same reason that teenagers make good soldiers and take unnecessary risks, they may behave promiscuously. This may be true even when they have adequate sexual information.

Teenagers who are angry with their parents may act out sexually. When there is stress in the home and when the family provides little warmth and understanding, there may be a strong motivation to find immediate gratification from sexual encounters. Many early teenager girls who find themselves pregnant moan that all they wanted was a little hugging and tenderness. A baby was a little more than they bargained for. Almost all pregnant teenagers report that they received little pleasure, support, or understanding at home, especially from their fathers.

Reasons to Delay Sexual Intercourse

It is important for you to realize that the normal adolescent, especially the middle-school or high-school adolescent, is intensely concerned with developing love relationships. For the young person, showing love to and feeling love from a person of the opposite sex are important developmental tasks. Crushes and love are preparation for more intimate mature relationships. However, parents are concerned with how the young person will act on these intense feelings.

There are many good reasons to delay sexual intercourse until later adolescence (age eighteen and up). For most early adolescents, sexual experiences are relatively exploitative. Partners are often not interested in giving pleasure to each other, but only in experiencing their own sexual release. Early experiences may have long-lasting effects on later sexual pleasure. Problems sometimes result from unsatisfactory, painful, and exploitative early heterosexual encounters. Some lesbians have reported that they felt more comfortable with women than with men after painful, embarrassing, or abusive sexual experiences too early in their lives. Similar statements have been made by homosexual males.

Early adolescents may not be mature enough to effectively deal with birth control devices and procedures. They often feel embarrassed about being careful and may not have the confidence to provide protection for themselves. They may not want to interrupt the flow of erotic feelings and use contraceptives, which may intrude on spontaneous sexual impulses. For girls, the less mature tissues of the vagina are more sensitive to infections and cell changes.

Parents need to be aware that if their teenagers have not been provided with an adequate amount of sexual information in the elementary-school years, it is necessary to provide that information during early adolescence. For guidance, see Chapter 5, Dealing with Sexual Issues.

Menstruation

It is helpful for a mother to share more specific information about menstruation with her adolescent daughter. (Fathers can communicate this information as well.) Even though the teenager may protest and say, *"I know all about it,"* repeat some basic information. Girls need to know that pads and tampons are available, where to buy them, how to use them, where to carry them, how frequently to change them, and how to maintain general hygiene during menstruation. It is also important not to communicate negative admonitions. Most young girls can engage in almost any sport or other recreational activity during their periods. Cramping may occur for some, but certainly not for every teenager.

You can also reflect that having a period is a bother and at times can be messy or embarrassing. A little humor takes the grimness out of this new biological event. Simply reminding an early adolescent that she is now a women and should be delighted to reach this milestone is often not enough. It may leave her feeling that no one understands the inconvenience of the whole experience. It may be helpful to also explain that she may feel more moody and irritable just before her period begins. But don't say, *"You're upset because you are getting your period."* This can enrage any female. It may be better to bite your lip and say nothing, recognizing that you need not take explosions personally when they occur at that time of the month.

Nocturnal Emissions

If parents did not explain the possibility of nocturnal emissions to their sons in elementary school, (see Chap. 5) it is appropriate to mention this during the early teenage years. The early adolescent needs to understand the terms *erection* and *ejaculation* and when and why they occur. Often, these topics are not covered in health classes. If a mother or father have trouble talking directly about these loaded matters, they can present their teenager son with a book or pamphlet dealing with sexuality. It is a better alternative than ignoring these important issues. It also expresses a respect for your son's need to understand his body and its functions.

Masturbation

Many adolescents stimulate themselves by masturbating. Many children have found masturbation to be a source of comfort. It is important not to create guilt feelings or increased anxiety by implying that masturbating is unhealthy, sinful, and dangerous. *"You can go blind if you keep on playing with yourself"* echoes in many adult memories. Of course, some young people do not participate in erotic play. But it is often far healthier for teenagers to give themselves sexual release through masturbation than to participate actively in sexual intercourse.

It may be hard for parents to suggest this. However, masturbation has so long been taboo that adults have no vocabulary or ability to comfortably discuss this possibility with their teenagers. But it may be worth a try. You can explain that knowing what parts of the body are sensitive and erotic and being able to comfortably explore helps in developing a satisfactory sexual life later. Locating the clitoris and finding it as a source of pleasure may be an important discovery for any female at any age. The ability to communicate to a partner what feels good often does not happen spontaneously during early sexual experience. If parents find this information too hard to communicate personally, books on the subject can be provided. In this way, the child may realize that masturbation is an acceptable release for erotic tension.

Birth Control and Unwanted Pregnancies

Parents are often terrified by the possibility of early unwanted pregnancies. What an awesome responsibility it is to bring a child into the world! For the mature adult, it is one of life's most stressful events. For an early adolescent who has barely completed childhood, there are serious personal, social, emotional, health, educational, and economical consequence. Young girls who become pregnant have difficulty completing the important developmental tasks of adolescence, such as remaining in school and dating, so necessary in preparing them for their adult roles.

The young girl who becomes pregnant is often uninformed about her body and usually had little information about methods of protecting herself from an unwanted pregnancy. Others may have such a poor relationship with their parents that they unconsciously fulfill the parents' worst nightmares and act promiscuously. Some teenage girls are so desperate for affection that precocious sexuality seems a solution. A few become pregnant when there is a strong identification with their own mother, who had a history of premarital pregnancies. Often, adopted children will be promiscuous during their teenage years and repeat the sexual behavior of their biological mother—at least, what they imagine was their mother's behavior.

Parents need to be aware that they can play an important role in preventing unwanted teenage pregnancies. It is the parent's responsibility to see that the teenager is informed about sexual intercourse, types of birth control available, how to obtain contraceptives, and how to use them. This information is as important for boys as for girls.

It is amazing how many informed teenagers do not utilize birth control methods. Many parents are reluctant to provide the contraceptives to the adolescent. Perhaps some parents feel that adolescents who are mature enough to be involved in sexual relationships should obtain their own safeguards. However, if a parent knows that an adolescent is already sexually active, setting up doctor's visits or taking the teenager to a birth control center may help prevent an unwanted pregnancy.

You need to provide adequate adult supervision, especially when your teenager is in the company of the opposite sex. Just "being there" is a great deterrent and will help to prevent many pregnancies. Parents also need to make sure that the relationship between themselves and the child is not so hostile that the child feels no support within the family.

You need to provide family pleasures, warmth, and humor to indirectly help adolescents control their strong sexual impulses. This is no easy task when adolescents are provocative, sassy, abusive, and absent much of the time. It is well-known that most young girls who function well at school and who have good family relationships and adequate sexual information rarely become pregnant in these early teenage years.

Parents can also provide opportunities for the teenager to learn some of the difficulties of caring for an infant, toddler, or preschooler. Many teenagers associate having a baby with playing with dolls, dressing and undressing them but then returning to them to a cradle when they have had enough. How different this is from the realities of parenting an infant! Therefore, encouraging teenagers to baby-sit, help out in a daycare center or a nursery school, or be a counselor in a summer camp may help prepare them for some of the realities and stresses of bringing a baby into this world.

Abortion or Adoption?

Abortion and adoption are controversial issues. They involve religious beliefs, taboos, and cultural and personal values. Parents need to support the adolescent in exploring all the possibilities and alternatives when dealing with an unwanted pregnancy. This will likely be stressful for most family members.

It is easy for parents to become hysterical and enraged, pointing fingers of blame and shame at the teenager. Few parents can take their teenager's pregnancy lightly. However, as stressful as it is, this problem may provide an opportunity to open up communication, engage in real problem solving, and provide a sense of warmth and caring between the adults in the home and the adolescent.

Young teenagers are usually dependent on their parents for financial support, so parents will have to provide money for an abortion or for care and support throughout a pregnancy. Young people who decide to keep the baby are also confronted with the realities of infant care and providing a home and support for the new baby. Many times, the infant is thrust on the grandparents, who may be in no position either physically or financially to start the child-rearing process all over again. Young adolescents must also face problems associated with an interruption in school attendance when they decide to raise a baby. Future life choices are severely limited when high school is not completed.

Placing the baby for adoption may be another alternative. However, once a baby is brought to term, a bond may be created between the mother and child, and wrenching the baby away may be difficult. The adolescent who puts her baby up for adoption will eventually need to mourn the loss and may struggle with guilt feelings and fantasies about the child for many years to come. As difficult as this process is, it still may be less traumatic than trying to raise a baby without the supports of a stable family, maturity, and financial independence.

Going through an abortion may also be stressful. A young teenager can find it difficult to arrange for the medical procedure, deal with the physical discomfort and inconvenience, and struggle with feelings of shame and guilt that may be associated with the abortion. The young woman may need a parent to take her, stay with her, and drive her home, as well as provide emotional support through the recovery period. Some professional counseling may also be in order.

It is difficult to make a decision to end a pregnancy, to give a baby up for adoption, or to keep a baby. The choices need to be explored calmly and directly. The early adolescent must consider all the family members involved, as well as the father of the unborn child, when making the choice. In the end, the young woman must make this decision herself, but her parents need to share their own feelings because they too are affected by the decision. It is easy to see why preventing an unwanted pregnancy is so important. The results of pregnancy are numerous; there are many emotional, social, financial, and legal implications involved, no matter what the choice.

Sexually Transmitted Diseases

Sexually transmitted diseases, or STDs, which include venereal disease, herpes, and the deadly AIDS virus, are frightening byproducts of sexual activity. As a result of the almost universal ability of teenagers to deny the possibility that anything bad will happen to them, many engage in sexual activity with little thought of the consequences. A surprising number have contracted herpes, chlamydia, gonorrhea, and syphilis. Some have little awareness of how and when they became infected. Nevertheless, their condition needs medical and educational attention. Too often, children are ashamed to talk about their symptoms with their parents or concerned adults, and the problems go untreated.

Parents need to provide regular medical checkups for teenagers. Adolescents often need reassurance, support, and information from doctors, but they are reluctant to ask for appointments. Questions that the young person may be afraid or too embarrassed to pose to parents may be easily answered by a professional.

> Jennifer was sure she had contracted a venereal disease by sitting on a toilet. Her doctor reassured her that unless she was having intercourse while sitting on the toilet, it would be next to impossible to get a disease. Was she relieved!

Health classes in junior high schools can provide some helpful sexual information. However, practical information about using condoms and practicing safe sex may not be explicitly presented in class. Nevertheless, sexually active teenagers need to be informed through discussion or books and pamphlets that deal with these intimate activities.

Parents who feel that school is not an appropriate place for sex education certainly need to take a more active and informed role in providing information about this important activity to their young teenagers. Simply admonishing young people that sex before marriage is sinful may not be enough to ensure that the teenager will abstain.

Most teenagers today have reasonably adequate information available about the spread of AIDS. But in the end, it is the parents' responsibility to provide the emotional supports within the family so that teenagers do not have to act promiscuously and find themselves vulnerable and involved in exploitative sexual situations and relationships.

Keeping the Teenager Off the Streets: Young Teenage "Run-A-Ways" are in Danger

Parents need to worry about any young person who is not living at home or in a supervised setting. Young people who are "on the streets" have few emotional and financial supports. They exist in an exploitative sexual world. In order to survive, they may be using their bodies promiscuously for emotional support as well as for financial gain. Casual sexual encounters, and life "on the streets" may predispose a young person to drug use (and addiction), as well as the AIDS virus and other communicable diseases, with obvious dire consequences. Drug use and their dangers may also be part of the street "scene".

Young people who aggressively reject their families are often feeling negative about themselves and are not functioning well in school or with peers. Their attacks on their parents act as an outlet for their many frustrations and disappointments. In response, it may be easier for parents to say, *"Get out of my house!"* than to try to deal with the stressful issues that both parent and child are facing.

More than any other time in history, it behooves parents to make sure the home is less stressful, tumultuous, and rejecting. The home should always attempt to provide a secure base to the out-of-control teenager. The prognosis is usually poor when young persons run away and try to live on the streets.

It may be important for parents to get professional help in creating a more harmonious household in which the adolescents feel they have a respected role and that they are not the only problem. Teenagers may also need similar help to find ways to get along with their family members.

Chapter 15

Drugs and Alcohol in Early Adolescence

It is not hard to see why teenagers may be seduced by drugs and alcohol. Advertising has made it clear that any discomfort can be eliminated quickly and easily with the ingestion of a pill. Stomachaches, headaches, backaches, muscle aches, menstrual discomfort, and bowel trouble all disappear when we take medicine. Adults are prescribed diet pills to control their weight, barbiturates to help them sleep, mood elevators to fight depression, and tranquilizers to assuage anxiety and tension. Children have grown up watching parents pop pills into their mouths at the breakfast table, pour themselves a drink when they come home from work, and hold onto a glass all evening long!

Research has shown that infants and toddlers who are deprived of adequate sensory stimulation find ways to sooth themselves. They learn to rock in their beds, bang their heads, suck their thumbs, masturbate compulsively, or pull at their hair. Children who experience early neglect and abuse are prime candidates for addictive behavior in their teenage years. Infants and toddlers who found such ways to bring pleasure to themselves will more likely look to drugs and alcohol to do the same thing to control the stresses of adolescence. Through the years, they have learned that adults will not be there when they need them. Drugs and alcohol help them feel soothed and comforted, just as during infancy they banged their heads or masturbated to ease their tension.

Why Teenagers Take Drugs

Teenagers often take drugs because they see the important

adults in their lives do the same. Teenagers are often depressed and anxious. Many of the changes of early adolescence create a higher level of anxiety and depression. Teenagers tend to experience loneliness more acutely than when they were younger. They are often left unsupervised after school and feel ignored by their friends. If teenagers are angry with their parents, they will more likely oppose their values and reject warnings about the use of drugs. What a good way to be oppositional!

Taking drugs may be one of the easiest ways to find acceptance with a group of young people. Not only do teenagers feel that their mood can be altered with these substances, but they enjoy the companionship and camaraderie of other teens who use drugs, so they join with them.

Young people who have a hard time finding satisfaction in school, sports, music, drama, or work often turn to drugs and alcohol to help them feel better, more grown up and less stressed. Those who cannot tolerate the anxiety connected with performance may take drugs. They may not be able to deal with the tension and stress of practicing, learning, or performing. Expectations to excel produce emotional strains that may be too intense for the already stressed out teenager. When feelings are so strong, drugs may dilute the pain. Unfortunately, after the effect of the drug or alcohol wears off, the young person is still confronted with the tasks and responsibilities he or she may have tried to escape.

Early adolescents who are heavily involved with drugs are more seriously affected by them than late adolescents or young adults. The young teenager's sense of self is still emerging, and the need to find satisfaction in competency and the mastery of skills is very important. Young teenagers who take drugs are derailed from their progress along a normal developmental course. It may be much harder to get back on track later.

Most teenagers use drugs experimentally, and drug use may be one of the delicious secrets that are kept from their parents. These young people may or may not go on to become addicted and use drugs in a self-destructive manner. Drugs can become addictive for teenagers who cannot soothe their anxieties and who have little capacity to emotionally restore themselves. As teenagers continue to use drugs, they often fantasize: "*I might die, and no one will care about me.*" "*Then they'll be sorry.*" "*At least I can trust these drugs or this alcohol to give me pleasure; no one else has.*" Heavy drug use often goes hand in hand with depression and any other unfulfilled needs or abusive conditions.

What Parents Can Do to Help

Parents must consider how much time the teenager is spending without adult supervision. That is not to say that young people should be denied privacy. Nor is there any real danger in allowing the young person to be alone in the house for short periods of time. But, the situation is much more dangerous when teenagers are left alone for long periods, as when parents do not return from work until very late in the evening or take long business trips or vacations. In these circumstances, it is easier for the teenager to look to peer groups for companionship. Trouble may also occur when a group of young adolescents are left at home with no supervision. The parent may feel that they are not needed since (they assume) the teenagers will take care of each other. However, fighting, aggressively "horsing around", and experimenting with drugs is more likely to take place when no adult is "there".

The use of drugs seems to counteract early adolescents' loneliness. They may feel angry at parents who, they feel, are not concerned enough with them to be present. Teenagers don't always want the company of an adult, but they want to know that they have not been abandoned and that their parents care enough about them to supervise and protect them. Parents who drive teenagers to after-school activities support their need for ego satisfactions. After-school activities help combat loneliness as well as depression.

Are you expecting too high a level of performance from your early adolescent? Do you expect your teenager to follow a script that has no hills and valleys in achievement? Often, adolescents shift gears and focus on body changes rather than academic accomplishments. Seventh and eighth graders are often difficult to motivate academically. However, by the ninth grade, most teenagers settle down, realizing that they have a future of more than just a day or so.

Are you caught up in annoying power struggles over chores and behavior, and do these conflicts often escalate into World War III? In such struggles, parents often feel that it is their last chance to correct and change the young persons' annoying habits. Parents forget that by creating these storms, they end up alienating the early adolescent, causing upsets that for some may be soothed only by drugs.

It is important to treat an early adolescent respectfully and politely, even when he or she is abusive. Perhaps this is the hardest thing for parents to do. It is very difficult for parents to see that stresses and physical discomforts may be causing the abuse. Parents are the safest person upon whom adolescents can vent their feelings. It may be too risky to blow up at their friends, teachers, or coaches. No one likes to be talked to in an insolent manner. But it is important to look at the larger picture and not overreact. You will need to extend broad shoulders to weather the often-abusive behavior of young adolescents.

Parents should be careful not to name call and model abusive behavior for adolescents. Does your early adolescent know what your values are and what you believe in concerning drugs, alcohol, and smoking? It takes time to share ideas and strong feelings with them. Use time spent relaxing around the dinner table and talking about neighbors, family, friends, and the news as a forum for communicating values. Tell your teenagers what you believe is happening in the world and how you judge and evaluate these events. It is much better to step back and talk about someone else who is having a drug problem that to preach at the young person. Young people often turn a deaf ear if they think that parents are preaching, talking down to them, or treating them like children.

Do your teenagers see you living up to the values you verbalize? Do you drink, take pills, smoke, and act irresponsibly? Do you pick them up on time, return home when you say you will, especially after you pontificated as to the need for them to come home on time?

Communicating About Drugs, Alcohol, and Smoking

In communicating with teenagers, a good maxim to follow is not to ask direct personal questions. Do not ask if the adolescent is taking drugs, smoking marijuana, or drinking. Most teenagers will tell you what they think you want to hear. They are great at shining you on and keeping this kind of information secret.

It is better not to try to frighten teenagers about the dangers of drugs, alcohol, and smoking. They probably know a considerable amount about the dangers. But often they feel invulnerable and immune to the perilous effects and enjoy the excitement of courting disaster.

Most young people experiment and occasionally indulge. These activities may not interfere with social or academic life. But if your children need help with substance-abuse problems, they will leave clues around, letting you know that they are using these substances. Their behavior may be extreme, or they may appear to be "out of it". It may be more helpful to talk about the young person's anxieties, worries, stresses, and pressures than to focus on addictive behavior. Listen, and ask how you could be of help.

It will not be easy to look at the underlying problems. It is easier for the parent to respond emotionally and lecture the teenager on the dangers of addictive behavior. Parents often react hysterically rather than focusing on possible problems in school or with friends or exploring what they, as parents, may be doing that upsets the teenager. It is more comfortable for parents to feel that it is the teenager who has the problem than to look at the more threatening and embarrassing issues within the family, which may be root causes of drug or alcohol use by the young person.

Family counseling may be a more effective way of dealing with the underlying issues than sending the teenager alone to a therapist. For some teenagers, group therapy may be helpful. A group experience may allow an adolescent to practice saying no or learn how to abstain when peer group pressures are great.

When one or both parents have a drinking or drug problem, it is often helpful for the teenager to be enrolled in a support group for children of addictive parents.

If you are aware that the subject of drugs or alcohol is being studied or the school is providing a lecture on this subject, take this opportunity to discuss the subject of substance abuse. *Ask what your son or daughter learned that he or she did not already know. Did he or she hear something that you might find interesting? Was it a good idea for the school to arrange for this kind of lecture? How did others in the class feel about the lecture? What made the teacher or lecturer become interested in substance abuse? Does your child have any suggestions to help Cousin Vicki, whose thirteen-year-old daughter is addicted to alcohol? It is important to express interest about what was especially meaningful to the teenager, not to give another lecture on the subject.*

Finding a time to communicate values and attitudes about drugs, alcohol, and smoking can be a real challenge for parents. One mother found that taking her daughter out to dinner once a month created a positive atmosphere so that they could talk objectively and calmly about this loaded subject.

Creating a positive relationship with your early adolescent is a challenge. It takes warmth, respect, understanding, and some humor during the short intervals that you are all together. No threats or scare tactics, or even the best education, will be as effective as creating a harmonious and supportive family environment. Threats to send a young person away to a juvenile hall or foster home simply confirm to the teenager that he or she is not valued. It also reaffirms the need for secrecy and vigilance in hiding the use of illegal substances from adults.

If a substance-abuse problem has become severe, it sometimes helps to change schools or move to a new neighborhood so that the teenager can start anew and play a different role with another group of peers. However, this is a drastic solution, and it may not be possible for many families.

Do What I Say, Not What I Do

It may be hard to model abstinence and provide a substance-free environment. When they were teenagers, many of today's parents experimented with drugs and alcohol. But it is important for adults in the household to avoid using illegal drugs or misusing prescription or legal drugs. If possible, adults should avoid taking medications to lose weight, to fall sleep, to relax, or to wake up. There should be no intoxication, nor should alcohol be allowed for underage children. When parents use drugs recreationally, it may be unrealistic to expect their teenagers to remain drug free. Many young people use their parents' supply of drugs or alcohol, locating their hidden supplies or taking their share from the bar.

You have a responsibility to see to it that drugs and alcohol are not provided to your teenage guests. This may be difficult for a parent who is anxious for a child to be popular. Parents may want their child's friends to have a good time at their home. As a result, they may be tempted to allow drugs and drinking to occur. Of course, this is illegal. Try to avoid such tempatations.

It may be wise for parents to provide their teenager with a ready reason to refuse any drugs or alcohol offered. For example: *"My parents are very anti-drug and will not hesitate to use their home testing kit on me."* It is wise to avoid such temptations!

Chapter 16

Middle School and Junior High

Junior high or middle school serves a very important function for the early adolescent. This larger institution acknowledges the young person's growing maturity and desire for independence and responsibility. In going from elementary school to junior high, there can be new stresses. Seventh graders do not have one teacher for most subjects, they do not have just one classroom serving as a secure base. They have to develop relationships with many teachers and many more students. The teacher may have as many as 150 to 200 students to relate to each semester. Not only is it hard to learn to know each child's name during a term, but it is next to impossible to establish a personal relationship with all of them. Many junior high school students feel that they are only a name on the seating chart and will only get recognition when there is a disturbance from that seat.

Problems Faced by Junior High Students (some "middle schools" now start in 6th grade)

6th and 7th graders are confronted with many of the same feelings that the kindergartner experienced when starting elementary school. 8th and 9th graders seem so large, sophisticated, and at ease! 7th graders are still trying to make an adjustment. They need to take responsibility for getting to each class on time, changing classes every period, storing possessions in a locker, changing clothes for physical education class, developing relationships with many different teachers, and finding a group of peers with whom to talk, eat, and hang out. All this, and they are still responsible for homework, class preparation, and tests!

In junior high school, teenagers are usually thrown in with a large variety of economic and social groups as compared with elementary school, which usually has a smaller and more homogeneous population. Initially, the seventh grader must identify with a group of peers who often have taken a special name, or an informal title. These groups change with generations and parts of the country. They often demand a certain pattern of speech, a special stride, and special clothing and hair styles. They have values about studying, school attendance, drugs, smoking, alcohol, sex, skateboarding, surfing, dancing, making music, drama, camping, and/or working out. Delinquent behavior may be a sign of status in certain peer cliques, while others are completely free of illegal activities.

The Impact of Junior High or Middle School

Ideally, the junior high school can provide a secure base from which the early adolescent can be distracted from the stresses of this tumultuous period of internal change. The teenager can begin to identify with adults who represent a variety of subjects, skills, interests, and passions. A teenager may connect with a shop teacher, health instructor, drama coach, or history teacher. This connection may provide a bridge to a particular subject or skill. At this age, it is important to a young person to relate to a teacher, who is usually more neutral, objective, and interesting than the parent with whom the teenager has a more emotionally complicated bond. It is important for teachers to understand the value of creating a personal relationship with each student. This is not easy to do. In a large and disruptive class, all students can become the enemy of the teacher.

Ideally, the junior high school will provide new and interesting curricula. Printing, cooking, sewing, drama, chorus, band, orchestra, languages, and assorted sports activities can all be opportunities for new learning and experiences. Challenging curricula are important to help distract adolescents from their obsessive introspection.

The traditional academic subjects often are not taught in ways that relate directly to teenagers. A common complaint is

"School is boring!" It may be more interesting to interrupt the teacher with a strange sound or provocative question. This will get a laugh in the classroom. An uproar may be more interesting than the drone of the teacher. Passing notes, staring at an admired classmate, shooting spitballs, daydreaming, and dozing may be common classroom distractions that are more fun than passive listening.

The school curriculum that includes field trips, performances, bake sales, parties, dances, sporting events, camping trips, and retreats may spice up the semester with change and excitement. Participating in events and having events to anticipate may help counteract the feelings of depression and isolation so pervasive in these years. In fact, involvement in school and extracurricular activities is probably the best medicine to avert depression and excessive use of drugs, alcohol, and sex. Unfortunately, school budgets do not always allow these participatory experiences, which may be costly to run. But these experiences are important motivators for school commitment and may prevent eventual drop out.

It is hard to find good junior high school teachers who enjoy their subjects, communicate them at a level young people can understand, enliven them with participatory experiences, humor, and firmness, and hold students' attention for the usual forty-five minute period. This is especially true when society gives so little respect and money to teachers. Often, the best candidates for inspiring young people do not go into teaching but select other fields of endeavor.

Choice of School

For children living in rural areas, there may be only one school available. But families in urban and suburban communities often have the option of selecting a school for their children. Teenagers are enormously influenced by their friends. They take on the values, attitudes, and commitments of the peer group, clique, or gang. Selecting a middle school may be the one thing you can do to help control the environment in which your teenager studies, plays, and socializes. It may also be important to find a school that specializes in the particular needs of your child.

Paying tuition to a private or parochial school when there is a public school available may seem like a waste of money. However, your teenager is educated only once. The junior high school experience may seriously influence the adolescent's life choices. Using some of the family income for this educational purpose may be a wise investment in the child's future. It also models that parents care enough about the teenager's school experience to put forth the effort to pay for education. Alternative schools may provide smaller classes and individualized teaching and give the young teenager an increased feeling of safety, protection, and security.

Early adolescents are in a state of transition and do not yet have well-formed notions about themselves and the world. They need a stable and enriched educational experience. In some ways, money spent on private education during these junior high school years have a greater effect on the adolescent than money spent for college tuition. If the teenager can find a personal connection with school and can identify with a group of friends who may be more motivated to learn and create, the chances are that the teenager will remain in school and look forward to college. On the other hand, the young person who becomes attached to peers who are turned off to junior high school may also have trouble relating to school. If classmates are more interested in using drugs, drinking, or participating in delinquent acts, it will be much harder for the middle school student to seriously commit to the educational experience. A poor academic experience in junior high school can set the stage for a similarly disappointing senior high record, which will affect college choices and influence the course of adult life.

Adolescent Fears and the School Experience

It is not unusual for some teenagers to be frightened of and exploited by peers. This may happen on the way to school, in the lavatory, between classes, or at lunch. Students may be so upset and frightened that they cannot concentrate on schoolwork.

They often feel that counselors and teachers have little power or interest in protecting them. Frequently, they are too frightened and embarrassed to complain, and they may expect retribution if they tell on their peers.

For these teenagers, school is a dreaded nightmare. Attendance may become spotty. Often, young people who spend time in the nurse's office or stay home with frequent illnesses are actually frightened of school dangers. The fear of being jumped or beaten up may be a realistic concern. Many urban public schools are warring camps, and some teenagers who are not allied to a group with power get caught in the crossfire.

Often, parents and counselors address only the issues of attendance and academic failure, seldom exploring the intense anxiety the student is experiencing in school. In some cases, teenagers can transfer to a different school. But most of the time, this is not possible. Helping a young person find a friend or establish a buddy system may diminish some of the tensions. This type of student support may help the teenager feel more protected and less vulnerable.

Parents may also consider other methods to physically protect their children. This can be done by concerted action both at the school and in the community. Money can be raised, where necessary, to provide guards and other supervisory personnel. Whenever there is a hint of problems, parents need to communicate with the school administration and teachers about the child's worries and concerns.

School Burnout

Children can experience school burnout in much the same way that adults experience job burnout. Schools are primarily academically oriented. In fact, there is increased pressure to teach high school material in junior high school and college material in high school. A small group of children may thrive on this increased stimulation. But there are many for whom the academic expectations and stress become overwhelming. Many hours of homework may be assigned. Children may feel that they are "drowning." Teachers may be unaware of the special difficulties a child is having. The young person finds it humiliating to ask for help.

Young teenagers may wake up dreading to go to school, find it easier to forget their books and homework in their lockers and not turn in assignments, which they may not have done completely or well. Children who are under academic stress and are floundering may also develop physical symptoms, including stomach aches, headaches, mononucleosis, ulcers, and colitis, and become prone to every virus that hits the community. These teenagers may be truly ill. Academic stress may lower their resistance.

Pressure from school expectations may also be a motivator for delinquent behavior, aggressive confrontations with other students, and vandalism. Seldom does a young person who is successfully sailing along in the academic mainstream or involved in activities like sports, drama, or music engages in extremes of hostile or antisocial behavior. However, today large numbers of children move through elementary school unable to read and write at grade level. They arrive at middle school or junior high school handicapped by their academic disabilities and overwhelmed by the curriculum. They are vulnerable

The use of drugs and alcohol can be another byproduct of school stress. Preparing for and taking tests and getting good grades are overwhelming tasks. Some students relieve this tension and anxiety with a joint, a downer, an upper, or alcohol. This often makes them feel competent and powerful. However, their report cards may tell a different story.

Children of academically successful parents may feel special pressure to achieve. The stress of upholding family expectations and academic traditions may be too difficult for some children, who may not have the intellectual potential to excel or may have emotional or social problems. Parents need to be sensitive to each child's intellectual level and not compound the pressure of school with unrealistic expectations.

On the other hand, some children whose families have never succeeded academically may feel guilty when surpassing the academic achievements of their parents or older siblings. These teenagers may feel programmed to continue a family script of school failure. The school needs to be sensitive to this conflict. Teachers can help by acting as alternative models with whom young people can identify. This kind of intervention does take time and effort on the part of the staff.

Of course, stress can also come from the school in terms of academic expectations that are too high or teachers who are not creative, are nonresponsive, or are downright mean and boring. But, it can also come from stress at home. Impending divorce or remarriage of a parent and the creation of a new family of stepparents and/or stepsiblings can put additional stress on a young teenager, as can illness within the home, parental unemployment, and parental substance abuse. Other sources of tension are moving to a new home and neighborhood and parents who are sexually, emotionally, or physically abusive.

Parents may blame the school or the child instead of accepting responsibility for the stress their home life creates. It may be possible for children under stress to participate in sports or other activities. But such children may not be able to learn, absorb, or integrate intellectual and academic materials while they are under stress. For almost everyone, it is easier to learn when in an emotional environment that is stable, with a minimum of anger, sadness, fear, and worry.

Cheating

School difficulties and stress stimulate the need to cheat, especially when parents demand high grades. In some families, children who do not excel academically may be punished and not allowed to go out on weekends, may be denied new equipment, or may be unable to obtain the approval of their demanding parents. When good grades become an end in themselves, some children may find it necessary to cheat to obtain these symbols of success.

Parents should keep in mind that it is more important to focus on the learning experience than on actual evaluation. Parents may find it easier to talk about a C grade than to explore what aspects of the course the teenager found stimulating, what was difficult, and what held little interest. Unfortunately, many children cheat and are never discovered. Then if they are caught later, in high school or in college, the effects can be most disastrous.

Talking about School Problems with the Early Adolescent

Report cards may be the first indication that a teenager is having problems at school. The teenager often dreads the parental reaction to D's and F's or U's. Comments such as *"I guess you feel pretty bad about this"* or *"Do you think this report card is fair?"* may open up communication. Of course, it is far easier to explode and to say *"You're lazy and never open your books,"* or *"No wonder you got so many "D's. You watch too much TV,"* or *"Why can't you be like your sister, who is such a good student, or your friend, Jason who would never get this kind of report card? He makes his parents proud."*

This tirade makes the young person feel worse and helps confirm the fact that he or she is a disappointment to mother and father. Castigating the teenager is not productive. Even telling teenagers that they are smart may not be encouraging because deep down they have their own doubts. It is important to try to find the source of the lack of motivation, and this is not always easy to do.

In reflecting what could be difficult for the teenager, you might say:

> *"I know it's hard to get off the phone to do homework when you're having such a good time talking with your friends."*
>
> *"Lots of kids find it hard to concentrate on a subject, especially when they don't like the teacher."*
>
> *"I can understand why it may be fun to get a laugh in class from your friends, rather than copy what is on the board."*
>
> *"Is there something that we can do to make it easier for you to do your homework and to listen more in school?"*

"We realize that you are spending most of the day in school, and we want your school experience to be a good one."

"Why don't you keep a record of how much TV you watch for a week?"

It is appropriate for parents to meet with a teacher, school administrator, or counselor to attempt to alter some of the forces that are disturbing the young person. The parents need to show commitment to the teenager's school by attending open houses, sporting events, plays, and concerts as well by providing a harmonious home environment free of television and other distractions during study times. Of course, parents are responsible for attending parent meetings as well as conferences whether their children are having trouble or not. It is respectful and supportive of the children's school experiences.

The Great Distracters

Television can absorb hours of time for any youngster. The creation of a television watching schedule at the beginning of the week may be important. Many families just say, *"no television after dinner on homework nights."* Of course the adults must respect this rule as well. It is very hard for the young person to turn away when one member of the family is engrossed in a television program. Listening to a radio or stereo may not intrude as much as television or videotapes, which demand watching as well as listening. But it is also a distraction.

Initially, announcing a change in family viewing policy may stir up loud protests. If so, you might say, *"Let's test this idea for the next two months and see what happens. At a later date, we can talk about whether this new plan made a difference in helping you get your schoolwork done, and we can then reevaluate the rule."*

Sidney was constantly upset that his mother was always out on dates. When he was home alone, television was his only company. No one was ever around to help him switch off the set and begin his homework. He was mad at his mother as well, which further eroded his resolve to do homework. If his mother had stayed home on weekdays, it may have helped Sidney focus on his school assignments.

The computer is both a positive and a negative force in the life of an early adolescent. As a word processor, it can make written assignments look professional and easy to read. Adolescents learn the keyboard without even being conscious of mastering the process of typing. Access to the Internet also opens up resources that may be useful for study and research. Contacting peers through computer chat rooms and e-mail may provide a constructive social avenue for a child who may be shy and unable to make more direct relationships. This certainly could be helpful.

Unfortunately, the Internet can also provide inappropriate material to young adolescents, particularly material related to sex and violence. A teenager may spend an inordinate amount of time in front of the computer. These after-school hours might be better spent by actively playing, reading, creating, or performing. Computer games also absorb a tremendous amount of time and may have limited value. Parents have little control over computer involvement. Some of it can be negative, and much can be positive, but parents cannot observe what the child is absorbing.

Identifying the Source of School Problems

Asking a young person what may be causing them concern or anxiety may be the best way to find the source of school problems. The goal is to create an atmosphere in which the teenager feels free to express worries to the parent.

When Christie started junior high, she felt that she was placed in a class that was much too easy for her. She was bored and wanted to be with her close friends. With her parents' support and the counselor's help, they were able to change her classroom. Christie's performance improved.

It seemed that Kevin frequently left his homework assignments at school. After some exploration, Kevin admitted that he was ashamed to do his work. His best friends were having trouble in class, and he felt disloyal to them if he buckled down and studied. The teachers assigned Kevin to work on a project with a top student. In time he became friendly with some other motivated classmates. And eventually he was able to perform up to his ability without feeling uncomfortable.

Charles felt that his parents were too rigid about bedtime. As a twelve-year-old, he didn't see why he had to go to bed at the same time as his ten-year-old brother. His parents agreed to let him stay up an extra hour. He felt that his parents were respecting his growing maturity. He more energetically participated in school and did not waste energy being angry at his mom and dad.

Carol needed a way to stay off the phone long enough to handle her assignments. Her mother could sense that Carol's friends were terribly important to her in her new school. Carol and her mother agreed to set up a schedule—one hour to talk on the phone, followed by one hour to study, until bedtime. Because Carol felt that her mother understood her need to talk with friends, she independently modified the time she spent chatting. Her assignments were finished without parental prodding and conflict.

Providing Tutoring

Providing tutors for a child who is having trouble in school may be advisable. If the underlying stress in not explored or handled, tutoring may have little effect. However, the tutor may be able to establish a special relationship with the young person. If the problem is essentially one of not understanding aspects of the curriculum, the tutor can serve as an important support system. In selecting a tutor, it may be helpful to find an older teenager or a young college student with whom the young teenager can identify and who doesn't act too parental or too authoritarian.

Assuming there is an academic problem that can be helped, it is important to locate a tutor who not only relates to the teenager but also understands the subject. Furthermore, the tutor needs to be able to teach and explain as well as encourage and motivate. Some tutors simply help the student do the homework and fail to teach the concepts involved. Teaching skills are not easy to find, particularly in young student tutors.

It may be difficult for many parents to actively involve themselves in their child's homework. The junior high school curriculum may far surpass the understanding of the parents. Furthermore, children and parents often irritate one another. This is particularly true when they are struggling with difficult subjects and the parent does not fully understand what the teacher expects. Teenagers may explode and even become abusive with parents in such situations. In contrast, teenagers seldom respond to tutors with insolent or extreme behavior. Consequently, it may be well worth the effort to attempt to find a competent tutor.

Summer Camp

Middle school students need adventure. By the time they reach early adolescence, children have learned an enormous amount. They need to test their understanding, strengths, and skills independently and courageously. Young people in rural areas can pit themselves against their natural surroundings by hunting, fishing, climbing, boating, farming, and caring for animals. In many cases, young people in the country can be alone, unsupervised, and safe for long periods of time. This may not be true in the bigger cities, where teenagers may not be able to safely experience independence away from adult supervision. The city streets may not be safe for boys and girls to walk or bike alone. Parks, which used to provide a country environment within the city, may now be unsafe for adults, let alone individual teenagers. Often, malls or shopping centers are the only place teenagers can go by themselves. But, mall experiences are limited, and adventure is scarce.

Summer camps may be an important part of the educational and social experience of young people ten to fifteen years of age, especially those who live in urban areas. Day camps with special activities are appropriate for children six to ten years old. Overnight camp serves an important function for the early adolescent. Spending time away from home and parents, managing clothes and possessions independently of parents, and taking care of bodily needs may be a maturing experience.

It is important for the young person to deal with homesickness and the discomfort of separation from a secure, familiar home base. For a few weeks, the teenager will be required to cope with a new and different environment. Working through sad and anxious feelings is a maturing experience, especially if the young person finds a few friends and can develop a positive relationship with a counselor or another teenager.

Camp is especially crucial for children who find little satisfaction in academic areas. At camp, a young person can be valued for skill in sports, games, hiking, or mountain climbing. In some camps, the focus may be on farming, horseback riding, or the care of animals. Other camps stress music and art, and teenagers can perform in plays and talent shows. They can get recognition for sculpting, potting, painting, weaving, sewing, cooking, or woodwork and learn the skills needed in these activities. Some young people enjoy a survival experience in which they have to sleep out doors, cook, bathe, and keep warm without the usual urban supports.

Summer camp experiences can develop other kinds of learning and are not to be underestimated. Often, children who are having academic trouble are enrolled in summer school. It may be more helpful for these children to find satisfaction in other activities rather than to be thrown back into a school environment that is difficult for them. Providing a camp experience before or after a short summer academic session may provide a good balance.

Parents need not feel that camps are only for the wealthy. There are many camps sponsored by nonprofit organizations that offer a summer experience away from home at a modest cost. Boy Scout and Girl Scout camps are examples. Adults often look back on camp experiences with pleasure. Years later, they use skills they learned at camp for their own recreation.

Of course, camps, like schools, differ in their ability to provide positive age-appropriate experience for young teenagers. Children who hate camp and who call or write that they want to come home must be taken seriously. They may feel unprotected and alone. Sometimes, the new camper is worried about what is happening at home and wants to touch base with the parents. Other times, the young person has not made a friend and feels lonely, sick, isolated, and abandoned—and sometime they truly are in an abusive situation. However, before the young person gives up on the camp experience, the reasons for the unhappiness need to be explored by the child, the camp administrators, and the parents. If the problem is truly not fixable and the child continues to be miserable, he or she should return home, perhaps to try another camp at a later date.

Work Experience for Young Teenagers

Many years ago, children apprenticed with their parents. They learned by observing and participating on the farm or in a shop, watching their father repair shoes, bake bread, cut meat, or wait on customers. By the time they were fifteen, many adolescents could almost run the family business. Many were as strong as their fathers, even if not quite as skilled. Girls participated competently in all aspects of their mother's work, like cooking, cleaning, sewing, childcare, and animal care.

Watching Parents Work

Today, many young people have no contact with their parents' employment. Both parents may go off to offices, factories, or stores far removed from the family home. Often, young people are deprived of the many learning experiences connected with watching their parents work.

Not only are the teenagers deprived of observing the parents perform, but they are also denied the opportunity to see how parents handle other adults, respond to problems, and handle disappointments and failures. Often, a father or mother will brag about exploits and successes. The young adolescent often sees the father or mother as larger than life and feels unable to measure up to the parent's accomplishments.

When young people are involved with their fathers or mothers at their places of employment, they usually experience the parents' vulnerabilities and difficulties as well as their successes, and they feel less unworthy: "If my father can lose a sale or make a mistake, it may not be so disastrous if I cannot always get A's." Parents seldom share their disappointments and failures with their family. But, watching an adult deal with these stresses may be of enormous benefit for the young person. It models how people cope with ups and downs, successes and failures, in life. Children who never observe their parents working are deprived of the opportunity to see them solve problems, handle conflicts, and be assertive and polite or aggressive and rude. In other words, they are deprived of seeing the parents respond realistically in an environment away from home. These observations may conflict with the verbal reports of success in court, a miracle on the operating table, a promotion at the office or factory, or an incredible sale.

Since adolescence is a time between childhood and adulthood, it is important for the teenager to have some preparatory experience in the adult world. In primitive cultures, the adolescent has to function as a man or woman in formal rites of passage. When a teenage boy has succeeded in killing his first deer or has survived alone in the forest for many days, he knows that he can cope as other adult males do.

In the past, teenage girls observed and participated in many of the household duties performed by their mothers. However, today, the working mother may be spending less time at home. Many homemaking skills are seldom observed by the teenager and therefore neglected in her informal education.

As a result of being separated from their parents' work environments, young people may have little idea how to function as adults. Of course, they do watch television and can learn how doctors, lawyers, private investigators, secretaries, oil moguls, and police function. But it is hard to identify with these and other professional and occupational roles without firsthand experience. In addition, professional roles as portrayed on TV are often idealized and stereotyped.

Work Experience Possibilities

It is extremely important for early adolescents to be provided a window into the adult world by having a variety of work experiences. Young people can help out in nursery schools, at construction sites, in garages and gas stations, on farms, and in stores and restaurants. They may be able to do secretarial or clerical work in an office and help with mailing and filing. At times, two teenagers can be hired to clean a house, garden, or wash cars. It may be easier to motivate a pair of teenagers than to assign one's own child to do routine tasks around the house. Some young people can get paid for many things they do. However, it is the work experience that should be valued, not the money alone. It is amazing how much can be learned by working a job for even a month or two.

Finding a way for young people to participate in the adult world takes time and creative planning. Parents need to explore what work situations are available and safe for their teenagers, either at their own places of employment or with friends and relatives. It may be hard for young people to find their own jobs, although it is not impossible.

A summer or after-school job does not necessarily have to be intense or demand many hours of work. But it should hold some interest and provide the young person with some feelings of success. For example, an attorney's teenage daughter came to help out in the office. Not only did she help him stamp and seal the mail, but he also took her with him when he interviewed witnesses, and he let her observe some interesting court proceedings. Parents who do not earn much money or achieve high-status jobs can still serve as an excellent model to their teenagers, especially if they take time to include the young person in some aspect of their work experience, even if it is just conversation.

Young people need to be around adults to learn about their future world. Otherwise, most of what they know is what they glean from their peer group, pop idols, or television. This may not be the most desirable way to prepare for their adult lives.

Chapter 17

The Middle Adolescent

Middle adolescence lasts from age fifteen to age eighteen. It is this period that most people associate with the word *adolescence*. Most remember their senior high school days, while the anguish of the bodily changes and emotional stress of earlier adolescence frequently fade from adult memories.

Parents need to acknowledge the fact that unique stresses and tensions are characteristic of these adolescent years. The tensions may be directly related to the developmental tasks of fifteen- to eighteen-years-olds. Parents also must prepare themselves for the eventual separation that occurs at the end of this period.

Tasks of Middle Adolescence

There are two main tasks of middle adolescence. The first is that the young person must experience desire and attraction to a member of the opposite sex and feel that he or she too is desirable. This is important to confirm and solidify sexual identification and self-esteem. The second task is for middle adolescents to establish expectations for their own futures. These might include occupational or professional goals as well as family and community roles.

These tasks are difficult to master because the young person basically handles them alone. The peer group is still important, but high school students must now meet their own specific goals, obtaining a high grade-point average so that they can enter a particular college or reaching out to develop an intimate relationship. These cannot be done as group endeavors. The athlete, actor, debater, dancer, drummer, poet, artist, or surfer is showing individual competencies and skills. Teenagers may be competing against their best friends for a position on the team, a role in a play, a partner at the prom, or a class office. This is indeed stressful. It may seem simpler to merge with a group, as they did in early adolescence, and function within its supports—or to not risk participation at all. Having to compete and put their own interests ahead of their friends is difficult and stressful.

The middle adolescent is not as preoccupied with his or her changing body as the early adolescent. Middle adolescents have generally become accustomed to how they look. There is a greater need to create their own style of dress, hairdo, or form of dancing, and to exhibit the more unique aspects of their identity. Pulling away from rigid peer group expectations and creating an identity is part of what middle adolescence is about. This throws middle adolescents into treacherous waters, where they may be swimming alone without the group as a life raft.

Middle adolescents can legally drive, which affords them mobility and increased independence. Obtaining a driver's license is perhaps the most specific rite of passage into adulthood in our culture. Using the family car and paying for gas and insurance or having one's own car may be a cause of strain within the family, especially when traffic tickets and accidents complicate the picture. When the teenager can legally drive, the parent is freed from the chore of driving. For the adolescent, driving is an important step in the process of separation and independence, allowing the young person to be in much greater control of comings and goings.

Paid work experience may be an appropriate part of the young person's life at this point. Paying jobs can add to ego satisfactions, but can also provide other stress for the teenager.

Formal dating may begin, and young people spend increased amounts of unsupervised time together. Interactions with the opposite sex are central to the life of the middle adolescent. Are they going with anyone? Who they are going with? How far to go sexually? These are central concerns in the daydreams and discussions of this age group.

High school pressures can be enormous for young people who want to attend specific colleges. They must work for good grades, compete in nationwide exams, and excel in some form of extracurricular activity. They may be indirectly competing or trying to fulfill rigid academic scripts of parents or older siblings. They may be pioneering their own educational course. Often, they are competing against their best friends.

High school students begin to develop their own approaches to life. They are often critical and abrasive with parents, no matter how understanding and accepting their parents may be. They may argue about politics, religion, morality, and values. They seem to create skirmishes and confrontations, as if to say, "You are not as perfect as you think you are. I can go off and make a better world and a more satisfying life than you have." Frequently, the parent is more than ready for the teenager to leave home and try!

The High School Experience

Entering high school may be another important transition for the teenager, although certainly not as stressful as entering kindergarten or junior high. Today, most high schools sit on large campuses and have thousands of teenagers enrolled. The young person is confronted with a larger variety of students. Many high schools are impersonal and forbidding. However, they do offer many arenas in which to function. There are drama clubs, debate teams, cheerleading, sports competitions, bands, and glee clubs, among many others.

Because of the great variety in the student population, there may be a large number of students who begin to cut classes, neglect homework, and eventually drop out of high school. The causes are many. Some students come from dysfunctional families. Some have learning problems that were never diagnosed or helped in the elementary and junior high school years. Teenagers may have strong attachments to peers with negative school attitudes. There may be addictive involvement with drugs and alcohol. Becoming stoned or loaded may be the most important goal for some young people at this time. Students may feel that no one in school cares about them or that there is no intrinsic satisfaction in any school activity. They may be expressing anger arising from within the family and acting it out by failing and dropping out.

There are also many teenagers who manage to stay in school by the skin of their teeth, but who are unable to make a positive commitment to the school experience. These young people somehow obtain degrees, but they are not motivated to go on with additional education after high school.

By contrast, there are teenagers who are strongly motivated to go on to college and graduate school. These young people often have goals relatively early in their teenage years. They populate honor classes and strive for A's and high grade-point averages. They may have intense extracurricular interests or may just participate in some activity in order to eventually impress a college admissions office.

Family expectations play an important role for highly motivated students. They are often trying to please their parents by living out a successful academic script. Some can do this easily, but others may feel the pressure intensely, either because of lower intellectual capacity or other environmental pressures. In some families, acceptance into an Ivy League school may be expected. Attending any other college is looked down on as failing. This may be especially true if parents have invested in costly tuition payments for elementary and junior high school to ensure a prestigious academic future.

For some young people, academic excellence may be the only way to obtain a scholarship that can pay for their academic careers. This is also true of athletes who feel they must excel in a particular sport to obtain scholarship money for their future education. They also need to achieve minimum grade-point averages to stay on teams.

The school experience is fraught with these and other competitive tensions and the need to exhibit competence in every school arena. There is little time, except perhaps lunch and between classes, to relax and unwind. School may be a serious and grim business from the high school student's point of view.

Even becoming a cheerleader, obtaining a part in a play, being selected for the student council, or playing on the basketball team can put a young person in a state of tension. Though there may be rewards, the stress to obtain these rewards can be very difficult to face.

The selection process for participation in extracurricular activities may be dependent on the young person's popularity, as well as on the partiality of the teachers in charge. Often, young people feel unfairly victimized when risking participation in some high school endeavor.

> Marina desperately wanted to be on the tennis team. Her coach consistently bypassed her for another young athlete whose mother frequently helped out at the school and was friendly with the coach. Marina's parents had come from Europe and felt they couldn't communicate effectively with those in a position of power. Marina never did play on a high school tennis team, but she was motivated enough not to give up and did well in park competitions.

High school teachers play an important part in motivating young people. Teachers' influence is even greater than it was in junior high. In junior high, teachers are competing with their students' intense peer group loyalties. But in senior high school, teachers truly represent an identifiable bridge into the adult world.

The teenager usually relates well to a teacher who has enthusiasm, competence, and passion. Teachers seem more interesting to adolescents than their own parents, from whom they feel they have learned all the parents have to teach. A teacher introduces a new way to look at life, with new ideas, concepts, and information, which is enormously appealing to the ever-expanding intelligence of the young person. Of course, there are also teachers who are indifferent, cruel, or rigid and make no attempt to relate to their subject in an appealing way or to make contact with their students.

Parents can feel threatened when their teenagers quote teachers or idolize them. They feel jealous of the teenager's newfound attachment and fear the increased loss of respect and control. It may be hard for parents to see enthusiasm for a teacher's ideas as a healthy step in the process of becoming a more independent thinker. It is not only the academic teachers who function as an important part of the school experience. Other adults involved in the arts, trades, sports, and school administration who interact with and influence young persons can also be inspirational and effective models.

Friendship

One of the stresses of the high school years may be the breakup of old friendships and the development of new ones, as well as changing peer group alliances.

> Marcy and Lisa had been close friends since fifth grade. In tenth grade, Lisa was asked to join the swim team. Her after-school hours were devoted to practice and intramural meets. She had little time for Marcy. Marcy was jealous of Lisa's newfound interest and her new friends on the swim team. Marcy experienced a personal loss until she eventually became close friends with a girl with whom she played in the band.

Friendships are important at the high school level. It is with close friends that personal experiences are validated, enemies verbally torn apart, and future goals are discussed. Sometimes friendships arise from a mutual trauma. Friends may have shared interests or talents, or they feel close to one another because of opposite traits and strengths. These friendships are not sexual, but they serve as an important adjunct to the dating process. Young people who are only children or whose siblings are much older or much younger especially need the support and companionship of good friends.

Teenage Siblings

Middle adolescents may look on their teenage brothers and sisters with both pride and pleasure. Often there is a decrease in tension between siblings during this middle adolescent period.

The parents and authority figures become the enemy, and the children become allied against this mutual oppressor. Thus can parents fall from the highest point on the totem pole to the bottom. The siblings find enormous pleasure in confirming and sharing their perceptions of mother or father. Siblings may also have common struggles with forces of authority in the home that deny them freedoms and material possessions or are constantly irritable and nagging.

However, there can still be unresolved sibling rivalries from early childhood. Parents may add to sibling tensions by playing favorites, comparing one sibling with another, or insisting that older siblings help care for younger ones. It is important not to require teenagers to baby-sit or supervise their younger brothers or sisters at the expense of their own social lives. Parents and teenagers should talk about what is fair and appropriate, so that teenagers feel that they are part of the decision-making process and do not feel exploited by the parents. Teenagers who are made to act as parents to younger siblings are deprived of carefree adolescent years and may delay having their own children or decide not to become parents at all. They can be burned out with too-heavy childcare responsibilities.

Dating

Today there is a tremendous variation in the way boys and girls get together. As more girls are able to drive and have the use of cars, they may not be so dependent on boys to formally ask them for dates and come their home to pick them up. It is common for young people to meet in designated places, each getting there independently. Pairing up may occur on the scene.

Parents often feel deprived when they do not meet the young person with whom their teenager is spending time. Also, they are not as able to relive their own dating experiences, which may have been more traditional. For some adolescents, formally asking a girl out to a movie or an event does not take place until after the high school years. For others, pairing off and officially going with someone may start as early as junior high school.

The process of dating or more formally relating to the opposite sex is a central developmental task of the middle adolescent. It is a way of learning to know the opposite sex, to experience warmth and sexual arousal, to feel valued and to risk rejection. It is a way of practicing the art of interaction between the sexes. It prepares the teenager for more intimate and prolonged relationships. It is fraught with tension as well as exquisite pleasure.

It takes courage to call and ask someone of the opposite sex to get together at a specific time. There is a risk that the person called will say no and that the young person will feel disappointed at the rejection. Waiting to be asked out and praying that the phone will ring is also difficult. It is complicated when a high schooler is asked out by the wrong person while yearning for another student to call to invite her out.

Unfortunately, there might not be a boy for every girl in a teenage girl's high school environment. (Or at least the boy she wants) Often, there is a small elite group whose members are popular and constantly sought after. Many girls may crave the attention of one cute guy. Or teenage boys feel drawn to a certain seductive creature. There may be many young people who are neglected in the process and who may have a hard time getting paired up.

There also may be a difference in what boys want out of a dating relationship and what girls want. Many boys want an outlet for their sexual longings. Girls may be less interested in the sexual aspect but need to date to feel valued, attractive, and lovable. Dating relationships and experiences intrude into much of the adolescent's daily life and psyche.

Many young people may be preoccupied not only with their own date behavior, but also with what they both did and said when they were together. They may constantly evaluate their date's reactions and responses. Talking about what happened on a date may provide much of the conversion between friends of the same sex.

Tensions arise over a young person's expectations of what is going to happen in the future with this relationship. *"Will he call again?" "Will she date anyone else?" "Is he too possessive?" "Can I trust him?" "Does he brag about what we do?" "Does she make fun of my penis?" "Will my friends like her?" "What will my parents think when they find out that he lives in that neighborhood?"*

Parents and the Dating Teenager

Parents can assume that a high school student who is going steady with someone or seems to have an intense relationship that lasts over many months is likely to be engaged in some form of sexual intimacy. Setting an early curfew does not guarantee that intimate sexual interactions will not take place. The car often provides the privacy necessary for sex to occur. When both parents are at work until late in the day or away on business or on vacation and their teenagers are unsupervised, they can more easily engage in sexual intimacies. Parents might consider some method of reasonable supervision between 3:00 and 6:00 p.m. Perhaps there is more pressure than in the past for teenagers to lose their virginity. Many teenagers feel inadequate and deprived if they have not experienced this monumental act by the time they finish high school.

Few teenagers share these experiences or feelings with their parents. Their intimate relationships are their private business, and most do not feel comfortable discussing these personal details. It may be important for parents to let their teenagers know their feelings about premarital sexual intercourse. Talking about the subject in general terms and discussing other young people's problems may be more effective than lecturing the teenager. Teenagers usually do not want to hear about their parents' own sexual experiences or to be reminded how sexually restrained the parents were as teenagers. If a teenager asks about sexual matters, it is important for the parent to make accurate information or literature available. Parents can also encourage adolescents to discuss personal matters with their doctors or other professionals, especially when the parents feel uninformed or are too embarrassed to handle specific questions. It may be important to schedule yearly doctor appointments just to provide a time for teenagers to discuss loaded or personal questions.

Parents experience varying degrees of tension when their

teenagers begin to date. Parents usually show less concern when they know the young person with whom their child is out. They also feel more comfortable if the date is close to the age of their son or daughter or if both attend the same school or come from a similar social and religious background.

Dating ground rules need to be discussed and agreed on. These include:

- Time to return from a date.
- Dating on school nights
- The number of consecutive nights out
- Drinking, drugs, and driving
- Parents' availability in emergencies
- Supervision at parties.

In high school, curfews need to be flexible and should be more responsive to what the young person is planning for the evening. Allowing an hour or an hour and half after the end of a movie may be appropriate if the young person is planning to get something to eat with friends. Young people should be expected to return from dances, parties, or just visiting at a friend's house at an agreed-on time. If for some reason the young person is more than a half-hour late, it is reasonable to expect a phone call that explains the problem. A high school student needs to know that it is better to wake the parent up than to allow the parent to lie in bed worrying.

The parent has the responsibility of not exploding when the phone call does come, so that this reaction will not cause the young person anxiety about calling the next time. Teenagers may resent getting yelled at when they are not on time. With the availability of cell phones and pagers, communication with family should be less of a problem.

Often teenagers will plan to sleep over at someone else's house so as to circumvent rigid curfew rules. In such cases, parents can check with the other teenager's parents about standards and expectations. The high school student may consider their mother or father's calling other parents to be intrusive and untrusting. A seventeen-year-old may exclaim, *"Do you think I'm a baby?"* But asking may be the only way a parent can feel less anxious and have some assurance that the teenager is in a safe environment.

On dates or group outings, designating one of the party-goers to be responsible for getting the group home safely is extremely important. Teenagers do need to know that the designated driver should not drink or take drugs. Calling home for assistance needs to be encouraged if there are no sober drivers available. There is little parents can do to ensure that this will happen, except by trying to keep a positive atmosphere in their home where communication is open and these expectations are discussed.

Parents must also advise their teenagers what time the parents will return from a night out. It is important to model consideration. Children need to know where their parents can be reached at all times, not only in emergencies. Again, cell phones or pagers can be carried by both parents and their children to facilitate communication.

Working

By the time the teenager has become a high school student, there may be many reasons to find a paying job. For many urban teenagers, the cost of entertainment is high. In some families, young people need to help pay for the gas they use and their own clothes and sometimes even help with family living expenses. The decision about where to work and how many hours to spend at a job is important. Working may conflict with school commitments. For some, the money and satisfaction of doing a job reasonably well can conflict with the less-relevant academic rewards of high school. Time commitments may be a concern, especially when the young person is involved with team sports or other extracurricular activities. Babysitting, which was a convenient and profitable job for the junior high school student, may begin to conflict with the teenager's own social life.

Summer vacation may be an excellent opportunity to experiment with a variety of job experiences. Working during vacation does not compete with school demands and pressures. However, teenagers and their families may require a regular year-round income to help defray expenses.

Counseling at summer camp may provide a wonderful opportunity for the high school student to learn about the care of young children, as well as to become a member of a youthful community of other counselors and camp personnel. The focus of most camps is recreation, and young people who work there can participate in the camp activities. Paying counseling jobs are often not available until the young person has graduated from high school. Assistant counseling jobs can prepare teenagers for this paying position.

Teenagers who work in stores, restaurants, gas station, hospitals, or amusement parks can experience many adult responsibilities. They are expected to arrive on time, work the prearranged hours, handle money honestly, and get along with other workers. When teenagers are paid in the coin of the realm, they must be accountable to employers. This is not simple, and many teenagers are fired for not fulfilling one or more of these responsibilities. It is possible to learn from work disappointments. Students who are not accountable at school for their homework or school attendance and who are not accountable at home for any regular chores may find the workplace quite different. It is usually much more difficult to con a boss than a teacher, mother, or father.

Some jobs are intrinsically stressful, and the young person may need to learn to deal with difficult personalities, tedium, and isolation. Others jobs are fun and pleasurable. If a coworker is sexually attractive, the job becomes associated with a pleasurable relationship and perhaps erotic feelings as well. The teenager can't wait to get to work!

High school jobs do not necessarily define the future occupations of the teenager, but they may increase the young person's ability to see the limitations as well as the opportunities of certain kinds of work. Such jobs may also increase teenagers' motivation in school and encourage them to seek more varied work opportunities in the future.

Parents who have professions or are in business may also provide work opportunities for their teenagers. This may afford unique benefits for the high school student. Or parents can also use their friends as resources for providing part-time employment. In fact, to work for someone outside of the family may be less emotionally complicated. In this situation, the young person is separated from the expectations and tensions of the family business as well as implicit parental pressure.

Money

In some families, it may be important to sit down and determine a budget that relates to the teenager's financial needs. These needs may include clothes, food, gas, car insurance, and entertainment. How much the parents are able and willing to pay varies. Other factors also may need consideration, including how much the teenager is earning and how much he or she is saving for future expenses, like college or a car. The budget should be decided at a time of reasonably good rapport. It should not be formulated when tempers are high and all parties feel deprived or drained. Money is related to security, nurturing, control, status, generosity, selfishness, independence, waste, guilt, shame, pleasure, and envy. It's no wonder that the spending of money can be an emotional issue between a teenager and the parents!

Every family approaches money issues differently.

Andrew came from a comfortable middle-class family. When he wanted money for a movie or an outing, he asked his mother, and she gave him what he asked for. Because his demands were reasonable and the family was financially secure, money never became a problem.

Heidi needed to buy, buy, buy. She was upset and depressed when she couldn't have the latest CD or the most fashionable clothes. Even though the family was financially secure, there was constant tension about

Heidi's whining for more. Giving Heidi a fixed monthly allowance from which to buy clothes and pay for entertainment provided her with some control, independence, and accountability. At the same time, this allowance freed her parents from feeling irritated at never being able to satisfy Heidi.

Carla's parents were divorced. Her mother told Carla that she was having a hard time with the household bills. Carla realized that her already stressed parents would not meet many of her financial needs. It was agreed that Carla's salary at the ice cream parlor would be used to pay for her clothes, lunch, and weekend outings. Her mother would occasionally buy her a surprise.

In the past, Lucy had never been demanding. She was relaxed about her allowance. Lately, Lucy's parents became concerned when money was missing from their wallets. In the last few weeks, Lucy kept asking for extra cash to pay for her needs. Eventually, her parents found out that she was using money for a growing cocaine habit.

Chapter 18

Stress and Anger in the Middle Adolescent

Parents can easily underestimate the intense stress that the high school student is experiencing. Much of the anger and abuse dumped on the parents has its roots in frustrations and disappointments at school. It is important not to add to the stress by reacting angrily to the student's irritability. You must also understand that you cannot rescue your child or spare him or her the normal anxieties of these high school years. Even children who attend small, protected, student-centered, and humanistic high schools are not immune from the pervasive social, academic, and emotional pressures of middle adolescence. Even those who sailed through elementary school experience tension and anxiety relating to all the competitive aspects of high school.

Teenagers between fifteen and eighteen have the capacity to become violent when upset. Their emotional reactions may be so intense that they are often frightening to experience. Their newfound strength coupled with a changeable emotional state and poor self-control can produce extremes of behavior. When their fragile emotional state is threatened, they can lose control, throw things, and physically attack anyone who upsets them. The victim is often the parent, but it can occasionally be a teacher or another teenager.

Most violent behavior occurs when the parent or another person humiliates, ridicules, criticizes, compares, belittles, shames, or embarrasses the young person. Violence can also occur if the parent slaps the teenager, who may then respond with unbridled strength and energy. Much of the energy that erupts is the stored-up rage that has lain dormant from the child's earliest years. Such negative experiences, that may occur in the home, in day care or nanny care, can generate extreme anger that seems to explode during adolescence. Early experiences of "abandonment", thought to be benign, fuel these violent eruptions, and can explode like a "time bomb" years later.

Parents need to be sensitive to the feelings of stressed-out teenagers and to avoid provoking them with intrusive, angry, or competitive responses. Of course, this is not easy, and it is especially difficult to step back when angry explosions take place. It is hard for parents to accept that they have ignited the fury of their children by making fun of their hair, criticizing their good friends, or bragging about how well someone else is doing. It is true that teenagers' reactions to the teasing are often out of proportion, but their responses are fueled by all the other stress in their lives. The teasing is often just enough of a spark to ignite an atomic blast. This explosion often takes place at home, where the teenager feels basically safe and accepted. Parents need to have broad shoulders to absorb this rage.

When dealing with adolescents, parents should tread carefully, be sensitive to their vulnerable egos, respect their opinions, and treat them politely. Careful responses will help avoid escalating the violent reactions of an already tense and reactive teenager.

Suicide

Suicide is one of the leading causes of death of teenagers. More school-age children take their own lives today than in the past. Parents have good reason to be concerned about prolonged bouts of depression. Many teenagers who are depressed have little ability to acknowledge and express their angry feelings. Some may feel that suicide is the best way to express their rage.

It may be hard to evaluate whether an adolescent is going through a normal mood swing or whether a more serious depression is involved. Young people who talk about killing themselves need to be taken seriously. They often require help dealing with their anger and the complicated personal problems they are facing. Often, they feel they are between a rock and a hard place. They may feel that there is no one who understands their conflicts or can help them find a solution. Some teenagers are intensely sensitive to disappointment, rejection, favoritism, and failure and feel that they cannot live up to parental expectations or even their own personal goals. They feel hopeless, alone, and often overwhelmed with intense feelings of sadness or anger.

Depression may be a result of feelings of inadequacy in school or in establishing close relationships with peers of the opposite sex. Suicidal feelings may also come from intense anxiety about homosexual attractions. Teenagers may be in profound conflict with their own and family expectations about their sexual identification.

A young person will often plan the suicide for a special day, like someone's birthday or a holiday, and may even seem less depressed before the actual attempt. Females will more typically overdose on pills or cut their wrists. Males will jump from a high place or shoot or hang themselves. For these young people, death seems the only solution. Suicide may be their only way to avenge themselves against the persons with whom they are angry.

By attempting suicide, some teenagers may want to frighten their families or those about whom they feel intense. They hope to communicate their desperate state. Unfortunately, many may die in the attempt, vainly hoping to be rescued, understood, forgiven, and loved.

Parents must be alert to any signs of continuing depression, threats about suicide, or dramatic acts of giving away personal possessions. There is a popular but very mistaken notion that people who talk about or threaten suicide will not actually do it. The fact is just the opposite; many persons who commit suicide do talk about it, sometimes over a long period of time. Therefore, any verbal threat or even discussion of suicide must be take seriously by the parent.

It may be important and necessary to secure professional help from a psychologist, psychiatrist, therapist, social worker, family doctor, tutor, or religious counselor. Friends and siblings can be mobilized to make more frequent contact with the teenager. Parents may need help themselves in responding to their child at this time. Family therapy may be important to create some changes within the family.

Medication may be prescribed by a psychiatrist or medical doctor to alter the intensity of the depressed state. However, it is a mistake to place too much reliance on drugs. Often, drugs are not consistently taken. In addition, drugs alone rarely deal with the underlying misery and stress which caused the depression. Other supportive measures are often necessary to deal with the profound anger and other intense feelings the young person is experiencing. If possible, parents can act as interested listeners, acknowledging the conflict the teenager may be experiencing, reaffirming their commitment to the teenager's life, and refraining from judgmental, critical, and preaching responses. Parents also need to acknowledge the part they have played in the teenager's stress and offer to work on changing their own attitudes and behaviors.

If teenagers are willing, include them in a family project. Planning a trip may provide some distraction and anticipated future pleasure for the young person. If such measures do not seem to be successful, as a last resort the family may be well advised to seek professional and consider hospitalization to prevent a would-be suicide. Treatment can continue in the hospital setting until the teenager has improved and imminent suicide risks have been abated.

Parents need to recognize how much anger they themselves experience when their child is suicidal. For a moment, any parent might wish the child would disappear or die. The time, effort, and expense to reach out to a depressed person may be great. Worry, anxiety, embarrassment, and a pervasive sense of impotence further complicate parents' angry feelings.

A child's death at any age has a profound effect on the whole family. Suicide creates feelings of guilt and shame that many parents and siblings cannot easily talk about. Family members are often denied the support they need after this kind of painful loss. Professional help may be necessary to handle the aftermath of a suicide.

Eating Disorders

Adolescents, whether early, middle, or late, are concerned with their physical appearance and their body image. Achieving an ideal weight is part of their physical image. In order to maintain or arrive at this ideal weight, some teenagers may develop anorexia nervosa (pathological fasting) and stop eating or diet severely, while others develop bulimia (bingeing on food and vomiting) or purging with laxatives. Still others may give up attempting to achieve to an ideal weight, overeat, and become obese. The young person may also swing from periods of overeating to fasting.

Eating disorders are more common in girls, but boys are by no means immune to these problems. All three conditions reflect the young person's obsession with food. All three can cause severe physical problems. Parents can be unaware of anorexia or bulimia for many months. Unfortunately, prodding, nagging, and cajoling by the parents seem to have little effect on the teenager's eating behavior. A young person's perception of her or his body seems to have little relationship to how the teenager is objectively perceived by others.

Anorexia Nervosa

The intake of food may be symbolically related to a teenager's anxiety about burgeoning sexuality or may reflect deep-seated anger toward a mother who has been associated with feeding and nurturing. Teenagers who stop eating are often unable to express intense feelings and may use food as a way to control their anxieties and hostile impulses. These teenagers may often be competent, hardworking, and responsible, and they seem to have been ideal children. The young person who has anorexia may have anxiety about separating from the family and yet feel trapped in family dynamics. Telling a young person that she or he looks thin or has a great figure has little effect on the eating disorder.

In anorexia, the body can become severely malnourished. Menstruation can stop with the loss of body fat. There may be hair loss as well. It is as if the young person is slowly committing suicide, although there is no one precipitating act to cause death.

When young people stop eating, start dieting to the point that they lose 25 percent of their body weight, or obsessively exercise, parents need to seek medical and psychiatric help promptly. Hospitalization may be necessary to treat the severe chemical imbalances in the teenager's body. Individual psychotherapy may not be as effective as family therapy, with all family members included. The parents can begin to take responsibility for some of the subtle problems affecting the teenager.

It may also be helpful for the teenager to join a group of young people with similar eating disorders. Support and understanding from peers can eventually be therapeutic. Therapy groups to help with anorexia and other eating disorders are available in most of the larger cities, but parents may need some professional help to locate and join them.

Bulimia

Parents may be the last to become aware that their teenager has bulimia. By bingeing, purging, and vomiting, the young person maintains a relatively constant body weight. In multi-bathroom households, it may be harder to come upon evidence of a bulimic condition, especially when young people are attempting to keep this personal behavior secret. Sometimes abrasions on the knuckles are the only telltale signs. Bulimia can come and go, but when forced vomiting or purging continues over many weeks, there can be serious abuse of the gastrointestinal tract. Serious medical problems can arise. Electrolytes may be out of balance, and dehydration and erosions in the esophagus can occur.

On the surface, bulimia victims seem to function very well. They are often attractive and energetic, with high expectations.

They desperately want to retain an ideal weight, yet they are obsessed with eating. After eating and ingesting large amounts of food, they feel depressed and guilty and this, in turn, is relieved by vomiting.

It is not easy for parents to confront a child when they suspect this eating disorder. Even though the young person feels an enormous amount of shame and guilt, he or she feels unable to control the bulimia. Eventually, the teenager may be relieved when encouraged to obtain professional help. With support, a teenager may be able to gain some insight into and control this compulsive behavior.

Obesity

Obesity is a serious social problem for the teenager. Young people usually wish to conform to an ideal image. Any abnormal state is perceived as unattractive. Overeating may be complicated by many factors, some of which may be related to the young person's physiology or body type, the number of fat cells, genetic determinations, or overweight parents. Food may have always been a source of pleasure, a form of reward, and a pervasive topic of discussion by most family members. Overeating and obesity can also be a defense against becoming sexual and entering the dating arena in which sexual contact is expected. Children who have been sexually abused may fear further sexual activity if they become attractive. For them, remaining fat may feel like staying safe and separated from the opposite sex.

While obesity may not create the immediate health risks associated with anorexia or bulimia, there may be some long-term effects. These include high blood pressure and diabetes.

Obsessive eating frequently occurs when a teenager is lonely or isolated. He or she may come home from school and raid the refrigerator or eat all the available junk food. There may not be balanced family meals to rely on or anticipate. For many of these teenagers, the roots of their overeating usually lie in their toddler or preschool years, when food was not only a source of pleasure but was used as a reward and a stress reducer. Cookies may have been used to help soothe and regulate an irritable child. Other sweets may have been used as an easy pacifier. This practice may have continued, since there is immediate pleasure in eating; it removes the intense discomfort of hunger and creates positive feelings of satisfaction. Food, like alcohol and drugs, may substitute for social interaction, school success, athletic performance, or ego satisfactions from artistic or creative expression. As a result, there are many difficulties in treating overweight teenagers. An extremely large percentage of people who lose weight with diets or special programs gain back the weight. Diets may be effective initially, but the body metabolism slows down when calorie intake is decreased. Diets also demand constant focus on the food itself, talking about meals, shopping and planning for them, and controlling the special yearning for morsels and goodies that seem to abound.

It is especially difficult for a young person to have a controlled approach to eating when under emotional stress. Young people feel as if they have little willpower and are often discouraged when they find themselves bingeing after being relatively under control. Losing weight needs to be seen as a reward in itself. Feeling thinner, being able to wear more appropriate teenage clothes, and liking how one looks can be a motivation to change.

As with anorexia, families can unconsciously play into the young person's eating problems. This is why support groups for overweight teenagers and even special camps away from home may help these high school students. Parents need to find out what they are doing to complicate the problem. They may be nagging about weight, buying high-calorie food for easy snacking, or creating an unpleasant atmosphere within the home.

Drugs and Alcohol

Drugs and alcohol are used in varying amounts and for a variety of reasons by many high school students. Some never use them. Others may limit use to a weekend party or outing. For others, drugs and alcohol may be a part of their daily lives. Teenagers may feel a need to dilute their intense feelings of stress and depression. The experimental use of drugs is more common in the junior high school years, although it may still be a factor for some high school students, especially for those who are late bloomers or who had extremely protected junior high school environments.

The regular use of either drugs or alcohol should be a serious concern for parents. It may be indicative of a need to escape from problems within the home, with peers, or at school. It can also be used to cover up some sort of trauma or abuse that has never been resolved or examined. Preverbal neglect and lack of adult stimulation in the infant and toddler years can predispose a teenager to substance abuse. Sexual exploitation and molestation or physical or psychological abuse can predispose a teenager to drug or alcohol addiction. This is especially true if the teenager cannot share these experiences or look at them openly. And if abuse occurred before the child turned three, the teenager may not be able to even retrieve these memories. All of the reasons discussed in the section "Why Teenagers Take Drugs" in Chapter 15 play a role in the middle adolescent years.

Unfortunately, the parent may be the last one a young person can talk to about these personal events. Finding a supportive listener or a therapist may be difficult for most high school students. Even with an understanding environment and parents who wish to help, many young people remain completely unaware of the causes of the addictive behavior.

Parents need to become more concerned when drugs or drinking become the central focus of their high school student's life. When students are loaded, spaced out, or wasted, not much serious learning takes place. Furthermore, their bodies cannot perform or compete in athletics on a consistent basis.

Some drugs may temporarily allow a young person to feel more energetic, powerful, and competent. However, their continued use will increase the teenager's level of irritability and cause other problems. If uppers and other substances are taken for an extended time, the body eventually becomes exhausted and undernourished and breaks down.

Young people are seldom aware of the negatives in the use of alcohol and drugs. They feel that they are having a good time and are usually unconcerned about the physical consequences. Teenagers may have little understanding of how much to take or the quality of what they are ingesting. They are also unconcerned about how drugs or alcohol are affecting their future choices and options for school and career. They may spend many of their waking hours thinking about getting high, finding the money for the drugs or alcohol, and searching out these substances and using them, rather than trying to directly deal with their tensions.

When a young person is involved in substance abuse, there is little ego satisfaction or competence gained from doing well on an exam, performing on the athletic field, or being creative in art or music. The young person is left with the symptoms of crashing, which may include fatigue, irritability, depression, and other physical discomforts. The truly addicted young person returns to drugs to relieve these negative symptoms, and the vicious process of drug and alcohol consumption starts all over again. Unless positive action is taken, this downhill spiral continues, often with disastrous consequences.

Parents have little ability to effectively intervene in their teenager's use of drugs and alcohol, since the seeds of such problems are sown at a much earlier age. The investment of parents' time and effort and the creation of a positive atmosphere in the home must start much earlier. Research has shown that many addictions have their roots in the first years of life. It is at this time that the infant learns to trust the parent to responsively satisfy needs. An infant who cannot rely on parents or caregivers to satisfy and soothe pain and discomfort learns not to trust them or expect that they will provide pleasure. As a result the infant will have difficulty forming secure attachments. Early-deprived children often lack a sense of optimism. They do not feel the world is nurturing. When such infants become teenagers, they may feel that drugs and alcohol provide a source of pleasure they can control. These teenagers do not have to depend on a close relationship to provide a sense of well-being or pleasure.

Of course, other factors in the child's early life or inherited susceptibilities may encourage a young person to use drugs and alcohol. Parents may be open and regular users of drugs and alcohol. The family may be dysfunctional, with sibling tensions, divorce, or mental illness. Teens may feel lonely and isolated from family and peers. Personal traumas, including sexual, physical, or psychological abuse, may play a role, as may continuing pain from an accident or illness.

Parents should provide an opportunity for the young person to address problems with mental health professionals and/or in drug and alcohol programs. As with other problem areas, parents can also actively acknowledge their own role in the addiction. Parents must also show a willingness to seek professional help and concretely and specifically modify their own behavior.

This does not guarantee that the young person will give up the addiction, for drugs and alcohol provide their own exquisite pleasure, and the teenager may still desire companionship with other users. Substance abuse is a difficult problem. Parents can seldom deal with their teenager's addictive behavior alone. Professional help is essential.

For parents, the best investment in preventing substance abuse takes place much earlier in the young person's life. "Attachment Parenting" and being there as an available, responsive adult may not guarantee a drug-free teenager, but it can go a long way.

Delinquency

Delinquency in boys is often connected with aggressive and destructive acts. Stealing, vandalizing, fighting, and terrifying others are considered delinquent behavior. Young people may display poor school attendance and truancy at one end of the spectrum and murderous assaults at the other. Delinquent girls are less likely to burglarize, fight, and destroy property, but they are more likely to become sexually promiscuous, not return home when expected, or run away. Girls may be involved in shoplifting things that they want to use or wear, but do not want to pay for or are unable to afford.

Delinquent acts are not only enormously upsetting to the

family, but they have legal ramifications that affect the young person's future. Unfortunately, in many cases the teenager does not get caught immediately when committing delinquent acts. Antisocial behavior may continue unabated for a long period of time. It provides excitement and adventure and serves as an outlet for aggressive impulses.

The delinquent teenager often has much rage and engages in self-destructive acts to punish one or both parents. As with other disorders, the roots of this negative behavior may be found early in the child's life. The development of a conscience, positive values, and accountability are primarily learned between the ages of five and nine.

Many delinquent young people have long histories of neglecting responsibilities, conning adults, and lying or cheating at school. Even minor illegal acts, such as shoplifting, can begin in elementary school. Often no one is aware that a theft has taken place, as a result no one sees to it that the child returns or pays for the stolen merchandise. Worse yet, the child is deprived of learning positive moral values: telling the truth, learning right from wrong, not stealing, etc.

Often young delinquents feel anger, resentment, and a lack of self-esteem. They have minimal feelings of competence and lack realistic future goals. An amazing number of delinquent teenagers can't read, or read far below grade level. School has provided little satisfaction. Their families may be too punitive, rejecting, and rigid or provide little warmth, attention, or physical presence. Parents of a delinquent teenager may be so involved with their own personal lives that they have no energy left to sustain a relationship with the teenager. They may be substance abusers themselves, or may be in the midst of a divorce. Parents may be so committed to their professions or careers that teenagers do not feel valued or cared for. The anger the teenager feels towards the parents who are not providing a stable support system is turned against the outside world.

School dysfunction also provides fuel for many aggressive acts. Sometimes, other teenagers are identified as the enemy and become victims of the violence. School buildings and offices may be vandalized as a result of a teenagers' anger with and disappointment in the school experience. These acts can be planned, supported, and encouraged by other dysfunctional teenagers, whose status and friendships are needed by the young person. In recent years, the news has been full of acts of violence committed by students who use guns to kill and terrorize school populations.

Many delinquent acts have their roots early in the child's development. This is especially true when children have been treated aggressively by their parents. They may have been frequently spanked or beaten and responded to harshly, with little sensitivity to their feelings and concerns.

Serious teenage delinquency is a growing problem. The increases may be a result of

- The availability of guns
- Family breakup due to death, divorce, or desertion
- Pervasive use of alcohol and drugs by family adults
- High unemployment in certain sectors of the population
- Physical and psychological abuse, neglect and punitive discipline
- A lack of familial supports to help the teenager live by society's rules.
- Lack of peer support to help the teenager live by the society's rules.
- The media's love affair with violence.

When teenagers are caught, parents are usually shocked and upset. These crimes confirm their deepest fears that their teenagers are "no good." The first impulse may be to punish. Often, the parents condemn their children, calling them "every name in the book". They may be so overcome with anger and humiliation that they simply reject their children. All they can think about is how ungrateful the young persons are for all that has been done for them, how much money has been spent, all the past trouble they caused, and their insolent attitude. Other parents blame the authorities and try to protect the teenagers from taking responsibility for what they have done. Unfortunately, getting young people off the hook may deny them the important and constructive experience of being made to feel accountable.

It is a rare parent who can admit what part he or she played or that parental actions over the years helped create the situation. Most parents blame the teenager's friends for the troubles: "If only he hung out with better friends." It may be true that the teenager's friends are displaying many negative behaviors, but there are reasons why each young person finds a specific group of friends with whom to relate.

There are no magic words or simple approaches for a parent to take at this time. It can be helpful if a young person could become attached to someone who represents a more constructive approach to life. Such person might be a group leader, an inspiring teacher, an encouraging boss, or even a therapist. With the help of such adults, there is the possibility that a positive relationship will develop and that changes in behavior can occur. It may also be helpful to dramatically change the young person's environment either by moving to a new neighborhood or arranging for the teenager to join the armed forces or temporarily live with another family or family member. In this way, the young person may be able to more easily "put on a new hat" and find new friends with whom to relate.

When a parent discovers a delinquent act, it is easy to communicate feelings of rejection and rage. The problem is that young people are exquisitely sensitive to feelings of rejection and hostility on the part of their parents. Many want to leave home rather than continually face a hostile, negative environment. It is on the street that teenagers find a community of other " losers", substance-abusing dropouts or victims of tough love. The sale of sexual favors or other acts of delinquency may be the only way for these young people to obtain money to live.

Parents need to prevent constant confrontations. Continual conflicts can make it untenable for the young person to remain within the home. Driving young people to escape to the streets is no solution. It simply escalates the problem.

While there are no simple solutions, there are some ways parents can deal with chronic delinquency. They may work with legal authorities to arrange an appropriate consequence to the teenager's acts. This may mean incarceration or a period of probation. It may be important to arrange for the young person to make reparations as well as just be punished. Psychotherapy may be part of the sentence. Individual or group therapy, with or without family participation, can be arranged.

Sadly, some adolescents are beyond help in their own home environments. The whole family should not be required to suffer when a child is continually draining emotional and financial resources. Foster placement may be necessary as a last resort.

No matter how strained the relationship becomes between the parent and the teenager, the young person can be told that he or she will always be welcome back into the home when able to control antisocial behavior. Parents can also communicate that they will always be there for their children. They might admit that they are not being effective in helping the teenagers deal with their special delinquent problems at the time. As difficult as this may seem, parents are advised to never give up altogether. Miracles can and do happen, even in the most hopeless situations. Your child should be made to understand that he or she is valued and will be welcomed back at some future date.

Death and Divorce

Both the death of a parent and divorce create added upheavals in the already turbulent years of the adolescent. Any major disruption can be upsetting to young people who want to completely bury themselves in their own private concerns and problems. They do not want to be bothered with worrying about the adults or other siblings in their life.

When a parent dies or the parents separate or divorce, there are many changes that can occur. There may be enormous financial pressure and intense grief and anger resulting from the loss. There may be more demands on the young person to be helpful and cooperative, to work, and to provide companionship to fill the void in the home. Most teenagers resent these demands, although they may feel sympathy for the bereaved or separated parent. They may also feel guilty that they do not want to provide the companionship and help the parent requires. During these years, most high school students feel entitled to be self-centered and carefree. Their concerns are personal and intense.

Unfortunately, just when adolescents need to move away from a stable and secure family to be more independent and exploratory, their secure family base is crumbling around them. Teenagers feel that the rug has been suddenly pulled from under their feet, creating greater imbalance at this time of their own rapid transition.

Teenagers who deal with the problems of death and divorce during early and middle adolescence often need to grow up too fast. They must take on adult responsibility before they have finished their teen years. As a result, many such prematurely adult adolescents are confronted with early midlife crises when they reach their thirties. They may give up their jobs, change mates, or leave on adventures. They missed the normal self-centered and carefree years of adolescence, and they are trying to recapture and perhaps repair the damage done in this early period of their life.

Young people from divorced families are also confronted with parents who may be beginning to date and develop new relationships or remarry. For many young people, fantasizing that their parents are sexual can be truly disturbing. It is much more comfortable for teenagers to think that parents don't "do it" at their age. Young teenage girls may be thrown into competition with their mothers or their fathers' girlfriends and prematurely engage in sexual intimacies. This may be a result of a strong identification with the women who are playing out seductive roles with their father. Other young people may completely withdraw from boy-girl dating, feeling repulsed by their parents' behavior and being afraid to compete in this arena.

Teenagers can also feel the personal loss of a parent. They may not receive any help in dealing with these intense feelings.

Often they are afraid to talk about the loss, since they worry that the subject may cause pain to the surviving parent. The focus may be on the grieving mother or father. As a result, many teenagers may never go through the mourning process at the time of the loss. Many years later, they may suffer symptoms associated with unresolved grief.

Remarriage poses other complicated problems for the teenager. Sometimes new siblings enter the home, adding pleasure or pain. In some cases, adolescents feel sexually attracted to their teenage stepsiblings; in other cases, they feel intense jealousy and rivalry. Parents need to be aware of such pressures on the adolescent and acknowledge the difficulties the whole family is experiencing when a death, divorce, or new marriage takes place. There should be ample discussion surrounding the events and plenty of preparation for changes that may ensue. Young people can accept realities if they are honestly reported and respectfully acknowledged and discussed.

Inappropriate Adjustments in Middle Adolescence

Since these may be the last years their child lives at home, parents may experience concern when they observe their high school student dealing with the developmental tasks of middle adolescence with denial, isolation, or acting out. The parent may notice that the young person denies any interest in the opposite sex, has little or no concern for body appearance, and fails to acknowledge the usual bodily changes and social shifts from childhood. These teenagers remove themselves from most social interactions or sexual exposure. They may become extremely embarrassed when this loaded subject is discussed. Dirty, baggy clothes; greasy, unkempt hair; and offensive body odor may signal that sexuality may be a problem for the teenager. Parents may have cause to be concerned when they do not see any normal adolescent interests emerge during the high school years.

Other teenagers who are having problems with their emerging sexuality may become intensely preoccupied and focused on some aspect of their lives. They may become overly intellectualized, fanatically religious, obsessed with music or art, or engrossed in a hobby or sport. Peers usually identify these young people as eggheads, freaks, nerds, and weirdoes. They show little interest in interacting with peers unless it relates to their specific interest. They find emotional security and safety in their passions.

> Brad, age seventeen, was obsessed with coins. He spent hours pouring over his collection. He had few friends. He hung out at the coin dealer's shop after school and learned an amazing amount about this specialized subject. He knew the prices of rare coins, the names of all the big collectors, and historical and geographical facts about coins.

> Betty, age sixteen, studies classical piano. She practices four or five hours a day and is especially into Bach. She scorns and rejects contemporary music. She is attached to her piano teacher and occasionally plays duets with other music students, but her contact is limited. To many of her peers, she seems snobbish and aloof, but in reality she is terrified of feeling any sexual arousal or physical attraction. The intense need to practice and master her art blocks out anxiety and uncomfortable feelings.

Parents are less likely to be concerned with young people who seem to intellectualize and isolate themselves through practicing, studying, or becoming experts. Parents are often relieved that their teenagers are not socializing, staying out late, spending money on clothes or cosmetics, or becoming mixed up with the "wrong group." However, it should be a matter of concern when teenagers are not normally reaching out to their peers and do not risk the uncomfortable feelings of sexual arousal, attraction, and rejection. They are isolating themselves from dealing with an important developmental task. These young people set up an intellectual defense against their growing sexuality. Of course, some may be very, very late bloomers.

A third group of young people is unable to deal with the developmental tasks of preparing for their future and forming close heterosexual relationships. They fail to use their intellectual and introspective abilities. As delinquents, they usually act out sexually or aggressively. They are afraid to look at themselves and determine who they are. They avoid the anxiety of preparing for the future by refusing to study, practice, or create. They discharge uncomfortable feelings without much thought of the consequences. There is little ability to delay gratification. Sexual promiscuity may be involved as part of such aggressive and self-destructive behavior. Parents should not have much difficulty recognizing that their teenager is acting out.

> At age eleven, Sally had been a victim of sexual molestation by her uncle. She was left with many ambivalent feelings when she became a teenager. She liked the attention she got from her uncle; he was the only adult who gave her pleasure and praised her. She also knew that their relationship was a secret, and she felt guilty and worried. In her teenage years, she had no one with whom to discuss this experience, but she longed for the same good feelings of warmth and contact she remembered from her early sexual experience. Having sex with boys was what she knew she could do well. There was nothing at school that interested her, and she had little support from her parents, who were divorced.

> Jonathan felt he could never compete with his father and become a success. He needed to "score" with many girls. He was relatively nondiscriminating, and he seemed obsessed with each sexual conquest. Jonathan was unable to have a positive connection to school and was afraid to face his rage at his demanding father. He developed a sexually transmitted disease at a young age, which further complicated his sexual activity.

> Keith was part of a gang that was engaged in destruction and vandalism. He was terrified of facing his sexual impulses and was also unable to function well in school. Feeling too shy to become involved in a boy-girl relationship, and unable to find satisfaction in a more constructive way, he stole cars, got into fights, cut classes, and owned a gun to "feel more like a man."

What Parents Can Do

It is important for parents to understand the particular stresses their teenager may be dealing with as well as to observe how he or she is handling problems. This is not always an easy task. There may be times when parents need other professionals to intervene. Arranging for help for the young person is part of the parents' responsibility. Although there is no guarantee the teenager will take advantage of such help, it is advisable to make it available.

> Natalie's mother and father were worried by her inability to make friends or ever go out on a date. They had marital problems and seldom did anything as a family. Realizing that she didn't have the time or training, Natalie's mother located a therapist at a mental health center near the house. It was not easy to persuade Natalie to make the first contact and meet the therapist. After the initial session, Natalie continued willingly and was helped by the therapist to better understand her family, her friends, and herself. In the end, she was grateful that her mother took time to provide this professional support.

Parents must be able to allow greater freedom for their teenagers to relate to the opposite sex and should support activities where young people can learn to know one another. Parents must also be aware that vicariously living their lives through a teenager's talents, skills, and proficiencies may delay the development of the social and sexual side of their child's personality.

> Sixteen-year-old Sheryl was a talented and vivacious violinist. She had enjoyed lessons with a teacher for five years and had played first violin in her high school orchestra. She was popular with boys in her class and was beginning to go out with a group that hung out together after school. Her mother told her that it was more important to increase her practice to several hours a day so that she might be able to enter a national gifted teenager competition. Although she enjoyed playing her

violin, Sheryl told her mother that she also enjoyed going places and having fun with her friends. "*If I have to practice even an hour every day, I will miss out on a lot of after-school activities. I don't want to do it.*" Her mother, who had given up a promising career as a concert violinist, was distraught. She could not understand Sheryl's decision not to take her music seriously.

Parents must also take care not to live vicariously through budding sexual and romantic relationships. They must refrain from being nosy and prying. If they intrude on the young person's sex life, there is a danger that they will be psychologically present during their teenager's sexual encounters. In other words, the parental phantom will always be hovering. No teenager can feel relaxed and enjoy an experience while a fantasy parent is watching.

Parents can also be supportive, humorous, and fair. They need to be available to discuss consequences and answer questions when asked. This is different from being the ultimate authority. Parents need to refrain from expecting a young person to be their friend and share their private lives with them.

It is also important for parents to refrain from dumping all their intimate and life problems on their teenager. These can be intrusions for a teenager who may be having a hard enough time growing up without the added parental concerns. A good rule to follow is to be a friendly parent. Do not use your child as a friend.

Parents must remember to provide some relaxed time to have fun as a family. Designated meals during the week can help establish a positive family atmosphere. Birthdays and holidays are valuable family rites to be respected. It is the parent's responsibility to see that they are.

Even though rules, expectations, and chores need to be formally discussed and decided on, parents can show some flexibility when special occasions arise. Flexibility can be much appreciated by the stressed-out teenager.

Timothy was in a play, and rehearsal lasted well into the night. His father offered to take over Timothy's chores during the two weeks of rehearsal and performances. The father wisely modeled generosity of spirit as well as flexibility for his son.

Parents need to be sensitive to the moods, worries, and anxieties of their teenager and attempt not to complicate these already difficult times by nagging, name calling, criticizing, and condemning.

Parents can more enjoy these middle adolescent years if they are sensitive and can step back from their teenager's provocative behavior. Parents also need to control their own impulsive, aggressive, and intrusive responses.

Preparation for Late Adolescence

As young people approach the end of their middle adolescent years, approximately age seventeen or eighteen, the issues of separation and independence become a concern for them and their parents. Young people begin to plan their post-high school lives. For some, college follows high school graduation. The college may be a local community institution or may be located in another part of the country. Young people who attend schools a distance from home move into dormitories or share apartments. Others may continue to reside at home as they go on with their education. Some students may decide to delay returning to school. They may plan to get a job and work, or travel, or bum around. There is a tremendous range of emotional maturity on the part of young people seventeen or eighteen years of age. Many may not be comfortable living away from home until early in their twenties.

In any case, the decision may include moving out of the family home to live alone or share an apartment. It is important for parents to prepare themselves for the changes. Parents need to shift their attitudes and their parental patterns in relating to the young person, whether the high school student decides to stay at home or move out.

You may be exquisitely aware that your teenager's senior year may be the last year that the whole family is together, sharing birthdays and holidays or participating in school events. You may experience sadness that this feeling of togetherness and proximity with children may be altered. Some parents feel sentimental and savor culminating high school events for the last time, especially for the youngest child.

If the parents themselves went off to college or left home and lived independently after high school, there may be an easier acceptance of these changes. If however, these shifts and separations did not occur in the parents own lives until they were much older, it may be harder to deal with separations after graduation.

Parents may be more able to handle the upcoming separation when they feel that they have participated fully and responsibly as parents from infancy through adolescence. These parents feel at peace and satisfied with a job well done. However, if parents feel guilty and anxious about their past role as mother or father, letting go may be more difficult. Parents should be aware of these unconscious feelings.

Parents may evaluate the emotional, social, and academic maturity of their child and feel concern that the child is unable to handle the stress of independent living. However, they still need to prepare for changes that will occur after graduation, even if their child remains home. There may be a new set of expectations about household chores and responsibilities, curfews, eating together, and informing the parents of comings and goings.

Stay-at-home mothers may feel that they will suffer a loss when their children go off to school. When the mother's identification is primarily as parent and homemaker, the meaning and time commitments of her life may be altered. When the last child in the family moves out, painful feelings associated with other losses in the parent's life may be rekindled. A mother may need a period of mourning when all the children leave. Other mothers may feel liberated and relieved when parental responsibilities basically come to an end and they can finally take care of their own needs.

Both parents may need to start planning for their own commitments or work before the home empties. It is important for them to explore and train for their own futures. Involved fathers may feel the loss of the companionship with their children as keenly as mothers.

The marriage relationship comes more in focus when there are no children around. Parents can begin to look forward to more free time to play and interact with one another, and they can spend time with their own peers. Parental sexual lives may enter a new era.

Financial pressure may continue to be heavy as college tuition skyrockets and living costs escalate as well. In fact, many families feel an enormous money drain during their children's college years. *"My bank accounts are hemorrhaging,"* a father complained. Mothers who did not work while their children were home may feel that contributing to the family income is necessary. Also, once supervision of their children is unnecessary, full-time employment is open to both parents.

For some parents, having no children at home provides a sense of freedom and the ability to truly focus on their own playtime and/or careers. Many careers can be restarted or new careers can be generated in these years, but parents should not lose sight of the obvious: raising children successfully is usually the most important career of one's life.

As children leave home and responsibilities for childcare decrease, some parents are confronted with problems concerning their own parents, who may have become ill or more dependent. Parenting one's parents may begin just as mother and father are looking forward to a more carefree existence. This added responsibility complicates their lives when they expect to be free.

Parents may experience midlife crises at the same time their children are reaching out to broader horizons. They may feel jealous of their children's ability to explore career choices freely just when they are feeling trapped in their own mundane work and perhaps "burned out".

Some parents may also be envious of the sexual experiences of their teenagers. Their child's new-found relationships may stimulate their own sexual feelings, which may have been somewhat dormant. There may be a renewed commitment to the marriage, or extramarital relationships may begin. Fathers may find themselves sexually aroused by female friends of their children and long to recapture that erotic time in their own life. This may happen to mothers as well, with their children's male friends.

Parents may experience profound disappointment with the way the young person has turned out. They may not like the way their child looks. They may be upset with teenagers' grade-point averages or their scores on national tests. Their hairstyles, clothes, personal habits, weight, or sexual orientation may repulse the parents. Parents may be worried about signs of substance abuse or disapprove of the young person's friends. As a result of these disappointments, parents may have a harder time showing support, affection and respect.

It may be hard to have faith that, after the young person leaves home, he or she will basically identify with the parents' values and life patterns. A young person cannot give mother or father the satisfaction of identifying with his or her values while still living at home. Most high school students seem to need to create irritation and abrasion to make separation from the family possible. Generating turmoil helps motivate moving out. After spending eighteen years in a secure home environment, most children need new adventures and new ways to test their mettle and find out who they really are.

Graduation

Graduation is the official rite associated with the end of high school. Receiving a diploma catapults the young person out into the world more dramatically than any other event. This rite of passage tends to be the most significant celebration of the adolescent years. It is generally more meaningful than a birthday or holiday. Graduation time is full of exciting events—proms, parties, and the stress of finishing the academic year. Surrounded by family and classmates, the graduate receives a diploma. Graduation marks the transition to late adolescence and early adulthood.

For most young people, high school graduation is a more

intimate celebration than the culmination of college or graduate school. Most seniors know each other. Along with positive expectations, there may be tension and stress. The senior may wonder:

"Will I have a date for the prom? Who shall I ask? Who will ask me?"

"What shall I wear?"

"Who is going to pay for dresses, tuxes, shoes, corsages, tickets, transportation? Will my parents pay some or all of the costs? Do I need an extra job?"

"Will I pass all my courses and actually get a diploma?"

"Will I perform or speak well at the graduation itself?"

Parents need to be sympathetic to these concerns and help the graduating senior handle them. The goal is to create a positive ending to the high school and family years. To accomplish this, the parent can cooperate with the graduate, either emotionally or financially. Months ahead of graduation, it is helpful to anticipate the approximate amount of extra funds that will be required. Family dissension may be avoided if plans are made to provide for the necessary money ahead of time, either from parents' contribution or from some extra jobs. Such advance planning will free the student and family to fully enjoy and experience this culminating and important milestone. Parents can also take responsibility for helping to supervise post-graduation festivities and plan for a safe venue for all-night graduation parties.

Chapter 19

late Adolescence

Late adolescence begins at approximately seventeen or eighteen years of age. Usually, the end of late adolescence merges with young adulthood sometime in the early twenties. There is no specific event or rite of passage that separates one phase from another.

Most late adolescents are ready for serious adventure, which will prepare them for their future life commitments. Adventures can be academic, intellectual, physical, or interpersonal. Late adolescents begin to test their abilities, values, and strengths in the world, farther separated from the immediate family. They are usually dependent on some form of parental support, whether financial or emotional. This important transition period into adulthood has its own tasks as well as stresses.

Developmental Tasks of Late Adolescence

The developmental tasks of late adolescence include

- Creating future career goals and proceeding with education or training to achieve them.
- Creating more intense and intimate relationships with an increased focus on spouse selection, marriage, and a future family.
- Developing a personal philosophy and a set of values and standards to live by, focusing on religion, politics, group allegiances, and/or idealism.

Late adolescents are often away from home when struggling

with these developmental tasks. They are dealing with the stress of separation from their families plus the trials of independent existence.

The College Experience

As teenagers plan to leave high school, they are confronted with decisions about the next year of their lives. Many have already opted for more education, either away from home at a college or university or at a local community college.

Teenagers who go on to higher education are confronted with new challenges. College provides much more freedom, a more sophisticated and demanding curriculum with a diversity of classes, and students from other ethnic and religious groups and from elsewhere in the country or world. There is much more freedom of choice, especially in planning time commitments. There may be the pressure of reports, extensive reading, and exams. Usually there is no adult responsible for seeing that these academic commitments are met. College students are basically on their own to study, socialize, and take care of themselves and their belongings.

Initially, it may be hard for first-year college students to deal with the pressures. They may not know how to take lecture notes, write formal papers, or prepare for two and three hour exams. Of course, much will depend on the young person's academic preparation in high school. In large universities, freshman classes can be enormous, with up to six hundred young people attending a large lecture. Study sections may be smaller, allowing for more active participation by students, but many large, impersonal lower-division classes can be overwhelming.

Professors can be inspirational, and many students feel in awe of their intellectual ability and wisdom. They can truly be newfound idols. These teachers can profoundly influence some college students. Of course, there may be other professors who are distant, uninteresting, and impersonal, with whom few young people connect.

Intellectual stimulation can come from meeting students who are excited about new ideas and approaches to life and who express a variety of attitudes and philosophies. There is more time at college for informal discussions and the intimate sharing of points of view, approaches to life, and personal experiences. Dormitories provide an excellent opportunity for social and intellectual discourse, which may take place around the table at mealtimes, in late-night confabs, or any time students are hanging out in the common rooms. These special times of intimate sharing may not happen as often if the young person is living at home and commuting to school. It is more usual for relaxed conversations to occur after formal school hours.

Some students find their first year at college a humbling experience. After graduating in the top quarter of the class with a high grade-point average, a student may be surrounded by other competent scholars. A's and B's, which came relatively effortlessly in high school, may not be so easy to come by. Some students—and their parents—have high expectations for achievement. Grades can continue to be a concern and can create pressure, especially if graduate school is a goal. Worry over acceptance to graduate school, medical school, or law school may be pervasive. Instead of exploring a variety of intellectual experiences, some young people stay goal oriented and grade conscious, never taking time to smell the academic roses.

Many young college students are delighted by the freedom most colleges provide. Some date, party, and socialize excessively. They find it hard to balance their academic commitments with the newfound activities. These late adolescents may have come from strict and rigidly controlled homes or non-coeducational schools in which dating and social interaction were formalized and limited. Away from the watchful parental eye, they become more adventurous, testing out behaviors they would never try at home.

Some young people have difficulty connecting and making friends in high school, but find the college more socially accessible. They throw themselves into new relationships with enthusiasm, often at the expense of their grade-point average.

Homesickness may be experienced in the first month of separation. Young people differ. Some may call home as frequently as once or twice a day in the beginning, and others may not write or call for many months. However, almost all freshmen appreciate a regular call, letter, or package from home. Young people who are lonesome and having trouble adjusting to the social activities and academic requirements of this new experience may need to call home to be reassured that they are anchored somewhere and that their familiar support system still exists. If the child is not far from home, weekend visits may ease homesickness. As college students begin to find new friends, date, and become involved in school activities, their need for and contact with parents will lessen. However, during times of stress, illness, or academic disappointments, phone calls may occur more frequently. Adolescents who have previously spent summers at camp or on trips away from home may not find the transition to dormitory living as stressful as those who have never left the nest.

Some freshmen are not only confronted with the new academic experience, but may also suddenly be dealing with their own meals, laundry, room care, and money. They may also have to schedule in part-time work to help defray the costs of going to school. For many, these more independent responsibilities may not be new; but taking care of their physical and financial needs can add stress for other college freshmen.

Getting a Job

Many high school students feel burned out with school and studying and feel that their high school diploma is all that they want for now. They are simply not interested in continuing formal education at this time. They prefer to work and experience the outside world more directly. Some late adolescents will benefit from a regular salary, which will enable them to move out of the family home, away from intra-family pressures they find intolerable. Even if the home environment functions smoothly, they may want to be independent and test themselves out in the world.

There is a variety of paid work that late adolescents can do, whether or not they have graduated from high school. This includes office work, construction, and sales. They can work in restaurants, department stores, gas stations, auto shops, and warehouses. They can be housepainters, housekeepers, and mechanics as well as do babysitting, reception, customer service, and phone sales. In all of these jobs, a young person can earn the minimum wage or more. Commission selling may produce a very uncertain income (or none at all). For the late adolescent the valuable service of babysitting may be the poorest paid of all.

For some young people, such jobs serve as a transition between high school and college, in the same way that a stint in the armed service provides training as well as a break from academia. Starting on the ground floor and doing menial or mundane tasks affords a young person a foot in the door and the experience needed to make their way up the ladder in a business or service occupation. It is not unheard of for a stock clerk to become the president of a department store or a carpenter to finds his way to the head of construction company, although with competition from college and graduate school applicants, it may be harder to rise to the top these days.

Some teenagers can find pleasure in their work experiences, either from the satisfaction of doing a job competently or from interacting with coworkers. Of course, the opposite is true as well. Stress can come from being ill-suited for a job or unhappy with a boss or other members of the workforce. At times, the work environment can reflect the same kinds of pressure that exist in the home. Sibling tensions arise between coworkers vying for the bosses' appreciation. Employers often take the place of mother or father, and angers and irritations are experienced similar to those felt within the family.

Young people need to arrive on time, as well as stay responsible for the hours assigned. They may find a forty-hour week oppressive or be amazed at how much it costs to live independently. Young people usually have little idea of the hidden supports that the family provides; phone, utilities, insurance, food, clothes, transportation, laundry, and rent can easily absorb every penny. Most young people need some financial help in supporting themselves, at least in the beginning. They may need help paying the initial rent deposit or the downpayment on a car. When the financial umbilical cord is severed during these vulnerable years, it may be very difficult for the young person. Both the late adolescent and the parents have a responsibility to find a way to relate to each other so that he or she does not feel cast adrift financially. The young person needs to have a comfortable way to ask for help.

As in high school, drugs and alcohol can create problems. The use of these substances may sabotage smooth functioning on the job. Drugs and alcohol may also undermine the young person's ability to come to work on time or to get along with other workers.

Some of the same problems occur for young people who become enormously successful in a particular endeavor and receive large financial rewards. They may be young professional athletes, actors, and other performers who have achieved notoriety and are suddenly responsible for hundreds of thousands of dollars. These late adolescents may not have the emotional maturity to deal with a sudden surge of money and success. They may have difficulty sustaining relationships with their parents, siblings, and past friends. They may feel cut off from existing emotional supports. For these successful young people, paying for drugs and alcohol may be no problem, but having the strength and emotional maturity to resist using them may not be possible.

After exploring various jobs, many young people realize that they need to obtain additional education and training. Perhaps the years of working help clarify the limitations of their present employment and intensify the motivation for another diploma.

Intimacy and Love

One of the developmental tasks that confronts the late adolescent and young adult is the search for a mate. Of all the decisions the young person makes, this is perhaps the most important. The mate who is selected most likely will be an integral part of the young person's life. The stability and success of this relationship will influence their lives and their future enormously.

Even before choosing a spouse, young people are learning how to relate to one another. They are learning to share feelings and ideas; they may be exploring each other's past, childhood, and family. They may be sharing future goals. Marriage, children, careers, and religion are usually discussed. All of these factors should be considered by both partners-to-be.

When two people meet, there can be immediate feelings of attraction, revulsion, or neutrality. A second encounter can confirm or dispel a first impression. A physical attraction energizes the relationship, and there can be a surge of erotic feelings, which motivates a young person to continue to seek out a particular individual. As two people continue their relationship, they may find that the initial physical attraction is not enough to overcome other qualities.

> Maggie met Paul in the biology lab. He reminded her of someone she liked in high school but never dated, and she thought that he was adorable. Paul walked her home from class a few times, then asked her out. In the following weeks, Maggie found that she was uncomfortable with the long silences and lack of smiles when they were together. Paul seemed preoccupied and nervous. Even though she was attracted to him and he was affectionate, she felt he gave her little conversation and fun. The relationship soon ended.

> Bill was equally disappointed after finally getting up the courage to ask out a pretty girl who worked in an adjoining office. He kept bumping into her in the elevator, and she always gave him a friendly smile. After a few dates, he found out that she was a complainer and seemed terrified of any outdoor activities. For Bill, who had a passion for camping, this young woman was a real turnoff.

The physical attraction creates the initial energy to instigate a relationship, but in time the young person will find that other qualities are needed to sustain the relationship. Qualities of mutual respect, interests in common, and similar values and goals help keep the physical bond alive. Feelings of friendship and companionship (along with sensual feelings) are of the utmost importance. Irritations, disappointments, and loss of respect can dampen the fires of passion.

Late adolescence and young adulthood may be the best time to search for and explore intimate alliances that may lead to marriages. The pool of unmarried men and women is large, especially in college and university environments. Young men and women can socialize in many different ways while taking classes and studying. They can meet in libraries, work in labs, or participate in the many programs offered.

Many young people are not focused on selecting a spouse in these years. They have priorities that appear more important to them. At a future time, when they are ready to find a mate, the available prospects may be more limited. On the other hand, the spouse-seeker who waits may feel more mature and may be better able to make a wise decision. So, the timing of this important decision involves balancing these two factors. In addition, women face the "biological clock" problem: If they delay marriage and procreation into their thirties, they may face increasing difficulty in their ability to become pregnant and bear children.

Homosexuality

Late adolescence is the time when gay and lesbian lifestyles emerge. Such life style choices may be difficult for many parents to accept. And while discussion of this complex subject is beyond the scope of this book, here are some guidelines that parents can consider:

- Do not allow this lifestyle to become a point of contention with the child.
- Let your child know that he or she remains a welcome family member.
- Extend and maintain emotional support just as you would have if your child had chosen a traditional lifestyle.

- Be respectful and courteous to your child's choice of partner.

For many parents, following these guidelines may be a real challenge. It may be necessary to mourn the loss of a future traditional family and deal with those disappointments without destroying the relationship to your son or daughter.

Living Together

Young people may decide that sharing an apartment seems like a good idea, especially after a few months of dating. The rationale may be, "We are getting along, so why not spend more time together, save some money, and have more privacy for sexual activity." To the couple involved, the fact of living together may not mean they are engaged to be married. Nevertheless, the very act of living together usually takes them out of circulation.

An advantage of sharing an apartment may be that both young people have the opportunity to learn to know each other under more realistic circumstances. They are not always showered, shampooed, made up, and dressed. They may be thrown into ordinary conflicts about spending money, doing chores, shopping, partying, and even using the same bathroom. Also, work and study schedules may conflict, as can the difference of sexual rhythms.

Even though young people are not legally married while they are living together, there may be many of the same conflicts and stresses that exist in marriage. Getting out of these informal couplings may be emotionally and financially difficult. There are no formal divorce proceedings. Young people may find themselves unable to separate and move out. They may ultimately drift into marriage, not because they have found the best possible person, but because they are not able to risk the emotional and (often) financial pain of a breakup. Inertia can be a powerful force!

While living together does provide an excellent window into the other person's personality, both young people are usually prevented from exploring other available men and women. Few relationships can survive the tensions and jealousies engendered when either person begins to date others when they are living together under one roof.

The most logical approach is to take this important step only after a couple has made the basic decision to marry. Living together for five or six months before marriage should help confirm the fact that they have made a good choice. It can also warn the couple that marriage is not a wise option.

Mate Selection

Many young people can create a list of characteristics that they want in a mate. Some of these qualities may be

- The capacity to give and receive affection
- Beauty, physical attractiveness, and that essential "mutual chemistry"
- Good health and vigor, freedom from serious illnesses, and the ability to have children
- Religious, political, or racial compatibility
- Similar interests and hobbies
- Roughly equal levels of education and intelligence
- Emotional stability; ability to control aggression
- Good relationship with family, especially with mother and father
- Generosity; capacity to be giving of time and money.
- Sexual compatibility
- Future occupational goals
- Future plans for children; the capacity to be a nurturing parent.
- Financial expectations; the ability to earn sufficient income.

Of course, each young person must decide what is important to include in his or her own list of criteria.

It is important to spend some time in this personal kind of exploration to help evaluate a potential partner. Rarely will any one person fit the bill perfectly. It may be that the politics of two young people differ, but there are many other things that prove to be compatible in their relationship. While political affiliation may seem to be a " big deal" for the twenty-one-year-old, it may be less important to people in their thirties. On the other hand, religious differences may not be a problem for the young adult but may pose a conflict once children enter the scene. Religious problems can be minimized if there is advance agreement about religious training and rituals.

It is also important to test a developing relationship under different circumstances and find out how each potential mate will react with one's own friends, alone or in private, in the morning, at the beach, at the theater, at one's own family home, on a camping trip, on a vacation, at a work-related gathering, during time of menstruation, on birthdays and holidays.

Young people also need to handle stress or pressure from their parents about their choice of friends or mate. Parents may have strong feelings and communicate them, adding another dimension of pressure or support to the developing relationship. Romeo and Juliet felt enormous pressure from the Montagues and Capulets.

Young people can be extremely idealistic and altruistic and may not take problems or conflicts in a potential mate seriously. Some tend to feel that they can change and rescue another person from their tragic history or difficult behavior. Many young men and women feel that their love and affection have the power to change their mate's character. They feel they can mold him or her into the person they dream of.

Also, young lovers often give to their potential mates what they, down deep, are yearning for. The girlfriend who is always sending sentimental cards and buying lavish gifts for her boyfriend may be hoping that he will come through with gifts and sentiment for her. Young people need practice communicating their own needs to each other in ways that aren't critical, demanding, or judgmental. They need to face all the realities, potentials, and limitations implicit in the developing relationship. This is no easy task when one is young and idealistic.

Parents have little control over decisions involving living together, mate selection, and marriage of their children. However, it is essential for the parent to maintain a positive relationship with their child, even if they disapprove of their choice. This may be a time when wise parents will bite their lip, grit their teeth-and smile!

Parents' Financial Involvement

As the last child flutters away from the nest to explore the outside world, parents are often surprised that the adjustment is easy. Compared to the intrusion and adjustments when a new baby arrives, this shift in the intensity of parental involvement is relatively simple. However, even when they are living away from home, most young people still need their parents to help provide financial support and encouragement. This support is much easier to give when the young person is acting appropriately and striving for realistic goals. It is also easier to be generous and encouraging when parents see their late adolescent successfully handling the college experience or job responsibilities. And parents may be able to more comfortably step back from parental roles when they are pleased with their child's friends and love relationships.

However, when their late adolescent decides to leave school, quit a job, or move in with an undesirable partner, parents may become angry and intrusively impart their own wisdom and mature suggestions. Their first impulse may be to remove financial support. But what young people do not need from their parents are threats of rejection, removal of economic support, and unsolicited advice.

> In her junior year of college, Priscilla decided that the college in which she was enrolled in was too isolated and too far from a large city. She decided to drop out, move to a larger city, and work for a while. Initially, her parents were appalled at this announcement. She had

always been such a serious and conscientious student. Their first impulse was to cut her off financially, which they hoped would force her to remain at school. However, they were able to listen to her multiple reasons for this change and decided to continue partial financial support for Priscilla as she began her new venture. By spring of the following year, Priscilla had applied to a college in a big city and was well on her way to obtaining a diploma. She was able to deal with her own conflicts and need for change without the complicating pressures from her family. Of course, she knew that they wanted her to obtain a college degree, and in the end she fulfilled their wishes.

Jerry's parents were almost hysterical when he announced in his senior year of college that he was going to live with a young waitress he had met. Jerry had planned to become a veterinarian, which demanded another four years of education and training. His parents were terrified that this relationship would lead to marriage or a pregnancy and undermine his commitment to his professional future. They threatened to stop his financial support if Sally moved in. Jerry had to make a choice between his parent's wishes and his affection for Sally. He chose Sally. As threatened, financial support was withdrawn. Jerry left school. He eventually finished college, but never went on for graduate training. It may have been wiser if Jerry's parents had not threatened such a severe alternative. In the end, they did not achieve their aspirations for their child or retain a positive relationship with him.

Kenny, age nineteen, was showing signs of drug and alcohol abuse. His parents had provided him with a monthly allowance, which he supplemented by working construction jobs. After several car accidents and traffic tickets, his parents decided to stop his allowance. They felt the money they were providing was paying for drugs and alcohol. They explained to Kenny that they loved

> him, but that they were not going to let their money be used for his destruction. Months later, when Kenny was desperate, they agreed to pay for a rehabilitation program. At present, Kenny is drug free and holding down a regular job.

In all these cases, the parents have reasonably comfortable incomes. Obviously, there are many parents who cannot provide economic support. But, for those parents who do have the funds, it is important to be supportive during these late adolescent years. An adequate allowance can free the young person to throw him or herself into the college experience, explore the variety of extracurricular activities available, and spend the time needed to build intimate relationships.

When a crisis occurs, it is hard to avoid acting omniscient and authoritarian. But although it is difficult, you and child should attempt to talk about the issue as calmly as possible and at an appropriate time and place. Discuss the adolescent's reasons for the decision. Ask if the young person understands why you are upset. In the end, the decision must rest in the hands of the adolescent, and you should usually support the decision, unless the funds will be used for drugs, alcohol, or other obvious self-destructive purposes.

It is easy for parents to feel they should control the money provided, but this erodes the relationship and prevents the young person from feeling like an independent adult. It may also be important not to tug on guilt feelings by constantly moaning about how much the tuition or rent is costing. Parents should not give what they cannot afford, and when they do help financially, the money should be given freely and without restrictions.

Since holding the purse strings is the only power parents feel they have during these late adolescent years, it is important to discuss limitations and expectations around the monetary support. If consulted, most young people will be responsive to the realities of the situation. They will usually accept what is given and augment it with their own employment if needed, or apply for loans to help sustain their living situation.

The Visitor

After a young person leaves home, there is a dramatic drop in the need to shop for groceries. The house stays in order much of the time, and the contents of the refrigerator are much more predictable. Parents need to learn how to shop for and cook for one or two people again.

Just when these adjustments are finally made, the young person may return home for a temporary visit. There are obvious re-entry emotions and tensions for all. During the first day or two, there may be increased irritability on the part of the returnee. Neither the late adolescent nor the parent is comfortable with old roles. No one is quite sure how to interact. Initially, the young person may need to be in bed until noon after being sleep-deprived during exam week. Adolescents may also stay out late visiting old friends, forgetting that the parents may have concerns about their whereabouts. They may use the family car or stay on the phone by the hour. Parents need to be understanding and tolerant. Remember, it is only temporary!

When the Visitor Brings a Friend

When a young person returns home, a friend may accompany him or her. The friend may be a roommate of the same sex or someone of the opposite sex with whom the son or daughter is having a relationship. Parents are suddenly confronted with some decisions. What room will each occupy? Who shall sleep in what bed? For the first time, the parents may realize that their child is sexually active. They wonder, "Who is this alien in our home?" They may also be looking at the visitor as a potential daughter-in-law or son-in-law.

Where a girlfriend or boyfriend spends the night may be more of a problem when there are younger siblings or no spare rooms or extra beds. It may be important to ask the returnee where he or she intends to have the friend sleep and discuss your own feelings. There are different ways to handle the situation.

Robin invited her boyfriend to come home with her for

the Christmas holidays. Her mother made up the sofa bed in the den for him. She also realized that Robin and her friend would spend most of their time in Robin's bedroom with the door closed. Robin's parents provided them with privacy and respected their time together, but were more comfortable not formally acknowledging that they were sexually active. Robin respected her parents' wishes. Her friend slept in the sofa bed at night.

Sharon called her mother and announced that Teddy would be visiting with her during spring break. She asked her mother if Teddy could sleep in her room. Her mother was aware that Sharon had been sexually active since high school and was reasonably selective about whom she was intimate with. Sharon's mother said she was looking forward to meeting Teddy and agreed to the sleeping arrangement. Her goal was to treat Sharon honestly and keep the relationship and communications open.

William's parents were uncomfortable with the idea that one of their children was sexually active before marriage. They made it very clear to William that Samantha could visit, but she would have to share a room with William's sister. William was annoyed by their old-fashioned values, but he wanted Samantha to meet his family. He reluctantly agreed to accept the sleeping arrangements, and the visit went smoothly.

The Returnee

After children have been away from home, some decide to move back on a more permanent basis. The reasons for the move home can be varied: For some, it may be financially unfeasible to live independently. Others may be recovering from a crisis, loss, or broken marriage and need the support of the familiar. Others may be waiting for acceptance to graduate school or are engaged to be married and do not wish to make temporary living arrangements. New guidelines for living together need to be discussed, including attendance at meals, financial contribution to the family budget, and chores and responsibilities.

Parents can assume that this child will be much like a boarder. They cannot expect to control the boarder's comings and goings. Every effort should be made to keep the relationship between the young person and the parents positive. There will come a time when this living arrangement will shift again, and the young person will move out to establish his or her own home.

Some young people need to move back home to repair a difficult and stormy relationship with their parents. Parents may need professional help to facilitate this reparative experience. Constant suggestions that the young person is a pain to have around and that the parents are tired of providing a home for him or her only retards the process of independence. It is like a mother's pushing a child off her lap when the child wants to be held and comforted. If instead the mother says, "I can hold you as long as you want, but when you are ready I will watch you go off to the sandbox," within minutes the child will scamper off. This same approach applies to the young person who returns home to become renourished or supported through a time of transition or stress. The more you urge them to leave, the more they may feel like clinging.

All through adolescence, parents need to increasingly step back from acting overly parental. It is important that they respect their adolescent's privacy, acknowledge the teenager's point of view, and refrain from making too many suggestions or recommendations. Parents need to provide emotional support when a young person comes to them for it, and to honor their financial commitments. In the end, mothers and fathers always need to feel free to communicate their own values and morality while modeling nurturing behavior with sensitivity and affection.

PART IV
PARENTING THE OLDER CHILD

CHAPTER 20
SUMMARY AND CONCLUSION

In this book, I have attempted to explore the developmental changes of children from kindergarten through the college years. I have also described parents' responsibilities, stresses, and pleasures during this period. Few experiences are so complex and frustrating, yet so rewarding. Even fewer experiences extend over two decades. What makes the process of parenting so challenging is the need to constantly shift one's understanding of the changing child as well as modify responses to the child's varied needs and demands.

The School-Age Child

As children enroll in elementary school, many of the custodial interactions between parent and child are greatly lessened. During these years, children generally take care of their own bodily functions and have learned to control some of their more primitive impulses and responses. The years from five to eleven are teeming with issues of mastery. The child is learning all kinds of skills, concepts, ideas, and facts. He or she is learning how to play by the rules, develop a conscience, and function independently.

Attachment issues are still important. The goal for parents is to provide a secure home base from which the child can go forth. Parents must provide increased freedoms and expect age-appropriate responsibilities from the growing school-age child. They must help the child become accountable. Parents must also provide supervision, stimulation, and some unwinding time for children during the after-school hours. The family is still an abiding force, and parents and child can enjoy mutually interesting activities. It is the parent's primary responsibility to create a sense of order and predictability, as well as some fun and joy. Family meals may be a time when all ages can interact, thus allowing the school-age child a window into the adult world.

Dramatic shifts take place from kindergarten through sixth grade. Children must be given more control as they approach the end of their school-age years. For some parents, relinquishing this control may be more difficult than taking on the initial responsibility of an infant. In any case, parenting the school-age child is generally an interesting and rewarding experience. Children should not be rushed or unduly pressured through these precious school-age years.

The Adolescent

It is easy for parents to make this period in the child's life stressful. The adolescent is going through enormous physical, emotional, and intellectual changes. He or she must say good-bye to childhood and enter the complex and challenging adult world. The transitional years between childhood and adulthood are full of turmoil and tensions. The home may be the only environment in which the teenager can fall apart. It is important for parents not to make matters worse by escalating punishments in response to the child's hostility or irritability. Parents must be careful not to intrude, control, irritate, compete with, or aggravate this young person. Parents often feel desperate during what they see as their last chance at being parental.

The goal for parents of adolescents is to learn to treat teenagers respectfully, allowing increased independence and privacy. Parents need to provide stability and continuity so that adolescents can focus on their own issues and are not distracted by parental concerns. Parents need to support the adolescent at school, at work, and in the important task of establishing intimate relationships.

Conclusion

A pervasive theme throughout this book is the need for parents to provide a positive and loving relationship with their growing children. Those who practice attachment parenting establish secure bonds and provide continuity of care and a parental presence through the important years. Unfortunately, this is not always possible, especially if death, divorce, separation, and/or economic disruption intrude on family life.

The job of parenting is never completely over. The years from infancy through late adolescence demand flexibility and constant shifts in intensity. From the twenty-four-hour job as infant nurturer to the unpredictable phone contacts from the older adolescent, an abiding bond is formed. The attachment between parent and child continues to be a vital force throughout life.

Parents are often needed when adult children face personal crises. Our homes and hearts should always be open for support and love, even when their lifestyles, achievements or behavior dissapoint us. The years ahead may be filled with the pleasures of weddings, a larger family, and eventually grandchildren. Then as a grandparent, you can experience the exquisite joy of revisiting infancy, childhood, and adolescence all over again.

A Parent Remembers

I was there to give a hug good-bye on the first day of school
    and to laugh at a knock-knock joke.
I was there to wipe away tears as her team lost by one goal
    and to clap hands as he jumped from the diving board.
I was there to rejoice when she rode down the street on her blue bike
    and to comfort him when his pet died.
I was there to help get supplies for a project
    and to get mad at the pile of dirty clothes.
I was there to read, to sing, to listen, and to hear the first notes from the clarinet.
I was there to help pack the duffel for a camping trip
    and explain what was so sad in the news.
I was there to drive to a party, a game, a performance
    and to buy new clothes for junior high.
I was there to tolerate new music and time spent privately.
    I was there to share a phone and to survive an irritable tirade.
I was there to feed new friends who invaded our table
    and see my son emerge as young man.
I was there to hug good-bye as she started her journey.
    What joy I felt because I was there.

Bibliography

Ainsworth, M.D.S. *Attachment: Retrospects and Prospect (In Parkes & Stevenson-Hinde) The Place of Attachment in Human Behavior.* Basic Books, NY, 1982.

Bettelheim, B. *Dialogues with Mothers.* Free Press of Glencoe, IL, 1962.

Bettelheim, B. *The Informed Heart.* The Free Press, NY.

Bettelheim, B. *Truants from Life.* Free Press, Glencoe, IL, 1955.

Block, Joel D., and Bartell, Susan. *Stepliving for Teens: Getting Along with Step Parents, Parents and Siblings.* Price Stern Sloan, 2001.

Bowlby, John. *A Secure Base.* Basic Books, NY, 1988.

Bowlby, John. *Attachment and Loss: Retrospect and Prospect.* American Journal of Orthopsychiatry 52(4), October, 1982.

Bowlby, John. *Attachment.* Basic Books, NY, 1969.

Bowlby, John. *Loss.* Basic Books, NY, 1980.

Bowlby, John. *Separation.* Basic Books, NY, 1973.

Brazelton, T.B. *Working and Caring.* Addison Wesley, Redding, MA, 1987.

Brindis and Jeremy. *Adolescent Pregnancy and Parenting in California.* Sutter Publications, 1988.

Brooks, J. *The Process of Parenting.* Mayfield Publishing Co., Mountain View, CA, 1987.

Byrne, K. *A Parent's Guide to Anorexia and Bulimia.* Henry Holt, NY, 1987.

Cobain, Bev *et al. When Nothing Matters Anymore: A Survival Guide for Depressed Teens*. (Paperback) Free Spirit Publisher. July 1998.

Cole and Rodman. *When School Age Children Care for Themselves: Issues for Family Life Educators and Parents.* Family Relations, 1967 (36:92-96).

Cooper and Wanerman. *Case Book of Child Psychotherapy.* Brunner, Mazel, NY, 1984.

Dobson and Bauer. *Children at Risk.* Word Publishing Co., Dallas, TX, 1990.

Droz and Rehmy. *Understanding Piaget.* International Universities Press, NY, 1972.

Elkind, A. *The Hurried Child.* Addison-Welsey Reading, MA, 1981.

Erickson, Eric. *Childhood and Society.* W.W. Norton, NY, 1950.

Frankel, Fred and Wetmore, Barry (Illustrator). *Good Friends are Hard to Find: Help your Child Find, Make and Keep Friends.* Perspective Publishing, 1996.

Giannetti, Charlene C., and Sagarese, Margaret. *Cliques: 8 Steps to Help your Child Survive the Social Jungle.* Broadway Books, 2001.

Ginott, Haim. *Between Parent and Child.* MacMillan, NY, 1965.

Goldstein, Freud and Solnit. *Before the Best Interests of the Child.* MacMillan, NY, 1979.

Haffner, Debra. *Beyond the Big Talk: Every Parent's Guide to Raising Sexually Healthy Teens.* New Market Press, 2001.

Haffner, Debra. *From Diapers to Dating: A Parent's Guide to Raising Sexually Healthy Children.* New Market Press, 1999.

Harrison and McDermott. *Childhood Psychopathology.* International Universities Press, NY, 1966.

Ilg and Ames. *The Gesell Institute's Child Behavior.* Dell Publishing Company Inc., NY, 1955.

Jacobvitz and Sroufe. *The Early Caregiver – Child Relationship and Attention-Deficit Disorder with Hyperactivity in Kindergarten.* Child Development, 1987 (58:1496-1504).

Karen, R. *Becoming Attached: What Children Need.* The Atlantic: February 2, 1990.

Leach, P. *Your Growing Child.* Alfred Knopf, 1986.

LeShan, E. *How to Survive Parenthood.* Random House, NY, 1965.

Magid and McKelvey. *High Risk Children without a Conscience.* Bantam Books, NY, 1988.

McBride, A. *The Growth and Development of Mothers.* Harper & Row, NY, 1973.

Meyer. *Death and Neurosis.* International Universities Press, NY, 1975.

Miller, Alice. *Prisoners of Childhood.* Basic Books, NY, 1981.

Murphy, L. Colin. *A Normal Child.* Basic Books, NY, 1956.

Musser, Conger and Kagan. *Child Development and Personality*. Harper & Row, NY, 1956.

Parkes and Steveson-Hinde. *The Place of Attachment in Human Behavior.* Basic Books, NY, 1982.

Pipher, Mary, Ph.D. *Reviving Ophelia: Saving the Selves of Adolescent Girls.* Ballentine Books, 1994.

Pittman, Frank, M.D. *Man Enough: Fathers, Sons and the Search for Masculinity.* Perigee Books, 1993.

Pollack, William, Ph.D. *Real Boys: Rescuing our Sons from the Myths of Boyhood.* Random House, 1998.

Postman and Weingartner. *Teaching as a Subversive Activity.* Delacorte Press, NY, 1969.

Powell, Douglas R. *After-School Childcare.* Young Children, March, 1987.

Pruitt, David, M.D., Anthony, Virginia Q. and Pruitt, David B. (editor). *Your Adolescent.* American Academy of Child and Adolescent Psychiatry. Harper Collins, 2000.

Ricci, Isolina. *Mom's House, Dad's House: A Complete Guide for Parents who are Separated, Divorced or Remarried.* Fireside Press, 1997.

Richard, E., Ph.D. Nelson, *et al. The Power to Prevent Suicide: A Guide for Teens Helping Teens.* Free Spirit Publishers, 1994.

Simmons, Rachel. *Odd Girl Out: The Hidden Culture of Aggression in Girls.* Harvest Books, 2003.

Sroufe, Cooper & DeHart. *Child Development.* McGraw Hill, Inc., NY, 1992.

Westheimer, Dr. Ruth K. *Sex for Dummies.* IDG Books, 1995.

Wolf, Naomi. *Promiscuities: The Secret Struggle for Womanhood.* Ballentine Books, 1997.

Zeligs, Rose. *Children's Experience with Death.* Charles Thomas, Springfield, IL, 1974.

Ziegahn, Susan T. *The Stepparent's Survival Guide: A Workbook for Creating a Happy Blended Family with Worksheet.* New Harbinger Publications, 2002.

INDEX

About the Author

Isabelle Fox, Ph.D. received degrees from Harvard/Radcliffe College and U.C.L.A. For the last 35 years, she has been a practicing psychotherapist specializing in parent-child relationships and developmental issues at the Western Psychological Center in Encino, California. She is the author of *"Being There: The Benefits of a Stay At Home Parent"* (Barrons 1996) and has lectured widely on this subject. For 10 years, she served as a Senior Mental Health Consultant for Operation Head Start. Dr. Fox and her husband live in Southern California and are the proud parents of two sons and a daughter and seven grandchildren.